LEARNING RESOURCES CTR/NEW ENGLAND TECH.
GEN   TK7868.P7 S63 1988
Sokolowski,   How to draw schematics and

3 0147 0001 3999 1

TK7868 .P7 S63 19

C0-AWI-978

Sokolowski, Steve.

How to draw schematics and
design circuit boards with your
IBM PC

How to Draw
Schematics
and Design
Circuit Boards
with Your
IBM PC

**This book is dedicated
to the memory of my father
Steve Sokolowski Sr.**

No. 3034
$19.95

How to Draw Schematics and Design Circuit Boards with Your IBM PC

Steve Sokolowski

TAB BOOKS Inc.
Blue Ridge Summit, PA

IBM and IBM PC are registered trademarks of International Business Machines, Inc.
Tandy 1000 is a registered trademark of the Tandy Corporation, Forth Worth, Texas.

FIRST EDITION
FIRST PRINTING

Copyright © 1988 by TAB BOOKS Inc.
Printed in the United States of America

Reproduction or publication of the content in any manner, without express
permission of the publisher, is prohibited. No liability is assumed with respect to
the use of the information herein.

Library of Congress Cataloging in Publication Data

Sokolowski, Steve.
How to draw schematics and design circuit boards with your IBM PC
/ by Steve Sokolowski.
p.   cm.
Includes index.
ISBN 0-8306-0334-4   ISBN 0-8306-9334-3 (pbk.)
1. Printed circuits—Design and construction—Data processing.
I. Title.
TK7868.P7S63   1988
621.381'74—dc19   88-20131
                                            CIP

TAB BOOKS Inc. offers software for
sale. For information and a catalog,
please contact TAB Software Department,
Blue Ridge Summit, PA 17294-0850.

Questions regarding the content of this book
should be addressed to:

Reader Inquiry Branch
TAB BOOKS Inc.
Blue Ridge Summit, PA 17294-0214

Contents

Introduction

For the past few years, engineers at modern electronics companies have been using computers to help design everything from space shuttle electronics to talking teddy bears. Advances in computer technology have produced computer software that automatically designs the most elaborate printed circuit boards and schematics when the proper data is placed into its memory. Software of this type costs hundreds or even thousands of dollars, not including the additional hardware needed for such a task.

    CAE (Computer-Aided Engineering) software is not available to the hobbyist of modest means. If you look through your local library or electronics store, you can see that many books have been written on the subject, but they all have one thing in common: the lack of actual programs to complement the technical language. There is a void between what's available to the high tech corporate engineers and the type of computer software that the kitchen table electronics enthusiast has access to. I plan to bridge this gap by introducing you to a new concept in Computer-Aided Engineering Software.

    This book presents two elaborate programs that allow you to lay out professional printed circuit board artwork as well as complete electronic schematics. Both programs allow you to design, edit, and print a complete electronics engineering package. Best of all, these CAE programs can be run on your IBM PC or compatible computer (using MS-DOS or PC-DOS) with as little as 128K of memory and one disk drive. No enhanced graphic adapters, mouse, or controller cards are needed.

The PC Board Designer generates printed circuit board artwork to a scale of 1:1 on an inexpensive graphics printer. Then just send this artwork to one of the PC board manufacturers that advertise in electronics magazines. Within two weeks, your finished board will be delivered to your door, ready for component mounting and soldering.

The Schematic Designer Program, with its 30 preprogrammed electronic symbols, will delight you with highly professional-looking schematics.

Drawing commands for both CAE programs are under the control of the user. Simply indicate where and what to draw and, at a touch of a button, your computer instantly displays the shape or pattern on the screen.

Both programs allow you to add additional electronic symbols and artwork patterns at any time, using an option called the Library feature. All Library patterns are saved on disk, accessible at any time.

Once you have mastered the available drawing commands, you are taken step-by-step from the drawing of a schematic of a working 12-volt power supply to laying out the artwork for the finished PC board.

This book was written with the novice electronic and computer hobbyist in mind. No confusing high-tech language is used. No assumptions of your programming abilities are made.

Books should be written to instruct and inform the reader. A book should not provide bits and pieces of information that confuse and frustrate. So take your time in reading this book and programming your computer and you too will not only be drawing schematics and designing PC board layouts just like the multi-million dollar corporations, but you will also be introduced to the fascinating world of computer-aided engineering.

HARDWARE NEEDED FOR THE PROGRAMS

- IBM PC or compatible computer
- 128K memory (or more)
- Graphics utility program
- Color monitor (used with PC board designer)
- Graphics printer
- Joystick or graphics tablet (optional)
- MS-DOS or PC-DOS (BASICA version 2.11 or later)

TAB BOOKS Inc. provides all CAE programs presented here on a standard 5¼ inch computer disk. Why waste time entering and de-bugging your programs when you can purchase a guaranteed working disk from a very reliable source? For information on purchasing the disk, refer to the purchasing coupon located in the back of this book.

Chapter 1
The Electronic Schematic
Designer Program

Before presenting the CAE programs, let's discuss the basics of how a picture is displayed on a computer monitor and printed on paper.

HOW GRAPHICS ARE DISPLAYED

A typical graphics printout is shown in Figs. 1-1 and 1-2. If these two figures were displayed on a computer monitor, they would appear as bits of light because a computer monitor is made up of very small dots located side by side. These dots can be turned on or off in any pattern. By lighting selected dots, pictures can be drawn. The total number of dots or pixels that are lighted to form a character (resolution) depends on a screen command or screen mode.

An IBM compatible has seven screen modes available, compared to only three screens available to the IBM machine (IBM screen modes are Screen 0 or Text mode, Screen 1, and Screen 2). Screen 0 to Screen 4 require the least amount of memory (16384 Bytes), while Screen 5 and Screen 6 (which may be available with IBM compatibles) require 32768 Bytes of memory. Due to the large amount of memory needed for Screens 5 and 6, a compatible computer containing just 128K cannot be used for designing PC boards.

To set the resolution of the monitor, all you must do is to incorporate into a program the statement SCREEN n, where n indicates one of the available screen modes. For example, to set the monitor to Screen 2, your BASIC program might include the line:

10   SCREEN 2

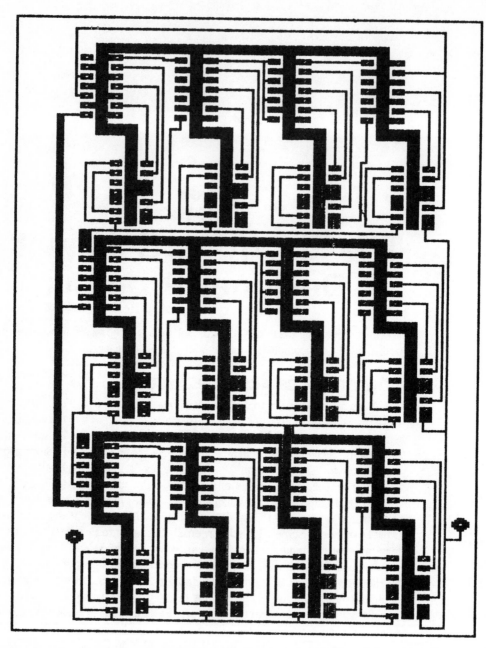

Fig. 1-1. Sample printout of a PC board using CAE software.

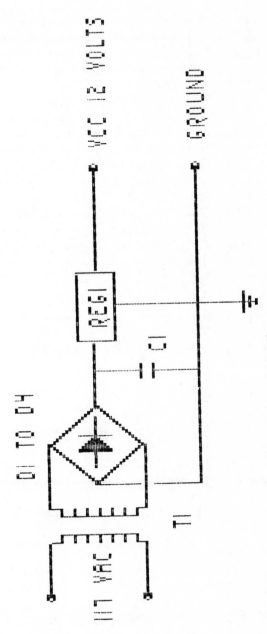

Fig. 1-2. Sample printout of an electronic schematic using CAE software.

Each screen mode has not only a resolution associated with it, but also a set of available colors.

Screen 0 (or Text Mode) has 16 available colors that can be programmed, but no graphic commands are available.

Screen 1 (Fig. 1-3) has four colors (with two palettes) and medium resolution graphics. The pixels are arranged in a format of 320 pixels across by 200 pixels down. Due to the unique elements of Screen 1 and also its availability on both IBM and compatible computers, this screen is used to display the artwork of the PC Board Designer program.

Screen 2 (Fig. 1-4) gives the highest resolution (640 pixels by 200 pixels), but there are only two colors available, black and white. Due to Screen 2's high resolution and its availability on both IBMs and compatibles, this screen is used to display all the graphic patterns of the Schematic Designer program.

Compatible computers, such as the Tandy 1000, offer additional screen modes. You can access these screens by typing SCREEN X, where X indicates one of the additional modes.

Screen 3 (Fig. 1-5) allows the use of 16 colors but the resolution is very low: 160 pixels by 200 pixels.

Screen 4 (Fig. 1-6) allows the use of only four colors. The resolution is 320 pixels across the screen by 200 pixels down. This screen has medium resolution.

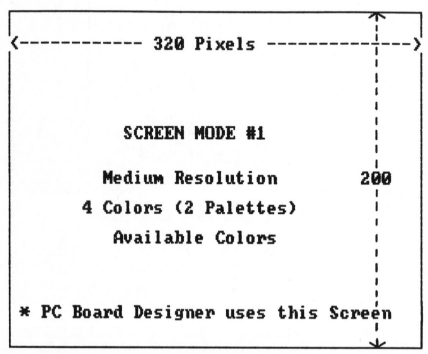

Fig. 1-3. Sample medium screen resolution (Screen Mode #1).

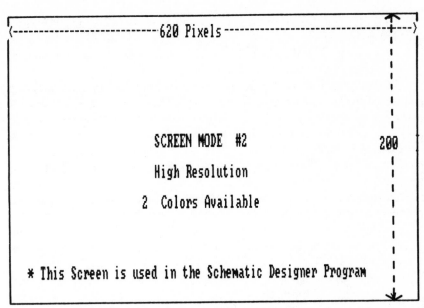

Fig. 1-4. Sample high screen resolution (Screen Mode #2).

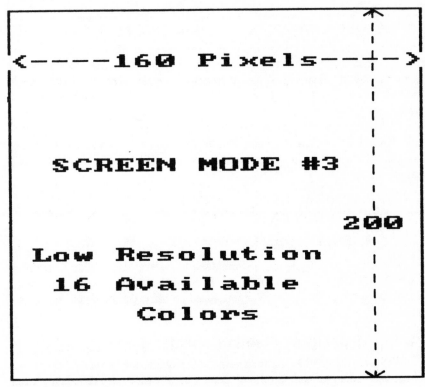

Fig. 1-5. Sample low screen resolution (Screen Mode #3).

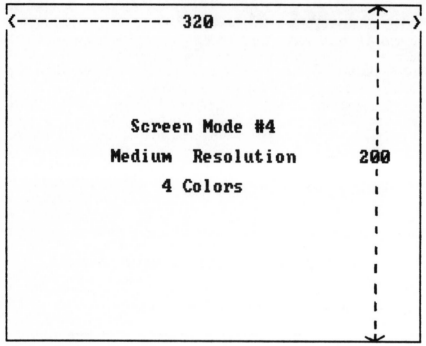

Fig. 1-6. Sample medium screen resolution (Screen Mode #4).

All patterns on the computer screen as well as computer text are made up by the lighting of specific screen elements or pixels. This can be easily seen by looking closely at the monitor while using one of the available screen commands.

Unlike the computer instructions contained within the Read Only Memory chips (ROMs) that cannot be changed or altered, all screen pixels are under the control of the programmer using the standard MS-DOS or PC-DOS BASICA commands as:

CIRCLE	GET	COLOR	LINE
DRAW	PAINT	PALETTE	POINT
PSET	PRESET	PUT	SCREEN

The above commands can be combined to control the lighting of monitor pixels to display a graphic image on screen. Using the DRAW command, electronic symbols, and printed circuit board patterns can be displayed on the screen.

PC Board Designer Screen Considerations

While writing the electronic Schematic Designer, the proper pixel spacing for the components associated with this program was not critical; my main concern was that the size of the symbols was pleasing to the eye.

The situation changed drastically while writing the PC Board Designer. The copper pads had to be properly spaced so that commercially available electronic components could be inserted and soldered on a finished PC board. I had to determine which of the available screen modes provided spacing of .1 inch between selected pixels. This spacing is critical for the proper drilling and installation of integrated circuits (ICs) and other components.

As previously discussed, Screen 1 has a pixel display of 320 by 200. If the resolution of Screen 1 were 320 by 320, our computer monitor would resemble a perf board (a board made from non-conductive material with holes drilled every .1 inch in both the horizontal or vertical direction) and an IC pattern could be drawn in both the horizontal or vertical position. Since this is not the case, all ICs drawn by the computer can only be placed in the horizontal position (Fig. 2-1).

The graph dots are spaced .1 inch apart horizontally. If vertical spacing was used for IC installation, the spacing between the pads would be too great, and the IC would not fit properly. Keep this in mind when designing a layout using the PC Board Designer.

Graphic Printing

Another concern with both the Electronic Schematic and Printed Circuit Board Designer was to convert the graphic material displayed on the monitor into a useful hard copy printout. Without a printed copy of the designs, this book would be just a collection of elaborate drawing programs, but this is far from true.

Using one of the many commercially-available graphic printers, a high quality schematic or PCB layout can be made.

All information sent to a standard graphic printer is in the form of numbers (0 to 255 decimal or OO-FF hexadecimal). The printer interprets these numbers according to the American Standard Code for Information Interchange, commonly referred to as the ASCII code. Most numbers (or codes) are printed as letters or symbols. However, the numbers 0 to 31, as well as some special sequences of code numbers, are used to control various functions of a printer. These control codes allow you to change character sets, select print modes, underline text, etc. Control codes have different meanings, depending on the current print mode. If a code is not recognized by a printer, an X is usually printed.

Graphic printing is the main purpose of the CAE programs, so I will discuss the graphics capability of standard printers. Additional information on character and graphic printing can be found in the instruction booklet that came with your printer.

Graphics Mode

Graphics mode does not provide pre-defined characters. If you program your printer using BASIC, you are responsible for the positioning and the action of the print head. Most printers allow the user direct programming control over all of the available graphic dots. With a printer using 800 available dot columns, you have BASIC control of up to 5600 individual graphic dots.

A standard sequence of BASIC commands to use the graphics capability of a printer is:

1. Send a control code which specifies the character set (normal, condensed, or compressed).
2. Send a control code to put your printer in the graphic mode.
3. Send a control code to tell the printer where you want the printer head positioned.
4. Tell the printer in which dot column you want to print.
5. Tell the printer what you want printed.

For example:

LPRINT CHR$(27);CHR$(16);CHR$(n1);CHR$(n2)

where n1 is a value between zero and three (0-3) and n2 is a value between zero (0) and 255.

As you can see, programming a graphic printer can get complicated. Also, the use of BASIC commands slows down the operation of the computer because all BASIC commands must be internally converted into a form understood by the computer before any execution can take place. (This is called machine language.) This conversion may take place in a fraction of a second, but printing the contents of an entire monitor screen can take about 5 to 10 minutes. A faster means of printing is to eliminate BASIC commands completely and load a program directly into the computer's memory.

Conversion and execution time now take place in micro-seconds. Printing speed, while improved, is limited by the time it takes to position the printer head and print. Now the average graphic takes about 3 minutes instead of 5 to 10 minutes to print. This machine language program is called a Graphic Utility.

For proper operation of both CAE programs, this utility must be loaded (while in MS-DOS or PC-DOS) within computer memory before any printing action can take place. A Graphic Utility program is usually supplied with your computer on the disk containing DOS and other programming material needed by the computer.

For example, when loaded, the Graphic Utility on the Tandy 1000 displays a number of printers supported by that version of the utility. Enter the number or letter that best describes the printer connected to the computer. This utility format depends greatly on the version and type of DOS and computer system you have. For additional information on loading a Graphic Utility, refer to the instruction booklet supplied with the computer.

ELECTRONIC SCHEMATIC
DESIGNER PROGRAM INTRODUCTION

Due to the investment of thousands of dollars required for a complete system, computer-aided engineering software is usually reserved for large corporations. Until recently, it wasn't practical for the small business or part-time electronics hobbyist to consider using a computer to produce high quality electronic prints. However, using the enclosed computer program, you can design, edit, save, and (using a dot-matrix printer) make hard copies of your efforts.

The program, Electronic Schematic Designer (Listing 1-1), is a CAE system that operates with only 128K of memory and one disk drive; you do not need an EGA (Enhanced Graphics Adapter) card.

Listing 1-1. Schematic Designer Introduction program listing.

```
10 REM                    * INTRODUCTION *
20 REM
30 REM                  (C)opyright 1987
40 REM
50 REM     This program is protected under the laws of
60 REM     the United States of America. Any
70 REM     publication or reproduction in any form -
80 REM     without the expressed written consent of
90 REM     the author or Tab Books Inc. is prohibited.
100 REM      ==> SAVE UNDER FILENAME "INTRO" <==
110 CLS
120 SCREEN 2
130 KEY OFF
140 FOR A=1 TO 100:NEXT A
150 SOUND 700,5
160 X=575:Y=170
170 PSET(X,Y):DRAW "R22;U5;D10;U3;F8;D5;U5;H8;U4;E8;U
    5":CIRCLE (X+23,Y),20
180 SOUND 600,5
190 X=50:Y=170
200 PSET(X,Y):DRAW "L16;U5;D10;U3;G8;D5;U5;E8;U4;H8;U
    5":CIRCLE (X-23,Y),20
210 SOUND 500,5
220 X=560:Y=10
230 PSET(X+10,Y-5):DRAW "TA-115;U30;TA115;U30;TA360;U
    25":PSET(X+10,Y):DRAW "L10":PSET(X+10,Y+14):DRAW "L10
    ":X=X+68:Y=Y+8
240 SOUND 400,5
250 X=35:Y=8
260 PSET(X,Y):DRAW "D1;L2;D1;L2;D1;L2;D1;L2;D1;L2;D1;
    L2;D1;L2;D1;L2;D1;L2;D1;L2;D1;L2;D1;L2;D1;L2;D1
    ;L2;D1;R2;D1;R2;D1;R2;D1;R2;D1;R2;D1;R2;D1;R2;D
    1;R2;D1;R2;D1;R2;D1;R2;D1;R2;D1;R2;D1;R2"
270 DRAW "U1;R2;U1;R2;U1;R2;U1;R2;U1;R2;U1;R2;U1;R2;U
    1;R2;U1;R2;U1;R2;U1;R2;U1;R2;U1;R2;U1;L2;U1;L2;
    U1;L2;U1;L2;U1;L2;U1;L2;U1;L2;U1;L2;U1;L2;U1;L2
    ;U1;L2;U1;L2;U1;L2;U1;L2":PSET(X+20,Y+15):DRAW "L38"
280 PSET(X+4,Y+15):DRAW "U1;L2;U1;L2;U1;L2;U1;L2;U1;L
    2;D10;R2;U1;R2;U1;R2;U1;R2;U1;R2;U1":PAINT (X-2,Y+13),
    1,1:PAINT (X-2,Y+17),1,1:PSET(X+6,Y+15):DRAW "U5;D10"
    :Y=Y+31
290 SOUND 600,5
300 LOCATE 5,22:PRINT "Computer-Aided Engineering Pro
    gram"
```

```
310 LOCATE 8,36:PRINT "for"
320 LOCATE 11,25:PRINT "Electronic Schematic Design"
330 SOUND 400,5
340 LOCATE 23,23:PRINT "(C)opyright 1987  Tab Books I
    nc."
350 FOR A=1 TO 5000:NEXT A
360 CLS
370 LOCATE 1,17:PRINT "Program designed for IBM PC's
    and Compatibles"
380 LOCATE 5,25:PRINT "Minimum Computer Requirements:
    "
390 LOCATE 8,28:PRINT "Black & White Monitor"
400 LOCATE 9,28:PRINT "128K Memory"
410 LOCATE 10,28:PRINT "One Disk Drive"
420 LOCATE 11,28:PRINT "Graphics Printer"
430 LOCATE 12,28:PRINT "Optional Joystick"
440 LOCATE 13,28:PRINT "MS-DOS or PC-DOS (Basica vers
    ion 2.11 or later)"
450 LOCATE 14,28:PRINT "620 x 200 Graphic Card"
460 GOSUB 1440
470 PRINT "In the DRAW MODE - you have the following
    options to input graphic"
480 PRINT "commands. They are as follows:":PRINT:PRIN
    T
490 PRINT "D=Draw R=Reset E=Erase I=Insert S=Save C=C
    ircle L=Load W=Wording P=Print Line"
500 PRINT "F=Filenames G=Get Section of Schematic  A=
    Put Graphic on Screen  T=Term.Point":PRINT
510 PRINT "DRAW - To activate, hit the 'D' key. This
    will allow you to draw a line.
520 PRINT "       To de-activate, just hit the 'D' a
    second time. You are now able to"
530 PRINT "        move the Drawing Cursor without lea
    ving a trace.":PRINT
540 PRINT "RESET - By hitting the 'R' key - you will
    clear the image on the screen."
550 PRINT "         The contents of the memory will re
    main.":PRINT
560 PRINT "Get Option - Saves desired graphic in comp
    uter memory. You are asked if this"
570 PRINT "             image will be saved in the Li
    brary File. You respond by typing"
580 PRINT "             Y (Yes) or N (No). If you ans
    wer Yes, you will then be asked to"
590 PRINT "             give this new image a name. R
    espond by entering a Filename. Then"
600 PRINT "             press the <ENTER> Key. The im
    age will now be saved on Disk. You"
610 PRINT "             may recall this image at any
    time by using the 'L' (LOAD) option."
611 PRINT "             This option requires you to i
    nput two X/Y diagonal locations."
612 PRINT "             Do this by pressing the 'G' k
    ey twice at the desired coordinates."
620 GOSUB 1440
```

```
630 PRINT "ERASE - This option erases a section of yo
    ur graphic. The 'E' option is used"
640 PRINT "         in the same manner as the 'G' opti
    on (two diagonal X/Y coordinates"
650 PRINT "         are needed). Instead of saving the
    image in computer memory, the"
660 PRINT "         ERASE option paints this graphic s
    ection to BLACK, thus erasing"
670 PRINT "         the image.":PRINT
680 PRINT "INSERT - Using the 4 ARROW keys - you can
    move the Drawing Cursor to any section"
690 PRINT "         of the screen. When in a section
    you wish a pre-programmed drawing to"
700 PRINT "         be placed - just hit the 'I' key.
    You will then be asked to enter the"
710 PRINT "         Item number that is associated wi
    th the electronic symbol. Then hit"
720 PRINT "         <ENTER>. The symbol chosen will b
    e drawn at that location.":PRINT
730 PRINT "FILENAMES - The 'F' option allows you to d
    isplay ALL filenames saved on"
740 PRINT "         Disk, which is located in Driv
    e A. You may also DELETE files"
750 PRINT "         just by typing KILL to the pro
    mpt <Hit Enter to Continue>."
760 PRINT "         Then type in the filename you
    wish Deleted - then press <ENTER>."
770 PRINT "         NOTE - This filename MUST cont
    ain the extension."
780 PRINT "         (ex. .LIB - .BAS ect.)"
790 GOSUB 1440
800 PRINT "SAVE - Used to SAVE the schematic shown, o
    n disk. You are asked to give your"
810 PRINT "         schematic a filename. When entered
    - hit <ENTER>. The disk drive starts."
820 PRINT "         Your drawing is now being saved for
    future use.":PRINT
830 PRINT "LOAD - LOADs a Complete Screen or Library
    symbol from Disk A. You enter"
840 PRINT "         the number 1 if you wish to LOAD an
    image from the Library, or"
850 PRINT "         enter the number 2 if you wish to L
    OAD an image from the Picture"
860 PRINT "         File. Then when asked, enter the FI
    LENAME of the image. When loaded,"
870 PRINT "         graphic will be displayed at the lo
    cation of the Drawing Cursor.":PRINT
880 PRINT "CIRCLE - This key allows you to draw any o
    ne of three programmed circles"
890 PRINT "         on the screen. These circles are
    used to draw additional symbols not"
900 PRINT "         included in the program library."
    :PRINT
910 PRINT "WORDING - Used to print letters & numbers
    at any location on the screen."
```

```
920 PRINT "            The ARROW keys can be used to mo
    ve the Drawing Cursor to any location"
930 PRINT "            so wording can be placed at a de
    sired point. To EXIT - just"
940 PRINT "            press the COMMA ',' Key. You wil
    l then be placed in the Draw Mode."
950 GOSUB 1440
960 PRINT "PRINT LINE - Used to Draw Diagonal Lines.
    This option needs two X/Y coordinates."
970 PRINT "            Move the Drawing Cursor to th
    e desired location. Then press the"
980 PRINT "            'P' Key once. Now move the Cu
    rsor to the second X/Y coordinate."
990 PRINT "            Press the 'P' Key again. The
    computer now connects these two"
1000 PRINT "            locations using a straight l
    ine.":PRINT
1010 PRINT "A Option  -  With an image in computer me
    mory, (placed there by using the 'G'"
1020 PRINT "            or 'L' option) the 'A' Key a
    llows the computer to Draw this in"
1030 PRINT "            memory graphic at the indica
    ted X/Y coordinates. By pressing the"
1040 PRINT "            'A' Key for the second time,
    the computer will Erase the image"
1050 PRINT "            just drawn but leaving any p
    reviously drawn material untouched.":PRINT
1060 PRINT "Termination - This option draws a small c
    ircle at the end of a line to indicate"
1070 PRINT "            a connection to this point
    from the outside world.":PRINT
1080 PRINT "Help     - This option saves the schema
    tic you are working on, under the"
1090 PRINT "            Filename 'DATA'. The screen
    will clear then the HELP program will"
1100 PRINT "            be LOADED. This program list
    s the Computer Key Options used with"
1110 PRINT "            the CAE Programs. When the n
    eeded information is known, your"
1120 PRINT "            computer will re-load your p
    resent schematic drawing."
1130 GOSUB 1440
1140 PRINT "Cursor Express - By pressing the 'J' Key,
    you are placed in the Cursor Express"
1150 PRINT "            Mode. If you have a Joys
    tick or Graphics Table connected to"
1160 PRINT "            the LEFT Joystick Port,
    you can now move the Drawing Cursor"
1170 PRINT "            around the screen faster
    then if the Arrow Keys were used."
1180 PRINT "            When at the desired loca
    tion, press the 'J' Key for the second"
1190 PRINT "            time. You will then be a
    ble to Draw, Erase or Insert Components"
1200 PRINT "            at the new coordinates."
    :PRINT
```

```
1210 PRINT "Print    or    -  Used to print your schem
     atic on a Graphic Printer."
1220 PRINT "                    Which button to press de
     pends on the type of computer you"
1230 PRINT "Shift/Print      have. Consult your BASIC
     Instruction Booklet for additional"
1240 PRINT "                    information.":PRINT
1250 PRINT "No. 1 Button  - Press this button to chan
     ge the color of the Drawing Cursor"
1260 PRINT "                    to WHITE.":PRINT
1270 PRINT "No. 2 Button  - Press this button to chan
     ge the color of the Drawing Cursor"
1280 PRINT "                    to BLACK. Use this button
     in conjunction with the 'D' key"
1290 PRINT "                    to erase lines by re-colo
     ring the line Black."
1300 GOSUB 1440
1310 LOCATE 6,1
1320 PRINT "To EXIT from any required keyboard input
     (ex. Entering a Filename or Component"
1330 PRINT "Number) just press the <ENTER> Key withou
     t entering any information. Your"
1340 PRINT "computer will cancel that input and retur
     n you to the Drawing Mode.":PRINT
1350 PRINT "When requested to enter a filename of an
     image that will be LOADED or SAVED,"
1360 PRINT "you are NOT required to add the extension
     (ex. .LIB or .PIX). These"
1370 PRINT "extensions are automatically inserted by
     the computer.":PRINT
1380 PRINT "The extension .LIB indicates ALL Files th
     at were SAVED as a LIBRARY File.":PRINT
1390 PRINT "The extension .PIX indicates ALL Files th
     at were SAVED as an IMAGE File."
1400 PRINT "An Image File is a file that has SAVED th
     e entire contents of the screen"
1410 PRINT "on Disk."
1420 LOCATE 24,1:INPUT;"Hit <ENTER> to Load your Comp
     uter-Aided Engineering Program ",AA$:CLS:RUN"DESIGNER
     "
1430 END
1440 LOCATE 24,1:INPUT;"Hit <ENTER> to Continue ",ZZ$
     :CLS:RETURN
```

Once loaded into computer memory, you can draw schematics using any of 30 pre-programmed electronics symbols. Refer to Figs. 1-8 and 1-9 for a complete graphic listing of these symbols.

Choose from resistors, capacitors, and coils, and at a press of a button these symbols are instantly drawn at any location on the screen. To produce quality drawings without the aid of a graphics card, the IBM PC computer command Screen 2 is used. This command produces a high-resolution graphic consisting of 12800 dots of light or pixels (picture elements) arranged in a pattern of 640

Schematic Designer

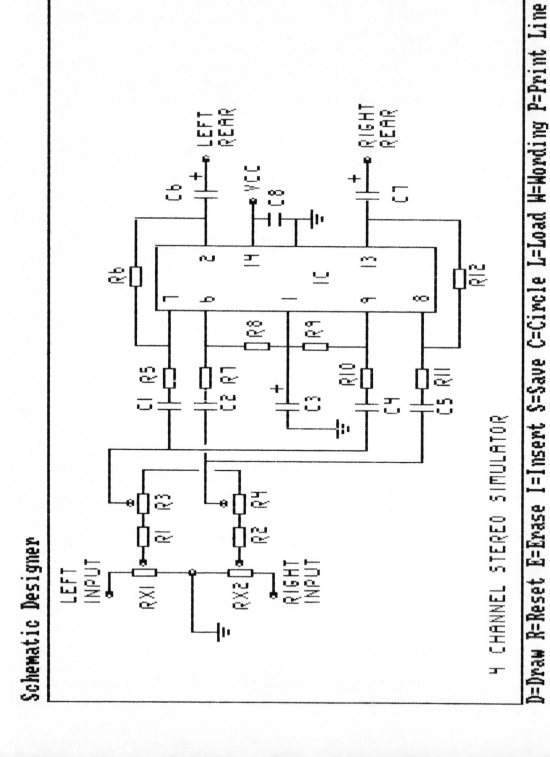

4 CHANNEL STEREO SIMULATOR

D=Draw R=Reset E=Erase I=Insert S=Save C=Circle L=Load W=Wording P=Print Line

Fig. 1-7. Sample schematic of a four channel stereo simulator.

pixels across by 200 pixels down. On the computer screen, each pixel appears as a dot. When printed, a string of dots is drawn as a continuous line.

Using the Screen 2 command, only two colors can be produced: black and white. Even if you own a color monitor, Schematic Designer produces a clear graphic display.

A sample schematic of a four channel stereo simulator is presented in Fig. 1-7. You are not restricted to graphic drawings; you can also incorporate any letters or numbers with the schematic. For example, this is used to indicate resistor values or designations (R1, C23, .002 μF).

The Electronic Schematic Designer is broken into four basic programming elements:

Introduction
Main Program A
Help Screens
Main Program B

The Introduction (INTRO)

The introduction acquaints you with the basic drawing commands available with the Schematic Designer Program. The introduction contains seven screens which can be easily displayed by pressing the <ENTER> or <RETURN> key.

When complete, the introduction automatically loads and runs the main Schematic Designer Program.

Main Program A (DESIGNER)

This is the main body of the Schematic Designer. It contains the BASIC commands necessary to draw or erase lines. Also included are the 30 pre-programmed electronics symbols that can be displayed at any location on the screen.

Help Screens (HELP)

The Help Screens can refresh your memory of the drawing commands used within Main Program A. The Help program contains five screens, which, like the introduction, can be displayed by pressing the <ENTER> or <RETURN> key.

Main Program B (DATA2)

This section is identical to the Main Program A except for the additional commands needed to re-load the screen graphic that was saved on disk before the help screen was displayed.

DRAWING ELECTRONIC SCHEMATICS

For the following refer to Main Program A starting at Listing 1-2.

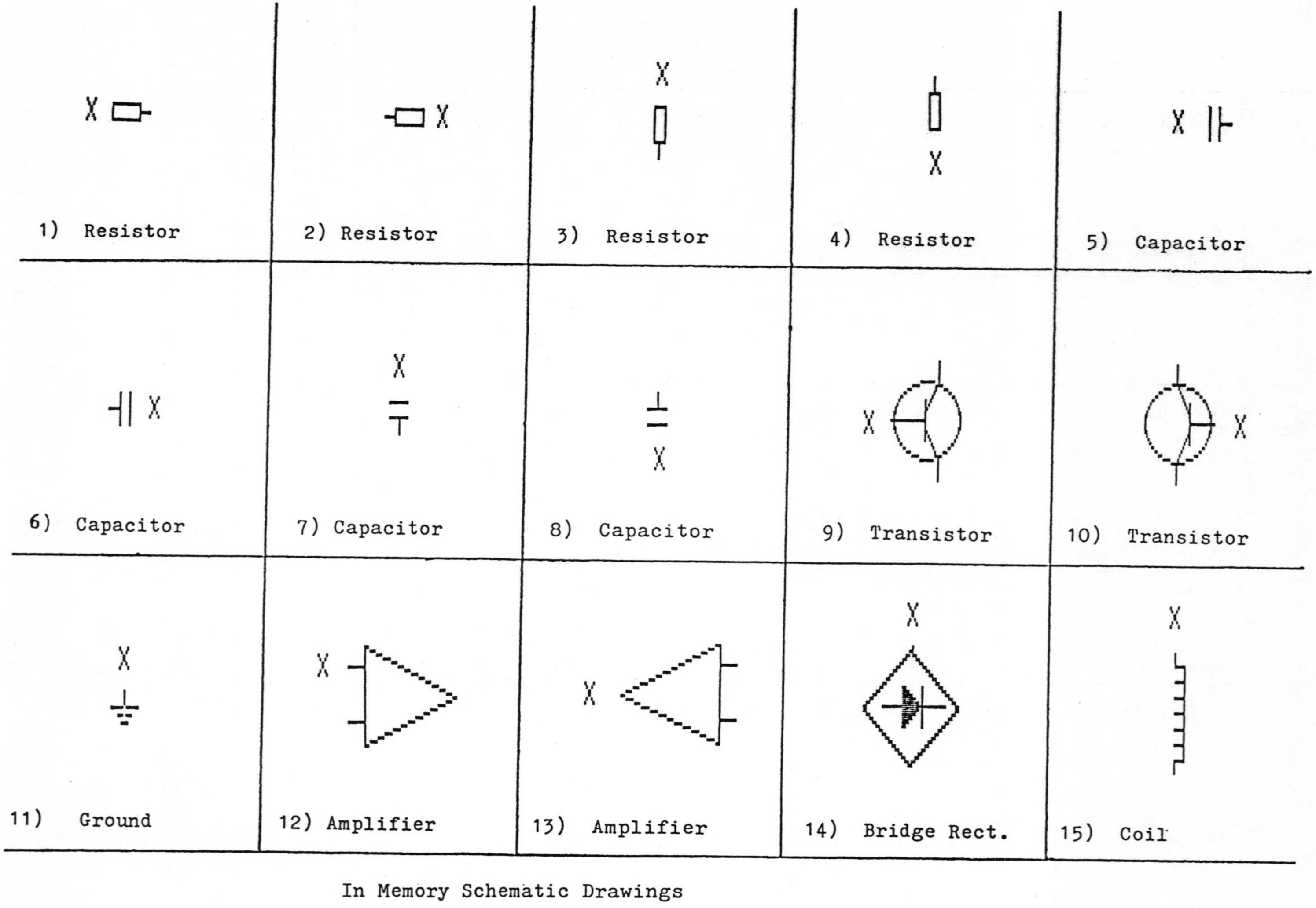
X
1) Resistor
X
2) Resistor
X
3) Resistor
X
4) Resistor
X
5) Capacitor
X
6) Capacitor
X
7) Capacitor
X
8) Capacitor
X
9) Transistor
X
10) Transistor
X
11) Ground
X
12) Amplifier
X
13) Amplifier
X
14) Bridge Rect.
X
15) Coil
In Memory Schematic Drawings

Fig. 1-8. Illustration of the pre-programmed electronic symbols (components 1 to 15).

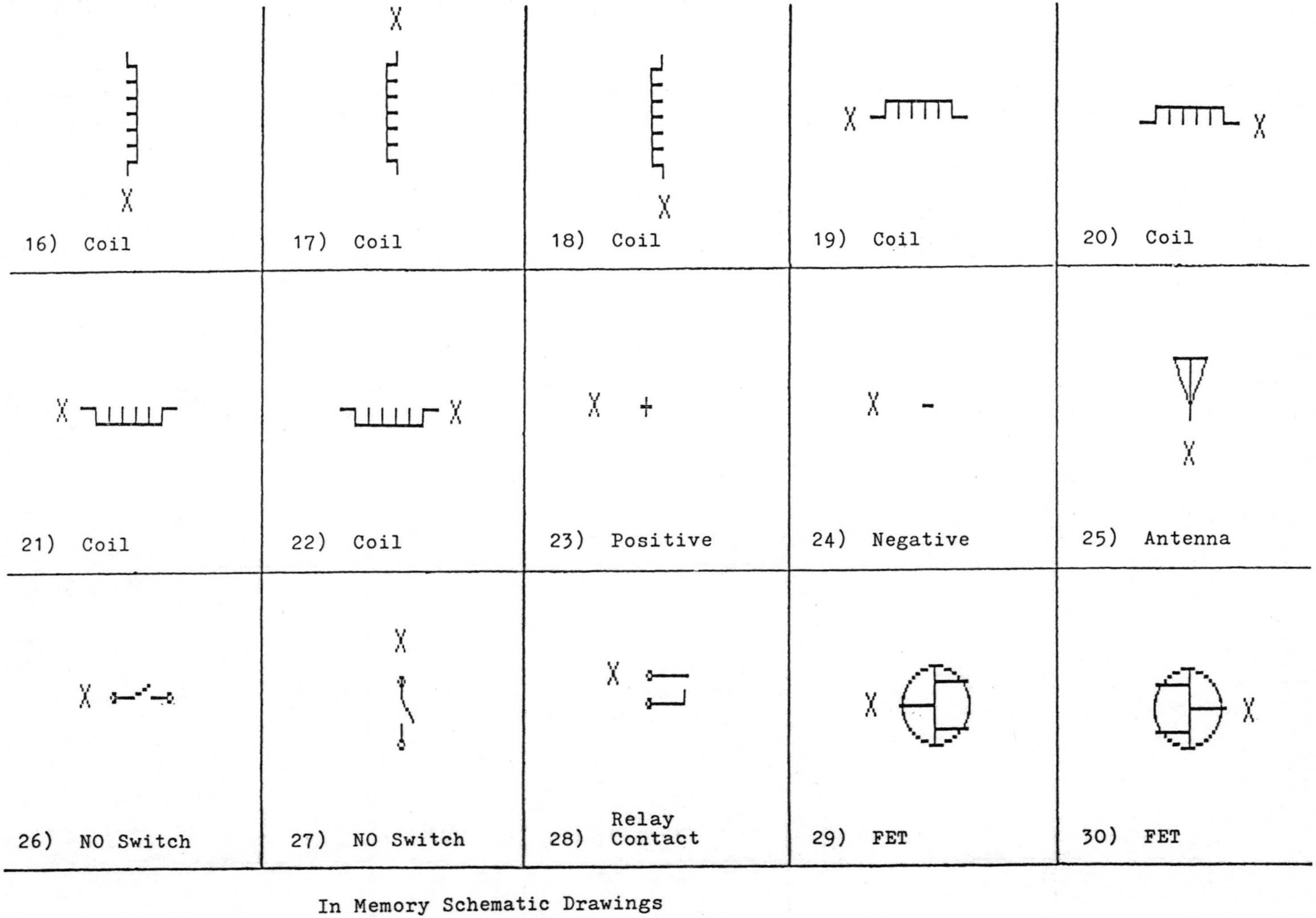

16) Coil 17) Coil 18) Coil 19) Coil 20) Coil

21) Coil 22) Coil 23) Positive 24) Negative 25) Antenna

26) NO Switch 27) NO Switch 28) Relay Contact 29) FET 30) FET

In Memory Schematic Drawings

Fig. 1-9. Illustration of the pre-programmed electronic symbols (components 16 to 30).

Listing 1-2. Schematic Designer Main Program A listing.

```
10 REM     Schematic Designer        MAIN PROGRAM "A"
20 REM
30 REM     This program is protected by the laws of
40 REM     the United States of America. Any
50 REM     publication or reproduction in any form -
60 REM     without the expressed written consent of
70 REM     the author or Tab Books Inc. is prohibited.
80 REM
90 REM                   (C)opyright 1987
100 REM
110 REM                   Version 5.10
120 REM
130 REM
140 REM     ==> SAVE UNDER FILENAME "DESIGNER" <==
150 REM
160 CLS
170 KEY OFF
180 SCREEN 2,,0,0
190 LINE(0,10)-(639,190),1,B
200 LOCATE 1,1:PRINT"Schematic Designer"
210 LOCATE 1,50:PRINT"(C)opyright 1987 Tab Books Inc."

220 DEF SEG=&HB800
230 DIM B(1500)
240 X=320:Y=90:C=1:L=1:S=1
250 GOTO 1230
260 A$=INKEY$
270 ON ERROR GOTO 650
280 IF A$ <>"" THEN SOUND 800,2
290 IF A$="H"OR A$="h" THEN GOTO 2030
300 IF A$="R"OR A$="r" THEN GOSUB 2300:S=1:LOCATE 25,
    1:INPUT;"REALLY ERASE (Y/N) ";Q$:IF Q$="Y"OR Q$="y"TH
    EN GOTO 1990 ELSE GOSUB 2300:GOTO 1230
310 IF A$="J"OR A$="j" GOTO 1830
320 IF A$="F" OR A$="f" THEN GOSUB 2300:GOTO 2070
330 IF A$="D"OR A$="d" THEN S=S*-1
340 IF A$="E"OR A$="e" THEN L=L*-1:IF L=-1 THEN A1=X:
    A2=Y: ELSE A3=X:A4=Y:LINE(A1,A2)-(A3,A4),0,BF
350 IF A$="T"OR A$="t" THEN PSET(X,Y):CIRCLE (X,Y),3,
    3:S=1
360 IF A$="P"OR A$="p" THEN L=L*-1:S=1:IF L=-1 THEN A
    1=X:A2=Y ELSE A3=X:A4=Y:LINE(A1,A2)-(A3,A4)

370 IF A$="G"OR A$="g" THEN L=L*-1:PSET(X,Y),0:S=1:IF
    L=-1 THEN A1=X:A2=Y ELSE A3=X:A4=Y:B=0:GOSUB 2300:LO
    CATE 25,1:PRINT"Recording Picture - Please Stand By";
    :GET(A1,A2)-(A3,A4),B:SOUND 800,2:GOSUB 2300:GOTO 232
    0
380 IF A$="A"OR A$="a" THEN  A1=X:A2=Y :PUT(A1,A2),B,
    XOR:SOUND 800,2
390 IF A$="S"OR A$="s" GOTO 1070
400 IF A$="L" OR A$="l" THEN GOTO 2340
410 IF A$="W" OR A$="w" GOTO 1240
420 IF A$="I" OR A$="i" THEN GOTO 670
430 IF A$="1" THEN C=1:F=0:S=1
440 IF A$="2" THEN C=0:F=0
```

```
450 IF A$="C" OR A$="c" THEN GOTO 1740
460 ON KEY (11) GOSUB 610
470 ON KEY (12) GOSUB 550
480 ON KEY (13) GOSUB 520
490 ON KEY (14) GOSUB 580
500 KEY(11)ON:KEY(12)ON:KEY(13)ON:KEY(14)ON
510 GOTO 260
520 IF X>=639 THEN GOSUB 2430;:RETURN ELSE P=POINT(X+
    1,Y):PSET(X+1,Y),C
530 IF S=-1 THEN PSET(X,Y),C ELSE PSET(X,Y),F
540 X=X+1:SOUND 200,1:F=P:RETURN
550 IF X=0 THEN GOSUB 2440;:RETURN ELSE P=POINT(X-1,Y
    ):PSET(X-1,Y),C
560 IF S=-1 THEN PSET(X,Y),C ELSE PSET(X,Y),F
570 X=X-1:SOUND 300,1:F=P:RETURN
580 IF Y>=190 THEN GOSUB 2420;:RETURN ELSE P=POINT(X,
    Y+1):PSET(X,Y+1),C
590 IF S=-1 THEN PSET(X,Y),C ELSE PSET(X,Y),F
600 Y=Y+1:SOUND 400,1:F=P:RETURN
610 IF Y=10 THEN GOSUB 2410;:RETURN ELSE P=POINT(X,Y-
    1):PSET(X,Y-1),C
620 IF S=-1 THEN PSET(X,Y),C ELSE PSET(X,Y),F
630 Y=Y-1:SOUND 500,1:F=P:RETURN
640 END
650 PSET(X,Y),0:DEF SEG=&HB800:IF ERR=53 GOTO 2460 EL
    SE RUN 230
660 END
670 LOCATE 1,37:PRINT SPACE$(44)
680 LOCATE 1,50:INPUT;"Enter Component # ",AA
690 IF AA>30 THEN GOTO 1720
700 IF AA=0 GOTO 1720
710 PSET(X,Y)
720 ON AA GOTO 730,740,750,760,770,780,790,800,810,82
    0,830,840,850,860,890,900,910,920,930,940,950,960,970
    ,980,990,1000,1010,1020,1030,1040
730 DRAW "U2;R17;D2;R6;L6;D2;L17;U2":X=X+24:GOTO 1720

740 DRAW "U2;L17;D2;L6;R6;D2;R17;U2":X=X-24:GOTO 1720

750 DRAW "R3;D9;L3;D4;U4;L3;U9;R2":Y=Y+14:GOTO 1720
760 DRAW "R3;U9;L3;U4;D4;L3;D9;R2":Y=Y-14:GOTO 1720
770 DRAW "U4;D8;U4;R1;C0;R5;C1;U4;D8;U4;R7":X=X+14:GO
    TO 1720
780 DRAW "U4;D8;U4;L1;C0;L5;C1;U4;D8;U4;L7":X=X-14:GO
    TO 1720
790 DRAW "L6;R11;L5;D1;C0;D3;C1;L6;R11;L5;D4":Y=Y+9:G
    OTO 1720
800 DRAW "L6;R11;L5;U1;C0;U3;C1;L6;R11;L5;U4":Y=Y-9:G
    OTO 1720
810 DRAW "R22;U5;D10;U3;F8;D5;U5;H8;U4;E8;U5":CIRCLE
    (X+23,Y),20:Y=Y-5:GOTO 1720
820 DRAW "L16;U5;D10;U3;G8;D5;U5;E8;U4;H8;U5":CIRCLE
    (X-23,Y),20:Y=Y-5:GOTO 1720
830 DRAW "D4;L8;R16;L8;D1;C0;D1;C1;L4;R8;L4;D1;C0;D1;
    C1;L2;R4;L2":Y=Y+9:PSET(X,Y),0:GOTO 1720
840 PSET(X,Y):DRAW"L6;U1;L6;U1;L6;U1;L6;U1;L6;U1;L6;U
```

```
    1;L6;U1;L6;U1;L6;U1;L6;U1;L6;U1;L6;D5;L10;R10;D
    14;L10;R10;D5;R6;U1;R6;U1;R6;U1;R6;U1;R6;U1;R6;
    U1;R6;U1;R6;U1;R6;U1;R6;U1;R6;U1;R6":GOTO 1720
850 PSET(X,Y):DRAW"R6;U1;R6;U1;R6;U1;R6;U1;R6;U1;R6;U
    1;R6;U1;R6;U1;R6;U1;R6;U1;R6;U1;R6;D5;R10;L10;D
    14;R10;L10;D5;L6;U1;L6;U1;L6;U1;L6;U1;L6;U1;L6;
    U1;L6;U1;L6;U1;L6;U1;L6;U1;L6;U1;L6":GOTO 1720
860 DRAW "D1;L2;D1;L2;D1;L2;D1;L2;D1;L2;D1;L2;D1;L2;D
    1;L2;D1;L2;D1;L2;D1;L2;D1;L2;D1;L2;D1;L2;D1;R2;
    D1;R2;D1;R2;D1;R2;D1;R2;D1;R2;D1;R2;D1;R2;D1;R2
    ;D1;R2;D1;R2;D1;R2;D1;R2"
870 DRAW "U1;R2;U1;R2;U1;R2;U1;R2;U1;R2;U1;R2;U1;R2;U
    1;R2;U1;R2;U1;R2;U1;R2;U1;R2;U1;R2;U1;L2;U1;L2;
    U1;L2;U1;L2;U1;L2;U1;L2;U1;L2;U1;L2;U1;L2;U1;L2
    ;U1;L2;U1;L2;U1;L2":PSET(X+20,Y+15):DRAW "L38"
880 PSET(X+4,Y+15):DRAW "U1;L2;U1;L2;U1;L2;U1;L2;U1;L
    2;D10;R2;U1;R2;U1;R2;U1;R2;U1;R2;U1":PAINT (X-2,Y+13),
    1,1:PAINT (X-2,Y+17),1,1:PSET(X+6,Y+15):DRAW "U5;D10"
    :Y=Y+31:GOTO 1720
890 DRAW "D4;R6;D4;L6;R6;D4;L6;R6;D4;L6;R6;D4;L6;R6;D
    4;L6;R6;D4;L6;D3":X=X+5:GOTO 1720
900 DRAW "U4;R6;U4;L6;R6;U4;L6;R6;U4;L6;R6;U4;L6;R6;U
    4;L6;R6;U4;L6;U3":X=X+5:GOTO 1720
910 DRAW "D4;L6;D4;R6;L6;D4;R6;L6;D4;R6;L6;D4;R6;L6;D
    4;R6;L6;D4;R6;D3":X=X-5:GOTO 1720
920 DRAW "U4;L6;U4;R6;L6;U4;R6;L6;U4;R6;L6;U4;R6;L6;U
    4;R6;L6;U4;R6;U3":X=X-5:GOTO 1720
930 DRAW "R9;U4;R8;D4;U4;R8;D4;U4;R8;D4;U4;R8;D4;U4;R
    8;D4;R10":X=X+59:GOTO 1720
940 DRAW "L9;U4;L8;D4;U4;L8;D4;U4;L8;D4;U4;L8;D4;U4;L
    8;D4;L10":X=X-59:GOTO 1720
950 DRAW "R9;D4;R8;U4;D4;R8;U4;D4;R8;U4;D4;R8;U4;D4;R
    8;U4;R10":X=X+59:GOTO 1720
960 DRAW "L9;D4;L8;U4;D4;L8;U4;D4;L8;U4;D4;L8;U4;D4;L
    8;U4;L10":X=X-59:GOTO 1720
970 DRAW "R7;L3;U2;D4":GOTO 1720
980 DRAW "R7":GOTO 1720
990 DRAW "U15;L10;R20":LINE(X,Y-3)-(X-10,Y-15):LINE(X
    ,Y-3)-(X+10,Y-15):X=X+3:GOTO 1720
1000 CIRCLE(X-1,Y),2,3:DRAW "R10":LINE(X+10,Y)-(X+20,
     Y-3):LINE(X+21,Y)-(X+32,Y):CIRCLE(X+32,Y),2,3:X=X+32:
     GOTO 1720
1010 CIRCLE(X,Y),2,3:DRAW "D4":LINE(X,Y+4)-(X+7,Y+10):
     LINE(X,Y+11)-(X,Y+15):CIRCLE(X,Y+16),2,3:Y=Y+16:GOTO
     1720
1020 CIRCLE (X,Y),2,3:DRAW "R22;L2;D1;C0;D3;C1;D3;L20
     ":CIRCLE(X,Y+7),2,3:GOTO 1720
1030 DRAW "R22;U9;D18;U3;R20;L20;U12;R20":CIRCLE (X+2
     3,Y),20:Y=Y+5:GOTO 1720
1040 DRAW "L22;U9;D18;U3;L20;R20;U12;L20":CIRCLE (X-2
     3,Y),20:Y=Y-5:GOTO 1720
1050 REM END OF PROGRAMMED ELECTRONIC SYMBOLS
1060 END
1070 REM SAVE SCHEMATIC
1080 PSET(X,Y),0
1090 GOSUB 2300
```

```
1100 LOCATE 25,1:INPUT;"Enter Filename of .PIX Graphi
     c to be SAVED (No extension needed) ",A$
1110 IF A$="" GOTO 1230
1120 GOSUB 2300
1130 BSAVE A$+".PIX",0,16384
1140 CLOSE:IF A$="DATA" THEN RUN "HELP.BAS" ELSE GOTO
     1230
1150 REM LOAD SCHEMATIC
1160 PSET(X,Y),0
1170 GOSUB 2300
1180 LOCATE 25,1:INPUT;"Enter Filename of .PIX Graphi
     c to be LOADED (No extension needed) ",A$
1190 IF A$="" GOTO 1230
1200 GOSUB 2300
1210 BLOAD A$+".PIX",0
1220 CLOSE
1230 F=0:LOCATE 25,1:PRINT" D=Draw R=Reset E=Erase I=
     Insert S=Save C=Circle L=Load W=Wording P=Print Line"
     ;:SOUND 800,2:GOTO 260
1240 GOSUB 2300
1250 LOCATE 25,1:PRINT "Character Insert Mode.       =
     => Hit COMMA ',' to Exit";:S=1
1260 B$=INKEY$:IF B$="" THEN 1260
1270 IF X>620 AND B$<>"," THEN GOSUB 2390:GOTO 1260
1280 PSET(X,Y)
1290 SOUND 800,2
1300 IF B$="1" THEN DRAW "U5":X=X+5:GOTO 1260
1310 IF B$="2" THEN DRAW "CO;R4;C1;L4;U3;R4;U2;L4":PS
     ET(X,Y-3),0:PSET(X+4,Y-3),0:PSET(X+4,Y-5),0:X=X+9:GOT
     O 1260
1320 IF B$="3" THEN DRAW "R3;U3;L2;R2;U2;L3":PSET(X+3
     ,Y),0:PSET(X+3,Y-3),0:PSET(X+3,Y-5),0:X=X+9:GOTO 1260

1330 IF B$="4" THEN DRAW "CO;U5;C1;D2;R4;U2;D5":X=X+9
     :GOTO 1260
1340 IF B$="5" THEN DRAW "R4;U3;L4;U2;R3":PSET(X+4,Y),
     0:PSET(X+4,Y-3),0:X=X+9:GOTO 1260
1350 IF B$="6" THEN DRAW "CO;U5;C1;D5;R4;U3;L4":PSET(
     X,Y),0:PSET(X+4,Y),0:PSET(X+4,Y-3),0:X=X+9:GOTO 1260
1360 IF B$="7" THEN DRAW "CO;U5;C1;R4;D5":X=X+9:GOTO
     1260
1370 IF B$="8" THEN DRAW "U5;R4;D2;L4;R4;D3;L4":PSET(
     X,Y),0:PSET(X+4,Y),0:PSET(X+4,Y-3),0:PSET(X,Y-3),0:PS
     ET(X,Y-5),0:PSET(X+4,Y-5),0:X=X+9:GOTO 1260
1380 IF B$="9" THEN DRAW "CO;R4;C1;U5;L4;D2;R4":PSET(
     X,Y-5),0:PSET(X,Y-3),0:PSET(X,Y-5),0:PSET(X+4,Y-5),0:
     X=X+9:GOTO 1260
1390 IF B$="0" THEN DRAW "U5;R4;D5;L4":PSET(X,Y),0:PS
     ET(X,Y-5),0:PSET(X+4,Y),0:PSET(X+4,Y-5),0:X=X+9:GOTO
     1260
1400 IF B$="/" THEN DRAW "R1;U1;R1;U1;R1;U1;R1;U1;R1;
     U1":X=X+9:GOTO 1260
1410 IF B$="-" THEN DRAW "CO;U2;C1;R4":X=X+9:GOTO 126
     0
1420 IF B$="A" OR B$="a" THEN DRAW "U5;R5;D5;U3;L4":P
     SET(X,Y-5),0:PSET(X+5,Y-5),0:X=X+9:GOTO 1260
```

```
1430 IF B$="B" OR B$="b" THEN DRAW "U5;R4;D2;L4;R4;D3
     ;L4":PSET(X+4,Y),0:PSET(X+4,Y-3),0:PSET(X+4,Y-5),0:X=
     X+7:GOTO 1260
1440 IF B$="C" OR B$="c" THEN DRAW "R4;L4;U5;R4":PSET
     (X,Y),0:PSET(X,Y-5),0:X=X+9:GOTO 1260
1450 IF B$="D" OR B$="d" THEN DRAW "U5;R4;D5;L4":PSET
     (X+4,Y),0:PSET(X+4,Y-5),0:X=X+9:GOTO 1260
1460 IF B$="E" OR B$="e" THEN DRAW "R5;L5;U3;R2;L2;U2
     ;R5":X=X+9:GOTO 1260
1470 IF B$="F" OR B$="f" THEN DRAW "U3;R2;L2;U2;R4":X
     =X+8:GOTO 1260
1480 IF B$="G" OR B$="g" THEN DRAW "C0;U5;R4;C1;L4;D5
     ;R4;U2;L2":PSET(X,Y),0:PSET(X,Y-5),0:PSET(X+4,Y),0:X=
     X+9:GOTO 1260
1490 IF B$="H" OR B$="h" THEN DRAW "U5;D2;R5;U2;D5":X
     =X+9:GOTO 1260
1500 IF B$="I" OR B$="i" THEN DRAW "C0;R1;C1;U5":X=X+
     6:GOTO 1260
1510 IF B$="J" OR B$="j" THEN DRAW "U2;D2;R4;U5":PSET
     (X,Y),0:PSET(X+4,Y),0:X=X+9:GOTO 1260
1520 IF B$="K" OR B$="k" THEN DRAW "U5;D2;R2;U1;R2;U1
     ":X=X+5:PSET(X,Y):DRAW "U1;L2;U1;L2":X=X+5:GOTO 1260
1530 IF B$="L" OR B$="l" THEN DRAW "U5;D5;R4":X=X+8:G
     OTO 1260
1540 IF B$="M" OR B$="m" THEN DRAW "U5;R3;D2;U2;R3;D5
     ":X=X+10:GOTO 1260
1550 IF B$="N" OR B$="n" THEN DRAW "U5;F5;U5":X=X+9:G
     OTO 1260
1560 IF B$="O" OR B$="o" THEN DRAW "U5;R4;D5;L4":PSET
     (X,Y),0:PSET(X,Y-5),0:PSET(X+4,Y),0:PSET(X+4,Y-5),0:X
     =X+9:GOTO 1260
1570 IF B$="P" OR B$="p" THEN DRAW "U5;R5;D3;L3":PSET
     (X,Y-5),0:PSET(X+5,Y-5),0:PSET(X+5,Y-2),0:X=X+9:GOTO
     1260
1580 IF B$="Q" OR B$="q" THEN DRAW "U5;R5;D6;U1;L5":P
     SET(X,Y),0:PSET(X,Y-5),0:PSET(X+5,Y-5),0:X=X+9:GOTO 1
     260
1590 IF B$="R" OR B$="r" THEN DRAW "U5;R5;D3;L3;F3":P
     SET(X,Y-5),0:PSET(X+5,Y-5),0:PSET(X+5,Y-2),0:X=X+9:GO
     TO 1260
1600 IF B$="S" OR B$="s" THEN DRAW "R4;U3;L4;U2;R4":P
     SET(X+4,Y),0:PSET(X,Y-3),0:PSET(X+4,Y-3),0:PSET(X,Y-5
     ),0:X=X+9:GOTO 1260
1610 IF B$="T" OR B$="t" THEN DRAW "C0;U5;C1;R4;L2;D5
     ":X=X+8:GOTO 1260
1620 IF B$="U" OR B$="u" THEN DRAW "U5;D5;R6;U5":PSET
     (X,Y),0:PSET(X+6,Y),0:X=X+10:GOTO 1260
1630 IF B$="V" OR B$="v" THEN PSET(X,Y),0:LINE (X,Y-5
     )-(X+2,Y):LINE(X+2,Y)-(X+4,Y-5):X=X+8:GOTO 1260
1640 IF B$="W" OR B$="w" THEN DRAW "C0;U5;C1;D5;R3;U2
     ;D2;R3;U5":X=X+10:GOTO 1260
1650 IF B$="X" OR B$="x" THEN DRAW "C0;U5;C1;F5":PSET
     (X,Y):DRAW "E5":X=X+9:GOTO 1260
1660 IF B$="Y" OR B$="y" THEN DRAW "C0;U5;C1;D2;R5;L2
     ;D3;U3;R3;U2":PSET(X,Y-3),0:PSET(X+6,Y-3),0:X=X+10:GO
     TO 1260
```

```
1670 IF B$="Z" OR B$="z" THEN DRAW "C0;R5;C1;L5;C0;U5
     ;C1;R5;G5":X=X+9:GOTO 1260
1680 IF B$="." THEN PSET(X,Y):X=X+3:GOTO 1260
1690 IF B$=CHR$(32) THEN:PSET(X,Y),0:X=X+9:GOTO 1260
1700 IF B$=CHR$(44) THEN:PSET(X,Y),0: GOTO 1230
1710 IF A$="W" OR A$="w" GOTO 1260 ELSE 1720
1720 F=0:S=1:LOCATE 1,50:PRINT"(C)opyright 1987 Tab B
     ooks Inc.":GOTO 260
1730 END
1740 GOSUB 2300
1750 LOCATE 25,1:INPUT;"Enter Size of Circle Desired
     (1/2/3) ",B
1760 IF B>3 OR B<1 THEN GOTO 1230
1770 PSET(X,Y)
1780 ON B GOTO 1790,1800,1810
1790 CIRCLE(X+6,Y),5:S=1:GOTO 1230
1800 CIRCLE(X+11,Y),10:S=1:GOTO 1230
1810 CIRCLE(X+21,Y),20:S=1:GOTO 1230
1820 END
1830 GOSUB 2300:LOCATE 25,1:PRINT "Cursor Express ON"
     ;
1840 PSET(X,Y),0
1850 A$=INKEY$
1860 IF A$="J" OR A$="j" GOTO 1920
1870 X=STICK(0):Y=STICK(1)
1880 IF POINT(X*6,Y*1.8)=0 THEN 1890 ELSE X=X+1:Y=Y+1
     :GOTO 1870
1890 PSET(X*6,Y*1.8):FOR AA=1 TO 100:NEXT AA:PSET(X*6
     ,Y*1.8),0
1900 IF X*6>=0 AND X*6<14 AND Y*1.8>=0 AND Y*1.6<5 TH
     EN LOCATE 25,1:PRINT"No Joystick Connected to Port";:
     FOR T=1 TO 2000:NEXT:X=320:Y=90:GOTO 1230
1910 GOTO 1850
1920 X=INT(X*6):Y=INT(Y*1.8)
1930 IF X>600 THEN X=620
1940 IF X<0 THEN X=1
1950 IF Y<11 THEN Y=12
1960 IF Y>180 THEN Y=185
1970 A3=X:A4=Y:PSET(X,Y),1:S=1:GOTO 1230
1980 END
1990 GOSUB 2300:A$="CLEARSCR":GOTO 1210
2000 END
2010 A$="CLEARSCR":GOTO 1130
2020 END
2030 PSET(X,Y),0:A$="DATA":GOTO 1120
2040 END
2050 SOUND 800,2:LOCATE 25,1:INPUT;"Hit <ENTER> to Co
     ntinue...",AA$:RETURN
2060 END
2070 PSET(X,Y),0:BSAVE"DATA.PIX",0,16384
2080 CLS:LOCATE 1,27:PRINT"Current Filenames on Disk"

2090 FILES
2100 LOCATE 25,1:INPUT;"When Ready - Hit <ENTER> ",ZZ
     $
2110 IF ZZ$="KILL" OR ZZ$="kill" THEN LOCATE 25,1:INP
```

```
      UT;"Which file shall I kill (must include extension)
      ",QQ$:IF QQ$="" THEN GOTO 2120 ELSE KILL QQ$:GOTO 208
      0:ELSE GOTO 2120
2120 CLS:BLOAD"DATA.PIX",0:CLOSE:RUN 230
2130 END
2140 DEF SEG
2150 GOSUB 2300:SOUND 800,2
2160 LOCATE 25,1:INPUT;"Enter filename of .LIB Graphi
      c to be SAVED (No extension needed) ",SS$
2170 IF SS$="" THEN DEF SEG=&HB800:RUN 230
2180 BSAVE SS$+".LIB",VARPTR(B(0)),5200
2190 CLOSE:DEF SEG=&HB800:GOTO 1230
2200 END
2210 DEF SEG
2220 GOSUB 2300:SOUND 800,2
2230 LOCATE 25,1:INPUT;"Enter filename of .LIB Graphi
      c to be LOADED (No extension needed) ",SS$
2240 IF SS$="" THEN DEF SEG=&HB800:GOTO 1230
2250 PSET(X,Y),0
2260 BLOAD SS$+".LIB",VARPTR(B(0))
2270 PUT(X,Y),B
2280 CLOSE:DEF SEG=&HB800:GOTO 1230
2290 END
2300 LOCATE 25,1:PRINT SPACE$(80);:RETURN
2310 END
2320 LOCATE 25,1:INPUT;"Do you wish this Image be SAV
      ED in the Library (Y/N) ",ZZ$:IF ZZ$="Y" OR ZZ$="y" T
      HEN GOSUB 2140 ELSE GOTO 1230
2330 END
2340 GOSUB 2300:LOCATE 25,1:INPUT;"Do you wish to LOA
      D from <1> .LIB (Library) or <2> .PIX (Picture) file
      ";ZZ$
2350 IF ZZ$="1" THEN GOTO 2210
2360 IF ZZ$="2" THEN GOTO 1150
2370 IF ZZ$<>"1" OR ZZ$<>"2" THEN GOTO 1230
2380 END
2390 FOR I=1 TO 10:SOUND 800,1:SOUND 0,1:NEXT:RETURN
2400 END
2410 Y=190:RETURN
2420 Y=10:RETURN
2430 X=0:RETURN
2440 X=639:RETURN
2450 END
2460 GOSUB 2300:LOCATE 25,30:PRINT"=> File Not Found
      <=";:GOSUB 2390:FOR I=1 TO 2000:NEXT:IF ERL=2110 THEN
      GOTO 2120 ELSE RUN 230
2470 GOTO 2120
```

Line 500 is a command that enables (turns on) a key trapping routine. This command instructs the computer to watch for a keyboard input (the pressing of any of the four arrow keys). These keys allow you to draw a line in the direction of the arrow key that has been pressed. Lines 460 to 490 are branching commands. For example, if the up arrow (key 11) is pressed the computer branches to program line 610. If the left arrow key (key 12) is pressed, the computer branches control to line 550, and so on.

The branching indicated within lines 460 to 490 instructs the computer to add or subtract one pixel element to the dot on the screen in either the X or Y positions. This addition or subtraction actually moves the dot (Drawing Cursor) around the screen.

Using Screen 2, you have 620 pixel elements in the X direction and 200 pixel elements in the Y direction (the X direction is on the horizontal axis of the computer monitor, while the Y direction is its vertical axis).

Program lines 670 to 1050 contain the pre-programmed electronic schematic symbols. These symbols can be placed at any screen location using the component insert (I) mode. Figures 1-8 and 1-9 display the 30 available symbols.

By using a Library feature (which can be seen in Lines 2160 and 2230) additional symbols can be added at any time. This is explained in greater detail later on.

To draw a pre-programmed symbol, you must first give the computer a reference point in the form of X/Y coordinates. This reference indicates where the symbol is to be drawn on the screen. This is accomplished by Line 710 (PSET (X,Y)), pressing the I (component insert) key.

SAVING AND LOADING GRAPHICS

To save and load schematic designs, two special DOS commands are used: BSAVE, used to save on disk the contents of the computer monitor; and BLOAD, used to load a saved graphic back onto the monitor. Unlike its BASIC counterparts (LOAD and SAVE) which can only load and save BASIC program material on disk, BLOAD and BSAVE can be programmed to store or load specific computer memory on disk. In the case of the two CAE programs, the memory to be saved or loaded is the video memory. This memory contains all the graphic information displayed on the screen. By doing this, you can save schematics and/or PC board designs on disk under a filename of your own choosing (using the "S" option). Then, by using the BLOAD command, the image can be displayed at any time (the L option), ready for additional printing or editing.

The BSAVE command is a one-line statement but very powerful. Refer to Line 1130 of the Schematic Designer Main Program A.

```
1100 BSAVE A$ + ".PIX",0,16384
```

BSAVE indicates to the computer that selected computer memory is to be saved on disk (Drive A). A$ is the filename of the design to be saved. This A$ was given a name by line 1100 which asked for this keyboard input. The string .PIX is a filename extension. It is placed automatically at the end of all filenames, indicating that these files are image memory files that contain a picture of the entire computer monitor.

The number 0 tells the computer to start saving the image file at the upper left hand corner of the monitor. By using the command DEF SEG = &hB800

(this command can be seen in Line 220) in conjunction with BSAVE and BLOAD, you are telling the computer that the video starting memory address is located at this point.

The number 16384 indicates the amount of memory that should be saved on disk. This memory location is for the lower right hand corner of the screen. Using the DEF SEG and BSAVE commands saves everything that appears on the screen from the upper left corner of the screen (Location 0) to the lower right corner (Location 16384). This saves the electronic schematic which just has been drawn.

Now, let's look at BSAVE's counterpart—the BLOAD command. The BLOAD command appears in Line 1210 of the Schematic Designer Main Program A.

```
1200 BLOAD A$+".PIX",0
```

BLOAD tells the computer to load a previously saved graphic back onto the monitor. A$ is the filename of the graphic to be loaded back into computer memory. This A$ was given a name in line 1180 which asked for this input. The variable 0, again, is the starting video memory address which was indicated to the computer by Line 220 (DEF SEG=&hB800). The ending address, the lower right corner of the monitor (16384 used in the BSAVE example), is not needed with BLOAD. The computer automatically loads the entire amount of memory that was saved using BSAVE.

PROGRAMMING

It's now time to put this theory into practice, and program the computer. Schematic Designer is broken into four parts. Program and save each section as it is presented in the following pages.

As you can see, Schematic Designer is a long program, so take your time. Follow each line and type it exactly as it appears. The time taken now will be time saved debugging the finished product.

The first program is the Introduction (Listing 1-1). It has 144 lines. Before programming, make sure any resident program (any program already in memory) is erased. To do this, type NEW and then press <ENTER> or <RETURN>.

You are now ready to program the Introduction. When finished, put an empty formatted disk into Drive A, type SAVE "INTRO" and press <ENTER> or <RETURN>. The Introduction is then saved on disk.

The second program to be typed is the Designer (see Listing 1-2). Before typing in the program, you must clear the Introduction program from the computer memory. Type NEW and then press <ENTER> or <RETURN>. The internal computer memory is now cleared, and ready for the Designer Program.

The Designer Program contains all drawing commands as well as the 30 programmed electronic symbols. The most complicated section of the program lies within lines 670 to 1050, which contains DRAW statements for the electronic symbols.

When you're finished typing the Designer Program insert the disk containing the Introduction (INTRO) into Drive A, type SAVE ''DESIGNER'' and press <ENTER> or <RETURN>. Main Program A is saved on disk under the filename DESIGNER.

With the Designer Program now saved on disk, type NEW and press <ENTER> or <RETURN> to clear the computer's memory. You can now type in the Help screens (Listing 1-3).

Listing 1-3. Schematic Designer Help program listing.

```
10 REM   CAE Program   Schematic Designer  * HELP *
20 REM
30 REM      ==> SAVE UNDER FILENAME "HELP" <==
40 CLS
50 KEY OFF
60 SCREEN 2
70 LOCATE 1,33:PRINT"H E L P"
80 LOCATE 5,1
90 PRINT CHR$(24);:PRINT" - - - - - Moves Drawing Cur
   sor in the UP Direction"
100 PRINT CHR$(25);:PRINT" - - - - - Moves Drawing Cu
    rsor in the DOWN Direction"
110 PRINT CHR$(26);:PRINT" - - - - - Moves Drawing Cu
    rsor to the RIGHT"
120 PRINT CHR$(27);:PRINT" - - - - - Moves Drawing Cu
    rsor to the LEFT"
130 PRINT
140 PRINT"Key Board LETTER KEYS":PRINT
150 PRINT"D - - - - - Press the 'D' key to draw lines
    on the screen. In this mode,"
160 PRINT"           you can press any of the four A
    rrow keys and leave a trace of the"
170 PRINT"           movement. To EXIT, press the 'D
    ' key again."
180 PRINT
190 PRINT"R - - - - - By pressing the 'R' key, you wi
    ll be able to Clear the screen of"
200 PRINT"           ALL graphic material. In the lo
    wer left hand corner of the screen,"
210 PRINT"           you will be asked again if you
    wish to clear the monitor. Respond"
220 PRINT"           by entering a Y for Yes or N fo
    r No. Then press <ENTER>."
230 GOSUB 1100
240 PRINT"G - - - - - Saves desired graphic in comput
    er memory. You are asked if this"
250 PRINT"           image will be saved in the Libr
    ary File. You respond by typing Y"
260 PRINT"           for Yes or N for No. If you ans
    wer Yes, you will then be asked to"
270 PRINT"           give this new image a name. Res
    pond by entering a Filename. Then"
```

```
280 PRINT"            press the <ENTER> key. The imag
    e will now be saved on Disk. You may"
290 PRINT"            recall this image at any time b
    y using the 'L' (LOAD) option."
300 PRINT"            This option requires you to inp
    ut two diagonal X/Y coordinates."
310 PRINT"            Do this by pressing the 'G' key
    twice when at the desired locations."
320 PRINT
330 PRINT"A - - - - - With an image in computer memor
    y, (placed there by using the 'G'"
340 PRINT"            or 'L' option) the 'A' key allo
    ws the computer to Draw this in"
350 PRINT"            memory graphic at the indicated
    X/Y coordinates. By pressing"
360 PRINT"            the 'A' key for a second time,
    the computer will Erase the image"
370 PRINT"            just drawn but leaving any prev
    iously drawn material untouched."
380 PRINT
390 PRINT"E - - - - - This option ERASEs a section of
    your graphic. The 'E' option is used"
400 PRINT"            in the same manner as the 'G' o
    ption (two Diagonal X/Y coordinates"
410 PRINT"            are needed). Instead of saving
    the image in computer memory, the"
420 PRINT"            ERASE option paints this graphi
    c section BLACK, thus erasing"
430 PRINT"            the image."
440 PRINT
450 PRINT"I - - - - - INSERTS component of your choos
    ing at any location on screen."
460 PRINT"            Enter number of component to be
    printer."
470 GOSUB 1100
480 PRINT"S - - - - - SAVEs Complete Screen on Disk A
    - You enter Filename when requested."
490 PRINT
500 PRINT"C - - - - - Leads you to a Sub-routine that
    allows you to choose any one of"
510 PRINT"            three pre-programmed Circle Siz
    es."
520 PRINT
530 PRINT"L - - - - - LOADs a Complete Screen or Libr
    ary symbol from Disk A. You enter"
540 PRINT"            the number 1 if you wish to LOA
    D an image from the Library, or"
550 PRINT"            enter the number 2 if you wish
    to LOAD an image from the Picture"
560 PRINT"            File. Then when asked, enter th
    e Filename of the image. When loaded,"
570 PRINT"            the graphic will be displayed a
    t the location of the Drawing"
580 PRINT"            Cursor."
590 PRINT
```

```
600 PRINT"W - - - - - Used to print letters and numbe
    rs at any location on the screen."
610 PRINT"          Hit the Comma ',' key to EXIT."

620 PRINT
630 PRINT"P - - - - - Used to Draw Diagonal Lines - N
    eeds two X/Y coordinates. Move the"
640 PRINT"          Drawing Cursor to the desired l
    ocation. Then press the 'P' key once."
650 PRINT"          Now move the Cursor to the seco
    nd X/Y coordinates. Press the 'P' key"
660 PRINT"          again. Your computer now connec
    ts these two locations using a"
670 PRINT"          straight line."
680 GOSUB 1100
690 LOCATE 2,1
700 PRINT"J - - - - - By pressing the 'J' key, you ar
    e placed in the Cursor Express Mode."
710 PRINT"          If you have a Joystick or Graph
    ic Table connected to the LEFT"
720 PRINT"          Joystick Port, you can now move
    the Drawing Cursor around the"
730 PRINT"          screen faster then if the Arrow
    Keys were used. When at the desired"
740 PRINT"          location, press the 'J' key for
    the second time. You will now be"
750 PRINT"          able to Draw, Erase or Insert C
    omponents at the new coordinates."
760 PRINT
770 PRINT"T - - - - - Draws a small circle - used to
    indicate a TERMINATION Point on"
780 PRINT"          the schematic. (ex. Connection
    to the outside world)
790 PRINT
800 PRINT"Print - - - Used to print your schematic on
    a graphic Printer."
810 PRINT"or          Which button to press depends o
    n the type of computer you have."
820 PRINT"Shift/Print Consult your BASIC Instruction
    Booklet for additional information."
830 PRINT
840 PRINT"F - - - - - The 'F' option allows you to di
    splay ALL filenames saved on Disk A."
850 PRINT"          You may also DELETE Files just
    by typing - KILL - to the prompt"
860 PRINT"          <Hit Enter to Continue>. Then t
    ype in the filename you wish to"
870 PRINT"          Delete - then press <ENTER>. NO
    TE - this filename MUST contain the"
880 PRINT"          extension (ex. .LIB - .BAS ect.)"

890 GOSUB 1100
900 LOCATE 3,1
910 PRINT"To exit from any required keyboard input (E
    x. Entering a Filename or Component"
```

```
920 PRINT"Number) just press the <ENTER> Key without
    entering any information. Your"
930 PRINT"computer will cancel that input and return
    you to the Drawing Mode."
940 PRINT
950 PRINT"When requested to enter a filename of an im
    age that will be LOADED or SAVED,"
960 PRINT"you are NOT required to add the extension (
    ex. .LIB or .PIX). These"
970 PRINT"extensions are automatically inserted by th
    e computer."
980 PRINT"Extensions are required ONLY if you intend
    to KILL a File when the 'F' option"
990 PRINT"is being used."
1000 PRINT
1010 PRINT"The extension .LIB indicates ALL Files tha
     t have been SAVED as a Library File."
1020 PRINT
1030 PRINT"The extension .PIX indicates ALL Files tha
     t were SAVED as an Image File."
1040 PRINT
1050 PRINT"An image File is a file that has SAVED the
     entire contents of the screen on"
1060 PRINT"Disk."
1070 GOSUB 1100
1080 GOTO 1120
1090 END
1100 LOCATE 25,1:INPUT;"Hit <ENTER> to Continue ....."
     ,AA$:CLS:RETURN
1110 END
1120 CLS:RUN"DATA2.BAS"
```

This is a 112 line program—it should not take you too long to type in. Be careful not to type any errors. When complete, type SAVE "HELP". With the disk containing the Introduction and the Designer Programs inserted in Drive A, press <ENTER>. The third of the four programs is now saved on the disk.

The fourth program is Main Program B (Listing 1-4). Since this program is almost identical to Main Program A, let's reload Main Program A. To do this, insert the program disk in Drive A, type LOAD "DESIGNER" and then <ENTER> or <RETURN>.

The Designer Program is loaded within a few seconds. When it is loaded, type DELETE 10-210 and press <ENTER>. Program lines 10 through 210 are erased from memory. These lines will be replaced by the 19 lines listed as the Main Program B. Type these additional lines as they appear.

When complete, save this entire program under the filename DATA2. This completes all the programming required for the Electronic Schematic Designer.

ELECTRONIC SCHEMATIC DESIGNER COMMANDS

Now with all the Schematic Designer Program material saved on disk, let's start doing something with it. This assumes that you have booted up your system with MS-DOS or PC-DOS and a Graphic Utility.

Listing 1-4. Schematic Designer Main Program B listing.

```
 1 REM     Schematic Designer       MAIN PROGRAM "B"
 2 REM
 3 REM     This program is protected under the laws of
 4 REM     the United States of America. Any
 5 REM     publication or reproduction in any form -
 6 REM     without the expressed written consent of
 7 REM     the author or Tab Books Inc. is prohibited.
 8 REM
 9 REM               (C)opyright 1987
10 REM
11 REM               Version 5.10
12 REM
13 REM
14 REM      ==> SAVE UNDER FILENAME "DATA2" <==
15 REM
16 KEY OFF
17 CLS
18 SCREEN 2,,0,0
19 BLOAD"DATA.PIX",0:CLOSE
```

With BASICA residing in computer memory, insert the Schematic Designer Disk into Drive A, then type RUN "INTRO" and press <ENTER>. Within a second or so, your computer displays the Introduction screen. This is the first of seven screens. To display each one of the seven, just press the <ENTER> or <RETURN> key.

For a printout of how your computer monitor should look at this stage, refer to Chapter 3. This chapter provides complete graphic display of each screen of both the Schematic Program as well as the PC Board Designer Program.

When all seven screens have been displayed, your computer automatically loads and runs the Designer Program (filename "DESIGNER").

Now with Schematic Designer loaded, it's time to discuss in detail each command available in the program.

Reset

Before using Schematic Designer, you must make a screen reset memory image file. (See Fig. 1-10.) This option clears the contents of the screen of all graphic material. Whatever is on the screen at this time is lost from memory.

When "DESIGNER" is loaded and running, a frame is drawn and copyright credits are displayed. The center of the display is empty. Press the "S" key (which saves the drawing on disk). In the lower left corner, you are prompted to enter a filename. Type "CLEARSCR".

With the Schematic Designer Program Disk in Drive A, press the <ENTER> or <RETURN> key. The drive turns on indicating that the monitor's contents are being saved. You can use the "R" (RESET) option any time you wish to clear the screen of all material (except for the program frame and credits).

With the screen cleared, you can now start drawing some kind of graphic.

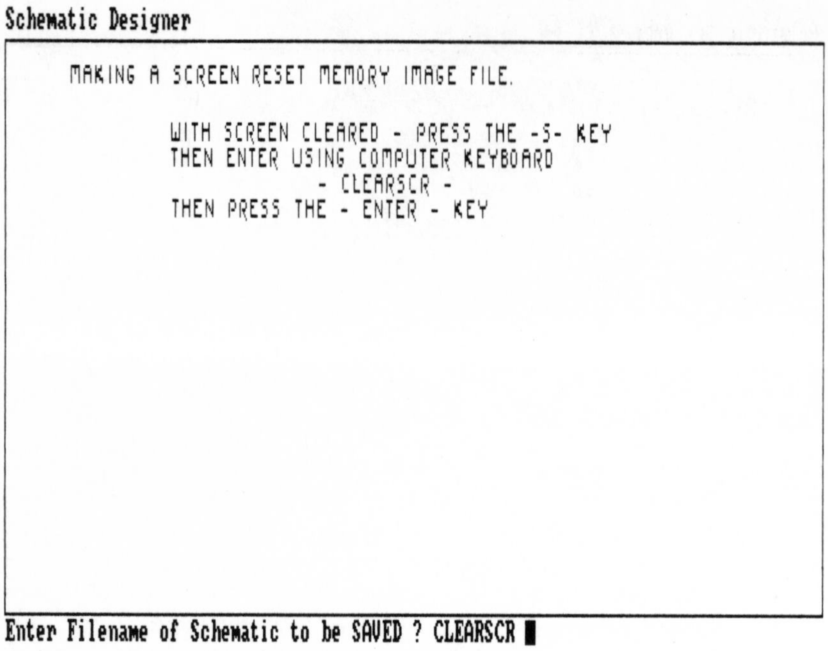

Schematic Designer

```
┌────────────────────────────────────────────────────────────┐
│                                                              │
│      MAKING A SCREEN RESET MEMORY IMAGE FILE.                │
│                                                              │
│              WITH SCREEN CLEARED - PRESS THE -S- KEY         │
│              THEN ENTER USING COMPUTER KEYBOARD              │
│                       - CLEARSCR -                           │
│              THEN PRESS THE - ENTER - KEY                    │
│                                                              │
│                                                              │
│                                                              │
│                                                              │
│                                                              │
│                                                              │
│                                                              │
│                                                              │
│                                                              │
│                                                              │
│                                                              │
│                                                              │
│                                                              │
│                                                              │
└────────────────────────────────────────────────────────────┘
```

Enter Filename of Schematic to be SAVED ? CLEARSCR ▮

Fig. 1-10. Making a reset screen for the Schematic Designer Program.

Arrow Keys

To move the Drawing Cursor to any location on the screen (within the limits of the frame) use the four arrow keys. (See Fig. 1-11.)

Go ahead—press the up arrow. The Drawing Cursor moves up. You will also hear beeps as the dot moves up the screen. The frequency of the beeps depends on the direction the dot is moving. Now press the down arrow. The cursor moves in the downward direction. The left arrow moves the cursor left, while the right arrow moves it right.

If you run this program with an IBM Computer, the volume of the beeps is soft and low, while for those who have a Tandy 1000 or some other type of compatible, very loud tones come from the speaker. The volume is dependent on a BASIC command that is used by compatibles but not by IBM computers. This is the Sound command. We'll discuss how to modify the program a little later.

Drawing a Line

To draw a line press the "D" key once. Now hit the arrow key for the direction you wish to draw a line (Fig. 1-12). The Drawing Cursor now leaves a trace. Try the other three arrow keys. The cursor moves in the direction associated with that key and also leaves a trace.

To exit from the drawing mode press the "D" key for a second time. Now press any of the arrow keys. The Drawing Cursor moves but does not leave any trace.

Schematic Designer

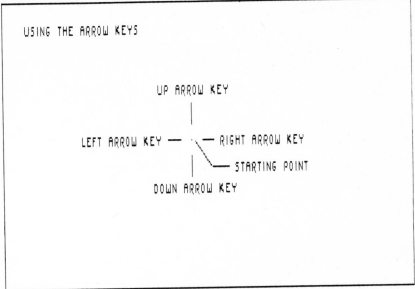

Fig. 1-11. Using the arrow keys to move the Drawing Cursor.

Schematic Designer

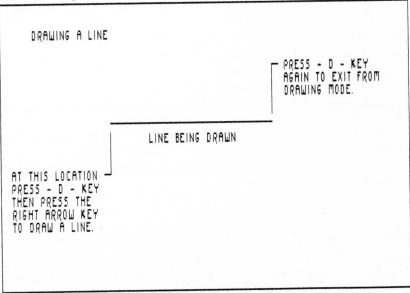

Fig. 1-12. Drawing a line with the Schematic Designer.

Schematic Designer

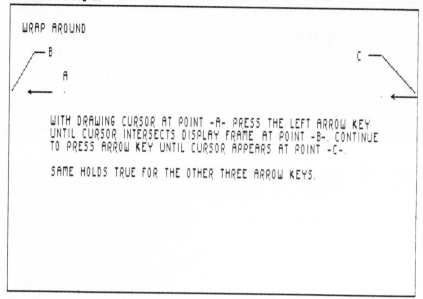

WRAP AROUND

B

A

C

WITH DRAWING CURSOR AT POINT -A- PRESS THE LEFT ARROW KEY
UNTIL CURSOR INTERSECTS DISPLAY FRAME AT POINT -B-. CONTINUE
TO PRESS ARROW KEY UNTIL CURSOR APPEARS AT POINT -C-.

SAME HOLDS TRUE FOR THE OTHER THREE ARROW KEYS.

Fig. 1-13. Drawing Cursor screen wrap around feature.

Wrap Around Feature

A very useful feature of the Schematic Designer is cursor wrap around. Wrap around describes a feature that allows the cursor to be driven to its outermost limits—in this case, the right display frame—and then be automatically returned to the left section of the screen without losing any display data or information.

An example of wrap around can be seen in Fig. 1-13. The Drawing Cursor can be moved to the left by pressing the arrow key. When it reaches the left display frame, it reappears at the right.

This feature can be used with any of the four arrow keys. For example, when you're drawing a schematic and the cursor is to the extreme left of the monitor, instead of waiting for the cursor to move to the right of the screen using the arrow keys, press the left arrow key until the cursor appears at the right side of the screen.

The Wrap Around feature can also be used when inserting text using the Wording Option.

Erasing a Line

Suppose you made a mistake. You pressed the up arrow key instead of the down. Recovery from this error is quite simple. (See Fig. 1-14.)

The Drawing Cursor comes in two colors, white (standard drawing mode) and black. To control the color of the drawing cursor, the number key 1 is used to change the color of the cursor to white, while the number key 2 is used to

Schematic Designer

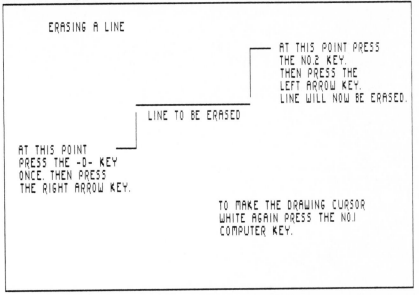

ERASING A LINE

AT THIS POINT PRESS
THE NO.2 KEY.
THEN PRESS THE
LEFT ARROW KEY.
LINE WILL NOW BE ERASED.

LINE TO BE ERASED

AT THIS POINT
PRESS THE -D- KEY
ONCE. THEN PRESS
THE RIGHT ARROW KEY.

TO MAKE THE DRAWING CURSOR
WHITE AGAIN PRESS THE NO.1
COMPUTER KEY.

Fig. 1-14. Erasing a line using the Schematic Designer Program.

change the color to black (background color of the monitor). To erase a mistake, all you have to do is to change the cursor's color to black by pressing the "2" key and then one of the arrow keys.

Clear the screen by pressing the "R" key. (Remember that the Designer Disk must be in Drive A for proper operation.) Draw a line to the right by pressing the "D" key once and then pressing the right arrow key. A line is drawn to the right. Remove your finger from the arrow key. Now press the "2" key. (Do not confuse this with the F2 key.) You can now erase the line by back tracking by pressing the left arrow key. Notice that the line is being erased.

To change the color of the dot to white again hit the "1" key.

Component Insert

Now that you know how to draw and erase a line, the time has come to insert components on the screen. (See Fig. 1-15.) The program has 30 preprogrammed electronic symbols in its memory. These symbols can be seen in Figs. 1-8 and 1-9, along with the component part number for each.

There are symbols for resistors, coils, and capacitors. Each is given a number. To draw a resistor, choose component number one (#1) to number four (#4). Components number three (#3) to number eight (#8) are capacitors.

The letter X appears in Figs. 1-8 and 1-9 to indicate the position where the symbol starts drawing.

Suppose a line has been drawn starting at the left and ending to the right. Let's draw a symbol of a resistor at the end of this line. Figure 1-8 shows that component number one (#1) is a resistor that is drawn from left to right. Press

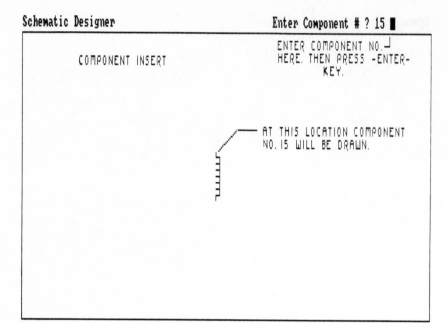

COMPONENT INSERT

ENTER COMPONENT NO. ⌐
HERE. THEN PRESS -ENTER-
KEY.

AT THIS LOCATION COMPONENT
NO. 15 WILL BE DRAWN.

Fig. 1-15. Having the computer draw a pre-programmed electronic symbol.

COMPONENT NO. 1 RESISTOR

Fig. 1-16. Drawing a wire and a resistor (from left to right).

the "I" key for Component Insert Mode. The upper right corner of the monitor reads "Enter Component Number". Type the number one (1). Then press <ENTER> or <RETURN>. The resistor is drawn at that location. (See Fig. 1-16.)

If a line has been drawn from the right to left component number two (#2) should be used, because the starting point of the drawing is at the right and ends at the left. (See Fig. 1-17.)

If a line has been drawn starting from the bottom of the screen and finishing near the top, and a resistor is needed, component number four (#4) should be chosen. Figure 1-8 shows that this resistor drawing starts at the bottom (note the location of the X) and finishes at the top. (See Fig. 1-18.)

If a line has been drawn from the top of the screen to the bottom, component number three (#3) should be used, because the computer draws the symbol from top to bottom. (See Fig. 1-19.)

Fig. 1-17. *Drawing a wire and a resistor (from right to left).*

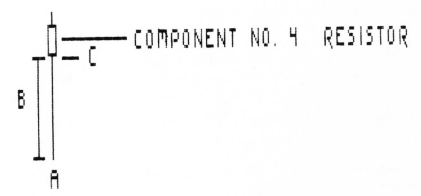

Fig. 1-18. *Drawing a wire and a resistor (from bottom to top).*

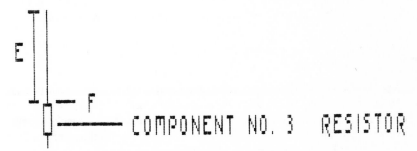

Fig. 1-19. *Drawing a wire and a resistor (From the top to bottom).*

Let's make a drawing together. (Refer to Fig. 1-20.) First, let's clear the screen by pressing the "R" key. Remember that the disk containing the Designer Program must be in Drive A. With the screen cleared and the Drawing Cursor at location A, press the "D" key once. This puts you into the Drawing Mode. By pressing the right arrow key, a line is drawn the length of line B. At location C, press the "I" key for Component Insert Mode. In the upper right corner of the screen, you are prompted to enter the component number

38

CLEAR SCREEN BY PRESSING THE R KEY.

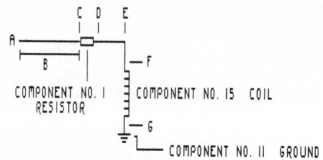

Fig. 1-20. Drawing your first schematic using a computer.

of the symbol you want to draw. At this time, press the "1" key. (This draws a symbol of a resistor which is drawn from the left to the right.) Then by pressing the <ENTER> key, this resistor is drawn instantly. The location of the Drawing Cursor is now at point D. To continue to draw a line, press the "D" key again. Now hit the right arrow key to continue the line.

At point E, press the down arrow key. This draws a continuous line in the downward direction. At point F, let's draw a coil by pressing the "I" key (for Component Insert Mode) and entering the component number of a coil. Type the number 15, then press <ENTER>. The coil is now drawn in the downward direction.

To top off our sample schematic, let's insert a ground Symbol. Using the arrow keys, position the cursor at point G. Then press the "I" key again, and at the prompt – enter number 11 (Component number for a Ground Symbol) then hit <ENTER>.Your finished schematic should look exactly as presented in Fig. 1-20.

Cursor Express

Due to the use of BASIC programming commands, it takes a bit of time to move the Drawing Cursor from one side of the screen to the other. If you have a joystick or graphics tablet handy and your computer is capable of using a joystick, you can take advantage of Cursor Express by connecting its DIN plug to the left joystick port of the computer.

To activate Cursor Express, press the "J" key one time. Now move the joystick handle (or press on the graphics tablet). The Drawing Cursor now moves in the direction you have chosen hundreds of times faster then if you used the four arrow keys.

To exit from Cursor Express just hit the "J" key a second time. You can then draw (using the "D" option) or insert components (using the "I" option) at the new location.

If you have an IBM Computer, an additional Serial Interface board must be purchased if you want to use the Cursor Express. This board plugs directly inside the main body of the computer. When installed, joysticks or graphics tablets can be used with your CAE programs.

If you have a Tandy 1000 or another type of compatible computer, this serial interface may already be factory-installed. Just plug the joystick or graphics tablet into the appropriate DIN socket.

Termination Point

Termination Point is easy to use. It draws a small circle at any cursor location. This circle indicates the end of a schematic line, or a connection to be made to the outside world.

To demonstrate termination point, first clear the screen. Press the "D" key once and use the left arrow key to move the cursor to the left. The cursor leaves a trace as it moves. At the end of this line, add a termination point by releasing the arrow key, and pressing the "T" key. A small circle is drawn at the end of the line.

With the use of Termination Point, pressing the "D" key for a second time to exit from the Drawing Mode is not necessary. (See Fig. 1-21.)

Circle

The Circle option is used to draw any one of three pre-programmed circles, each with a different diameter. Circle #1 is the smallest and Circle #3 is the largest.

To use the Circle option press the "C" key. At the lower left corner of the screen, you are asked "What Size Circle You Wish Drawn?" Respond by entering the number one, two, or three (1, 2, or 3). Then hit <ENTER> or

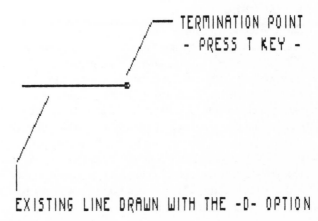

Fig. 1-21. Using the termination option.

CIRCLE OPTION - C -

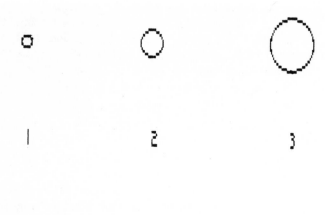

AVAILABLE CIRCLE SIZES 1 - 2 - 3

Fig. 1-22. Using the circle option.

<RETURN>.Your computer draws the circle of the chosen size at the desired screen location. (See Fig. 1-22.)

Save Graphic

Now that you have mastered Draw, Component Insert, Termination Point, and Circle, a means of saving the schematic on disk must be presented.

To save a screen graphic at any time, press the "S" key (see Fig. 1-23). In the lower left corner of the monitor, you are asked to give your schematic a filename. Using the keyboard, type the graphics name, but remember that this entry must be less than eight characters. (Also, do not use any of the reserved words. See the back of the book for a list of reserved words.)

With the Schematic Designer Disk in Drive A, press the <ENTER> or <RETURN> key and Drive A starts to operate. The computer is now saving your schematic on disk under the filename you have chosen with the extension .PIX (for Picture File). This process takes about 5 to 10 seconds, depending on the complexity of the graph.

Schematic Designer

SAVE GRAPHIC

    WITH THE SCHEMATIC YOU WISH SAVED DISPLAYED ON THE
    SCREEN PRESS THE -S- KEY.

    YOU WILL THEN BE ASKED TO GIVE THE IMAGE A FILENAME.
    WHEN COMPLETE PRESS THE -ENTER- KEY.

    IMAGE WILL BE SAVED AS A .PIX FILE..

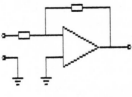

                ENTER FILENAME HERE ⌐

Enter Filename of .PIX Graphic to be SAVED (No extension needed) ∎

Fig. 1-23. Saving an image on disk.

A saved graphic requires a large amount of disk space. The average number of images that can be saved on one disk is approximately six. Keep this in mind when saving your schematic, so you don't run out of disk space.

Loading a Graphic

With a schematic already saved on disk, you can request that the computer instantly display any design at a touch of a button (see Fig. 1-24). To load a previously-saved schematic back into video memory, press the "L" key. Then in the lower left corner of the screen, you are asked if the graphic to be loaded is from the Library File or Picture File. For now, respond by entering the number 2 for Picture File. You are then asked the name of the .PIX (Picture) File to be loaded. Using the keyboard (see Fig. 1-25), type the name of the print. With the disk containing this graphic in Drive A, press the <ENTER> key. Drive A will load this .PIX pattern back into video memory within 2 to 4 seconds, ready for additional editing or printing.

Note: If you choose a filename not contained on the disk the computer is programmed to beep and display an error message within a fraction of a second after the <ENTER> or <RETURN> key is pressed indicating an error has occurred. The schematic already on screen remains with no changes, and the Drawing Cursor is then located in the middle of the screen.

Wording Option

Schematic Designer also allows you to enter any number of characters at any location on the screen (see Fig. 1-26). This is useful to indicate component values and designations. Schematic Designer supports the following characters:

A B C D E F G H I J K L M N O P Q R S T U V W X Y Z
1 2 3 4 5 6 7 8 9 0
– / .
space bar

To activate the Wording option, just press the "W" key. In this mode, you will still be able to use the four arrow keys to move the Drawing Cursor to the location on the screen that you want to print letters and/or numbers. To exit from Wording, just hit the comma key.

Schematic Designer is also equipped with an end of line alarm. While typing, if the printed letters or numbers come within half an inch from the right border of the screen, the computer sounds an alarm. This indicator has the same function as a bell on a typewriter.

When printing at the extreme right border of the screen, press the right arrow key to make use of the Wrap Around feature. The Drawing Cursor appears at the left side of the screen where you can continue entering characters until the comma or the alarm sounds again. Cursor Express does not function in this mode.

Print Line Option

This option allows a line to be drawn at any angle with respect to the horizontal axis. (For example, you can use this option to draw the contacts of an open switch.)

Schematic Designer

```
    LOADING A GRAPHIC




        WITH SCREEN CLEARED OR DISPLAYING AN IMAGE  PRESS
        THE -L- KEY.
        YOU WILL THEN BE ASKED IF THE NEW IMAGE WILL BE
        LOADED FROM THE LIBRARY -.LIB- OR PICTURE -.PIX- FILE.
                    SEE BELOW

        FOR THIS EXAMPLE  ENTER THE NO. 2



                    TYPE NO. 2. THEN PRESS ENTER ----
```

Do you wish to LOAD from (1) .LIB (Library) or (2) .PIX (Picture) file ? 2 ▌

Fig. 1-24. Indicating whether an image is to be loaded from the Library (.LIB) or Picture (.PIX) File.

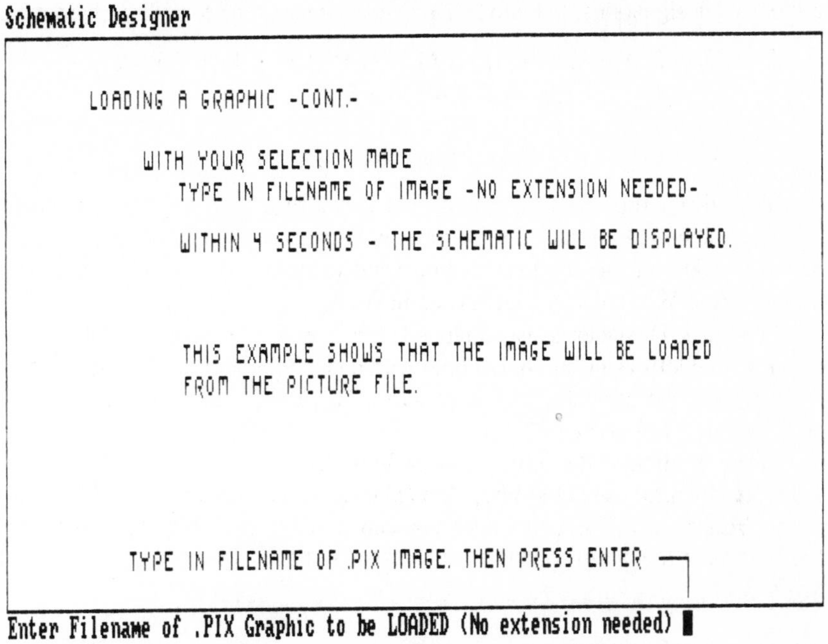

Schematic Designer

```
    LOADING A GRAPHIC -CONT.-

        WITH YOUR SELECTION MADE
            TYPE IN FILENAME OF IMAGE -NO EXTENSION NEEDED-

            WITHIN 4 SECONDS - THE SCHEMATIC WILL BE DISPLAYED.




            THIS EXAMPLE SHOWS THAT THE IMAGE WILL BE LOADED
            FROM THE PICTURE FILE.




        TYPE IN FILENAME OF .PIX IMAGE. THEN PRESS ENTER ─┐
```

Enter Filename of .PIX Graphic to be LOADED (No extension needed) ▌

Fig. 1-25. Loading an image from the Picture (.PIX) File.

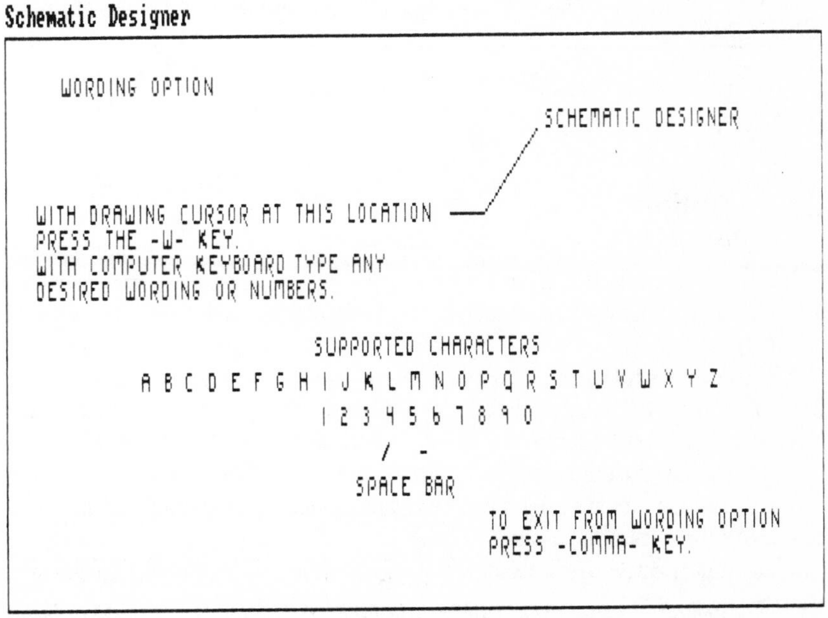

Schematic Designer

```
    WORDING OPTION
                                        ╱ SCHEMATIC DESIGNER


    WITH DRAWING CURSOR AT THIS LOCATION ──╱
    PRESS THE -W- KEY.
    WITH COMPUTER KEYBOARD TYPE ANY
    DESIRED WORDING OR NUMBERS.

                    SUPPORTED CHARACTERS
        A B C D E F G H I J K L M N O P Q R S T U V W X Y Z
                    1 2 3 4 5 6 7 8 9 0
                            /  -
                        SPACE BAR
                            TO EXIT FROM WORDING OPTION
                            PRESS -COMMA- KEY.
```

Fig. 1-26. Schematic Designer's Wording Option.

PRINT LINE OPTION

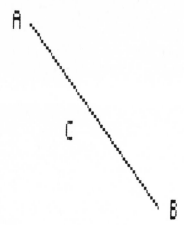

Fig. 1-27. Using the Print option to draw a line on any angle.

Two X, Y coordinates are required to be entered into the computer. This is done by pressing the "P" key twice. In other words, with the Drawing Cursor at the desired screen location, press the "P" key. (At this time no line is drawn.) Move the Drawing Cursor to the second position. Enter this second X, Y coordinate by pressing the "P" key again. The computer now connects these two locations with a solid line. For the next example, see Fig. 1-27.

With the Drawing Cursor at location A, press the "P" key. Now move the cursor to location B. By pressing the "P" key for a second time, line C is drawn connecting these two points.

Erase Option

The Erase option is used to erase any large portion of your schematic. Using the same principle discussed earlier with the Draw option, you can erase a section of the print by coloring that section black, which is the background color of the monitor.

With some kind of print on the screen, use the arrow keys to move the Drawing Cursor to the upper left corner of the section you want to erase. Then press the "E" key. Now move the cursor to a location that is on a diagonal to the first (lower right corner). By pressing the "E" key for a second time, two X, Y coordinates have been entered. The computer then draws an imaginary box using these two locations.

The print located within this imaginary box is then colored black, thus erasing it from the screen.

For a better understanding of the Erase option, let's examine Fig. 1-28. This is a schematic of a working integrated circuit amplifier. Suppose you want

Schematic Designer

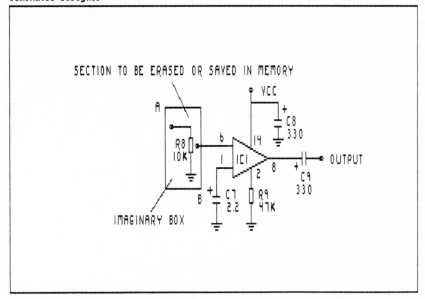

Fig. 1-28. Erase option being used to clear screen of component R8.

to erase the volume control connected to pin 6 of the IC. To do this, move the Drawing Cursor to location A, then press the "E" key. Now move the cursor to location B. Notice that location B is on the diagonal axis to point A. Using these two points, you can create an imaginary box. Located within this box is the volume control you want to erase. By pressing the "E" key for the second time, your computer colors this section black, thus erasing this portion from the screen.

Saving Graphic in Computer Memory

Using the same principle discussed with the Erase option (diagonal X/Y Location Points), a section of a schematic can be stored in computer memory so that it can be re-drawn at a later time.

This option can be used to move sections of a print to another screen location, or it can be drawn again with a completely different circuit. This option also allows you to save these schematic sections on disk as a .Lib (Library) file.

With your monitor showing a print, use the arrow keys to move the Drawing Cursor to the upper left corner of the schematic you want to save. Then press the "G" key. Now move the Drawing Cursor to the diagonal location (lower right corner) and press the "G" key again.

At this time, the computer saves the print located within the imaginary box drawn using these two X, Y coordinates.

Only a limited amount of memory is allocated for graphic Saving, so if the computer takes a split second to record the schematic, the layout was too large for the memory to handle. To compensate for this, break the layout down into a smaller area.

For a better understanding of the GET Option, refer to Fig. 1-28.

Assume you wish to save the 10KΩ volume control of the Integrated Circuit Amplifier. Using the arrow keys or Cursor Express, move the Drawing Cursor to location A. This time, instead of pressing the ''E'' key to erase the image, press the ''G'' key. Now move the cursor to location B. Press the ''G'' key for the second time. Instead of erasing the volume control, the computer now scans the image contained within an imaginary box drawn using coordinates A and B, and saves this graphic within memory, waiting to be placed elsewhere on the screen. Upon completion of this memory save, you are asked if this image should be saved in the Library File. Respond by entering ''Y'' for yes or ''N'' for no. At this time, enter ''N'' for no.

Note that this method of saving a print is volatile. This means that if the computer is turned off for any reason, the schematic saved in this manner is lost from memory. Also, if you save a second image, the first layout is automatically erased from memory to make room for the new one.

Placing Memory Graphic on Screen

With an image saved in computer memory, the A option is used to redraw the schematic elsewhere. Using the arrow keys (or Cursor Express), move the Drawing Cursor to any other section of the screen, being sure that the new location chosen has enough space to redraw the saved print. If not enough space is available, the computer beeps as soon as the ''A'' key is pressed. No graphic is printed; instead, it is lost from memory.

If the above conditions are met, press the ''A'' key. The computer draws the entire print saved in memory using the ''G'' (GET) Option. You can redraw this print any number of times without losing it from memory.

If you are not satisfied with the chosen location of an in-memory print just displayed, press the ''A'' key again, and the print just drawn is erased from the screen. Any previously drawn print is left untouched.

File Option

With a number of files on a disk, you may wonder which images are saved and how much disk space is available for additional files. This is the job of the File option. Without exiting from the Designer Program, you can have all files displayed on the screen along with the amount of available memory.

By pressing the ''F'' key, this can be accomplished. Figure 1-29 is a sample screen display of 19 files. From this display, you can see that there are ten .BAS (BASIC) programs, five .PIX (Picture) files, and four .LIB (Library) files. Also, there are 171008 Bytes of free disk space.

At the bottom of the screen, there is a display prompting you to press <ENTER> to resume the Designer Program. If you type the word ''KILL'' instead, you can delete unwanted or unused files from the disk. When using the Kill option, the extensions associated with the filenames must also be added or an error occurs. For example, if you see:

When Ready - Hit <ENTER>

type

KILL <ENTER>

If you see:

Which File Shall I KILL?

type

CLEAR.PIX <ENTER>

The disk drive starts to operate, and within a few seconds the disk files are displayed again, minus the CLEAR.PIX file.

To exit from the File Option, just press <ENTER> at the ''When Ready - Hit <ENTER>'' prompt.

Hard Copy Print Out

The final option supported by Schematic Designer is the Hard Copy Print Out. When a schematic is displayed on the monitor, press the <SHIFT> and/or

```
                   Current Filenames on Disk
A:\
INTRO    .BAS    DESIGNER.BAS    HELP     .BAS    DATA2    .BAS
DRAW     .BAS    GRAPH   .BAS    INTRO2   .BAS    PCB      .BAS
HELP2    .BAS    PCB2    .BAS    DATA     .PIX    SAMPLE1  .LIB
CLEARSCR.PIX     SAMPLE2 .LIB    CLS      .PIX    DATA3    .PIX
CLEAR    .PIX    SAMPLE3 .LIB    SAMPLE4  .LIB
  171008 Bytes free
```

```
When Ready - Hit <ENTER> ▮
```

Fig. 1-29. Sample computer display of the File option.

<PRINT> key(s) (used on compatibles) or the CTRL and/or PrtSc keys (used on the IBM computers), being sure you have a printer on line.

Within two to three minutes (this time depends on the type of printer used), you will have a high quality draft of the schematic. If you are in doubt which key to push, refer to the computer instruction manual that accompanied your purchase.

Additional Electronic Symbols

By referring to Fig. 1-30, you can see that additional symbols can be drawn using the 30 available drawings. To draw a diode, have the computer draw a resistor in the position desired and then, using the Draw ("D") option, add the cathode band.

To draw a variable capacitor, have the computer draw a capacitor symbol, then, using the Line Print option ("P"), draw a line at an angle through the capacitor.

To draw a transformer, have the computer draw two coil symbols back to back as shown.

By using your imagination, you can create any number of electronic symbols with the available programming.

DRAWING A POWER SUPPLY

By this time, you should have mastered the Schematic Designer commands that allow you to draw a line and insert various electronic components on the screen. So let's draw a complete 12-volt power supply. Figure 1-31 shows how the finished design will look. The following design procedure is listed step by step, so you should not run into any difficulties.

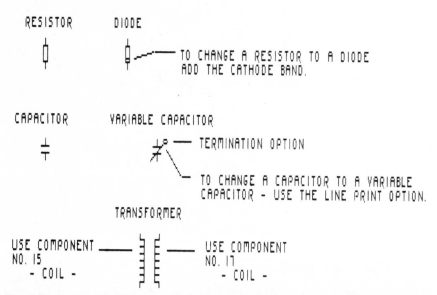

Fig. 1-30. Sample of additional symbols that can be drawn using the existing Designer commands.

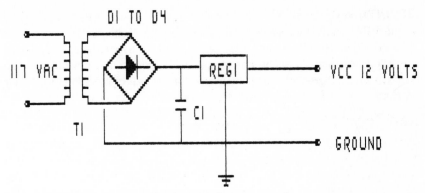

Fig. 1-31. Complete schematic of a 12-volt power supply.

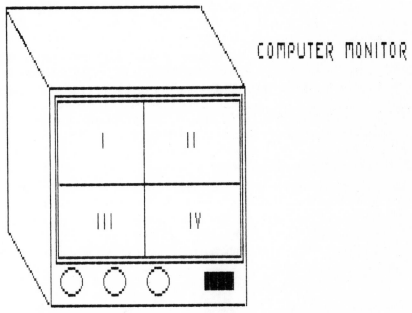

Fig. 1-32. Computer monitor divided into four screen quadrants.

The first problem you will encounter is the starting position, on the screen, of the design. Figure 1-32 shows a computer monitor that has been divided into four equal parts labeled I, II, III, and IV. To draw the power supply, position the Drawing Cursor in quadrant I.

For other, more elaborate designs, only drawing experience will allow you to make the logical decision on where to start. If you find that your design is not centered correctly on the screen, the Get ("G") option can be used to move any section of the layout to a new location.

With Schematic Designer up and running, use the arrow keys (or Cursor Express) to position the Drawing Cursor somewhere within the imaginary borders of screen quadrant I. When positioned, the power supply can be drawn.

Drawing a Transformer

Refer to Fig. 1-33 for the drawing of a transformer. With the Drawing Cursor at location B in quadrant I, press the "I" key. In the upper right corner of the screen, you are asked to enter the component number of the symbol you want to draw. In this case, using the computer keyboard, enter the number 17. This number draws a coil pattern. Hit the <ENTER> key.

Now using the left arrow key, move the Drawing Cursor to location A. Press the "I" key and enter the component number (#15); then hit <ENTER>. At this time, you will have drawn the electronic equivalent of a transformer. Press the "D" key (Draw Mode). Now press the left arrow key. At this time, your computer draws a line (Line A - G). At location G, press the "T" key (Termination Point). A small circle is then drawn indicating a connection to the outside world.

Using the down arrow key, move the cursor to location F. Press the "T" key again. A second circle is drawn. Press the "D" key, then hit the right arrow key to connect points F and E.

Press the "D" key again. (This prevents your computer from drawing any additional lines.) Now move the cursor to the bottom section of the transformers' secondary winding. Press the "D" key and draw a line to location D. Then press the "D" key again. Using the arrow keys, draw line B - C.

At this time, stop and examine your layout. Congratulations! You have drawn your first electronic schematic.

Drawing a Bridge Rectifier

Using the arrow keys, move the Drawing Cursor to location C, then press the "I" key. At this location, the computer will draw a bridge rectifier at the secondary windings of the transformer (see Fig. 1-34). Enter the component number for the bridge rectifier (component #14) then press the <ENTER>key. Upon entering this component number, the rectifier is drawn, connecting points C and D of the transformer.

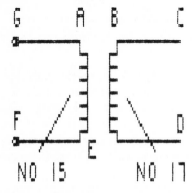

Fig. 1-33. Drawing a transformer.

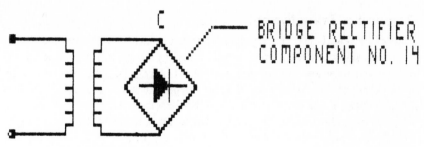

Fig. 1-34. Adding a bridge rectifier.

Drawing the Ground Connection

With the Drawing Cursor at point H, press the "D" key, then the down arrow key until the line reaches location I. (See Fig. 1-35.) You may have noticed that line H - I intersects the transformer's secondary connection to the rectifier. At a location just above this intersecting point, press the "D" key. (This disables the Drawing Mode.) Press the down arrow key until the Drawing Cursor appears at the other side of this transformer connection. Now press the "D" key (which enables the Drawing Mode), and then the down arrow key to continue drawing line H - I.

To draw line I - L, press the right arrow key. At point L, press the "T" key. A termination point is then drawn at the end of this line.

Now position the Drawing Cursor at point J. Press the "D" key and draw line J - K.

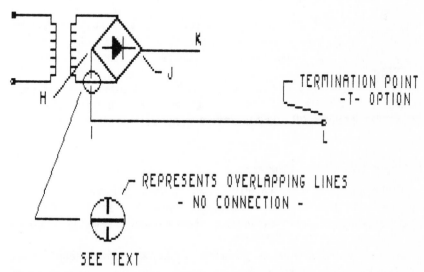

Fig. 1-35. Adding a ground connection to the power supply.

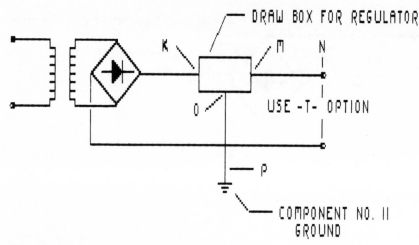

Fig. 1-36. Drawing a voltage regulator and adding the ground symbol.

Adding a Regulator and Ground Symbol

With your Drawing Cursor at point K, draw a box using the arrow keys. (See Fig. 1-36.) This box will represent the voltage regulator of the power supply. To draw the box, press the up arrow key, then the right, then the down, then the left arrow key. The size of the box is not critical, but remember that the Wording option will be used later to give the box a component value, so leave enough room inside for this wording.

Disable the Drawing Mode by pressing the "D" key, then move the cursor to point O. Hit the "D" key to draw line O - P. Notice that this line intersects line I - L. This is allowable, seeing that the voltage regulator must be connected to ground for proper operation. At location P, draw the ground symbol by pressing the "I" key and entering the component number 11. Then hit <ENTER>.

With the ground symbol now drawn, move the Drawing Cursor to point M, then press the "D" key. Using the right arrow key, draw line M - N. At location N, press the "T" key to draw a termination point.

Adding the Filter Capacitor

Using the arrow keys, move the cursor to point Q. Press the "D" key and draw a short line (Line Q - R) using the down arrow key (Fig. 1-37.) At point R, press the "I" key and enter component number seven (#7) to draw the filter capacitor. Hit <ENTER>.

When the capacitor is drawn, press the "D" key again and continue to draw line S until it intersects line I - L.

The drawing of the power supply is now complete.

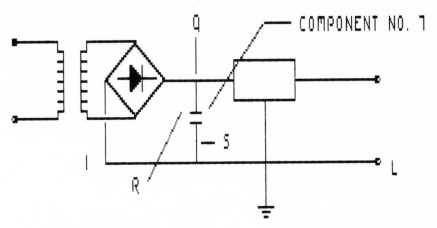

Fig. 1-37. Adding the filter capacitor.

Adding Component Values

Now that the schematic of the power supply is complete, let's start labeling the components and indicate the input and output connections using the Wording option (Fig. 1-38).

With the Drawing Cursor at location T, press the "W" key. Your computer indicates that you are in the Wording Mode by displaying this fact at the lower left corner of the screen. If you wish to exit from this mode, press the comma key.

At location T, type the wording "117 VAC" making sure there is enough room to the left of the schematic to prevent overlapping. Now, still in the Wording Option, move the cursor to location U. Then type "T1". This is the transformer label.

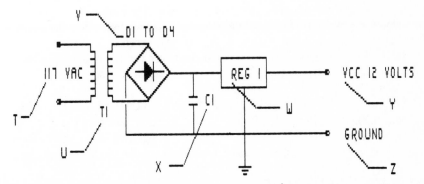

Fig. 1-38. Using the Wording option to label the power supply.

At point V, type "D1 to D4". This indicates the component labeling of the four diodes used to make up a bridge rectifier. At location X, type "C1" for the filter capacitor.

At point W (located inside the regulator box), type "REG1" to designate the voltage regulator.

At point Y, type "VCC 12 Volts". This is the positive voltage output of the supply.

Type "Ground" at point Z. This is the common connection point of the supply.

When complete, press the comma key to exit the Wording Option. You are now in the Draw Mode. You can now make any last minute corrections to the design using standard drawing commands before saving the print to disk.

When the schematic is to your liking, press the "S" key (for the Save option). With the Schematic Designer Program Disk in Drive A, type "PS12V". Then press <ENTER>. The schematic is then saved on disk under the filename "PS12V.PIX".

If you want, you can press the "F" key. This option displays all filenames contained on the disk located in Drive A. When displayed, look for the filename of the 12 volt power supply to make sure that it has been saved and notice the amount of remaining free disk space. If this amount should drop below 10000 bytes, it's time to insert another formatted disk. Remember that this new disk should contain the CAE programming material.

ADDING YOUR OWN ELECTRONIC SYMBOLS

If the 30 electronic symbols that are programmed in the Schematic Designer Program were all that you needed to draw any schematic, then this section would not be needed. But this is far from the case.

The number of electronic symbols representing components can run into the hundreds. To program all the possible combinations into the Schematic Designer would be a monumental task, not to mention the extraordinary amount of computer memory needed.

The next best thing is to draw and then save, on disk as a Library Image, the needed electronic symbols. When any of the extra images are needed in a design, all you must do is to recall the graphic by its filename. Then the image is instantly displayed at the proper location on the screen.

Symbols representing electronic components are not the only images that can run into the hundreds. Printed Circuit Board pads and spacing can also be represented many ways.

For this reason both the Schematic and the Printed Circuit Board Designing programs make use of the Library feature. This section discusses the drawing and saving (on disk) of Library Images for the two programs. The symbols may be different, but the procedure for saving and recalling the graphic is the same.

Adding a Symbol to the Library (Schematic Designer Program)

The illustration in Fig. 1-39 is an electronic schematic of the 12 volt power

Schematic Designer

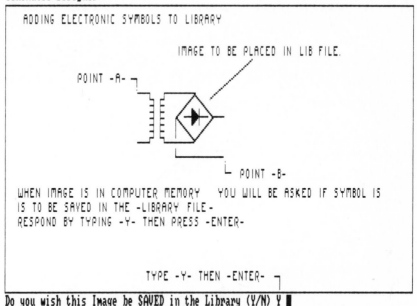

Do you wish this Image be SAVED in the Library (Y/N) Y ▐

Fig. 1-39. Adding electronic symbols to the Library (.LIB) disk.

supply, less the filter capacitor. Saving this image on disk for future use can be easily done by first drawing the required schematic. In this case, it is the power supply. Using the arrow keys or Cursor Express, move the Drawing Cursor to Point A. Then press the "G" key. Move the cursor to Point "B". Then press the "G" key again.

Please note that the image you want saved as a Library File must be fully contained within an imaginary box that can be drawn using these two X, Y coordinates. To refresh your memory, refer back to the Schematic Designer Drawing commands.

Upon pressing the "G" key the second time, the computer begins to scan the image located within the two X, Y coordinates. Depending on the complexity of the image, this scanning can take from ½ second to as much as 5 seconds. With the available memory allocated for image scanning, the area of the symbol can be as much as 3 inches square. If a larger area is to be scanned, refer to the "Program Modifications" section of Chapter 2.

When the computer finishes its image scan, you are asked (in the lower left corner of the screen) "Do you wish this Image to be SAVED in the Library (Y/N)". At this time, respond by entering "Y" for yes. When entered, you are then asked to give the image a name. Enter the filename "SAM1" (see Fig. 1-40). Then press <ENTER> or <RETURN>. Drive A will turn ON. Instead of saving the entire image on the monitor (as a .PIX File will do) the Library File ONLY saves the area of the monitor which contains the schematic of the power supply.

Schematic Designer

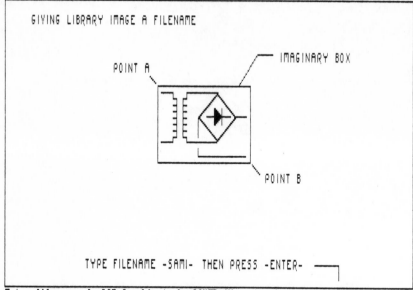

Enter filename of .LIB Graphic to be SAVED (No extension needed) SAM1█

Fig. 1-40. Giving the new image a filename.

Loading a Library Graphic

Now that the CAE disk contains a Library File, Fig. 1-41 demonstrates how to recall this image and place it back onto the screen. Using the arrow keys, move the Drawing Cursor to a location on the screen where you want the power supply to be drawn. Then press the "L" key. When pressed, you are asked:

"Do you wish to LOAD from <1> .LIB (Library) or <2> .PIX (picture) file?"

This time, respond by entering the number 1 for Library File. You are then asked to enter the filename of the Library Image. For this example, enter the filename SAM1 (see Fig. 1-42). Then press <ENTER> or <RETURN>. Note that no quotes or extensions are needed for this input.

Upon entering the filename, Drive A starts searching for the power supply image. When found, the computer displays the schematic at the X, Y location you have chosen.

If the location of the displayed image is not to your liking, press the "A" key. As discussed in the "Drawing Commands" section, the power supply image is erased, but any previously-drawn graphics are left untouched. At this time, you can use the arrow keys or Cursor Express to relocate the Drawing Cursor to another position, where you can press the "A" key again. The Library Image is redrawn at the new location.

This power supply image remains in computer memory until another Library File is called upon. Then, if you want to draw another power supply, you must again press the "L" key and respond with the proper filename.

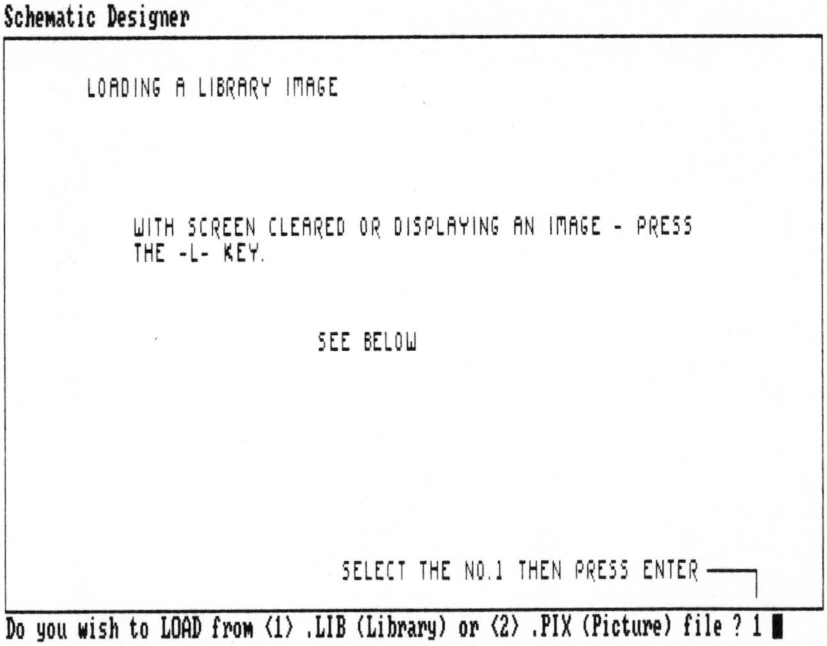

Schematic Designer

```
       LOADING A LIBRARY IMAGE




       WITH SCREEN CLEARED OR DISPLAYING AN IMAGE - PRESS
       THE -L- KEY.



                    SEE BELOW




                    SELECT THE NO.1 THEN PRESS ENTER ———
```

Do you wish to LOAD from <1> .LIB (Library) or <2> .PIX (Picture) file ? 1 ■

Fig. 1-41. Recalling a Library Image from disk.

Adding PC Board Patterns
(PC Board Designer Program)

Like the Schematic Designer, the PC Board Designing Program can save PCB patterns on disk to be recalled at any time. The procedure is the same as described above, so I won't go too deeply into its operation.

Figure 1-43 illustrates a 14-pin copper pattern for an integrated circuit. This image will be used in this example. As with the Schematic Designer, move the Drawing Cursor to Point A. Then press the "G" key. Now move the cursor to Point B. Press the "G" key again.

When the computer completes its scan of the image, you are asked if this image is to be saved in the Library File. In response, enter "Y" for yes. You are then asked to indicate the filename of this new image (see Fig. 1-44). Respond by typing the following:

14DIP <ENTER> or <RETURN>

When entered, this graphic is saved on Disk under the filename 14DIP.LIB.

To see if this is so, you can press the "F" key (FILE option). This feature displays all filenames located on Disk A. The name 14DIP.LIB should be in this list.

Loading a Library Graphic

Loading a graphic with the PC Board program is the same as loading an image using the Schematic Designer. Just locate the Drawing Cursor, using the

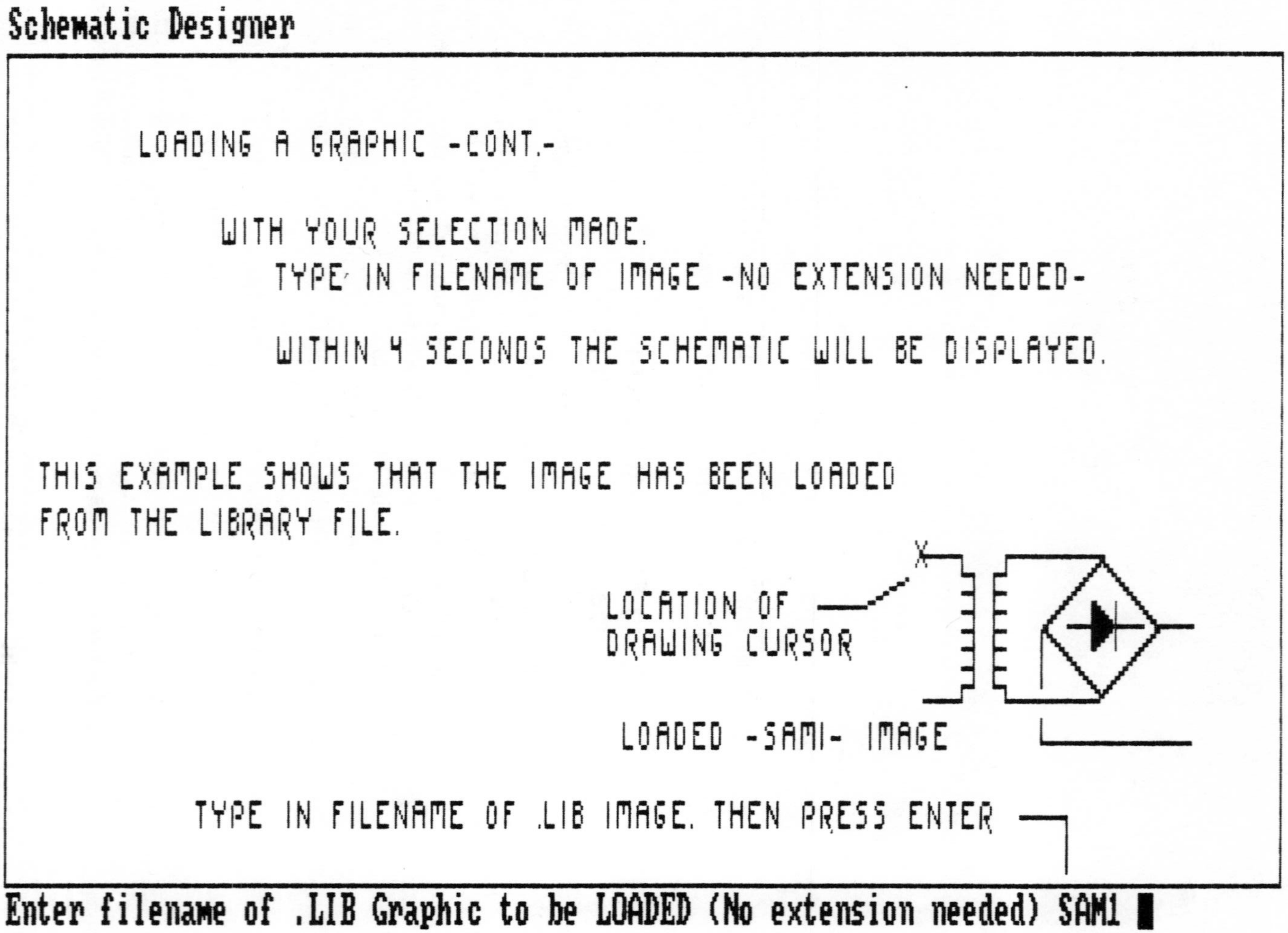

Schematic Designer

```
LOADING A GRAPHIC -CONT.-

    WITH YOUR SELECTION MADE.
      TYPE IN FILENAME OF IMAGE -NO EXTENSION NEEDED-

        WITHIN 4 SECONDS THE SCHEMATIC WILL BE DISPLAYED.

THIS EXAMPLE SHOWS THAT THE IMAGE HAS BEEN LOADED
FROM THE LIBRARY FILE.

                        LOCATION OF
                        DRAWING CURSOR

                    LOADED -SAM1- IMAGE

    TYPE IN FILENAME OF .LIB IMAGE. THEN PRESS ENTER
```

Enter filename of .LIB Graphic to be LOADED (No extension needed) SAM1 ▮

Fig. 1-42. Before the image can be recalled, you must indicate its filename.

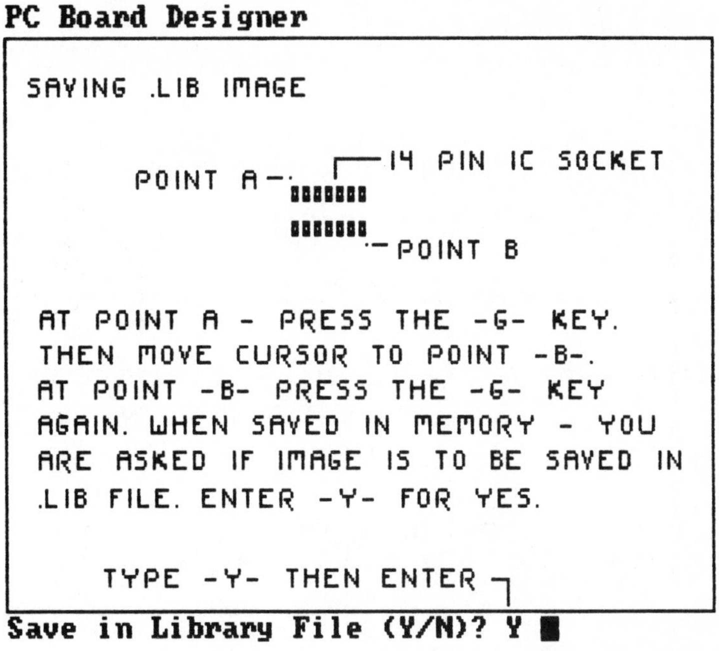

PC Board Designer

```
SAVING .LIB IMAGE


                              ┌─── 14 PIN IC SOCKET
        POINT A ─. ▪▪▪▪▪▪▪
                   ▪▪▪▪▪▪▪
                        .─ POINT B

AT POINT A - PRESS THE -G- KEY.
THEN MOVE CURSOR TO POINT -B-.
AT POINT -B- PRESS THE -G- KEY
AGAIN. WHEN SAVED IN MEMORY - YOU
ARE ASKED IF IMAGE IS TO BE SAVED IN
.LIB FILE. ENTER -Y- FOR YES.


        TYPE -Y- THEN ENTER ─┐
```
Save in Library File (Y/N)? Y █

Fig. 1-43. Saving an image in the Library using the PC Board Designer.

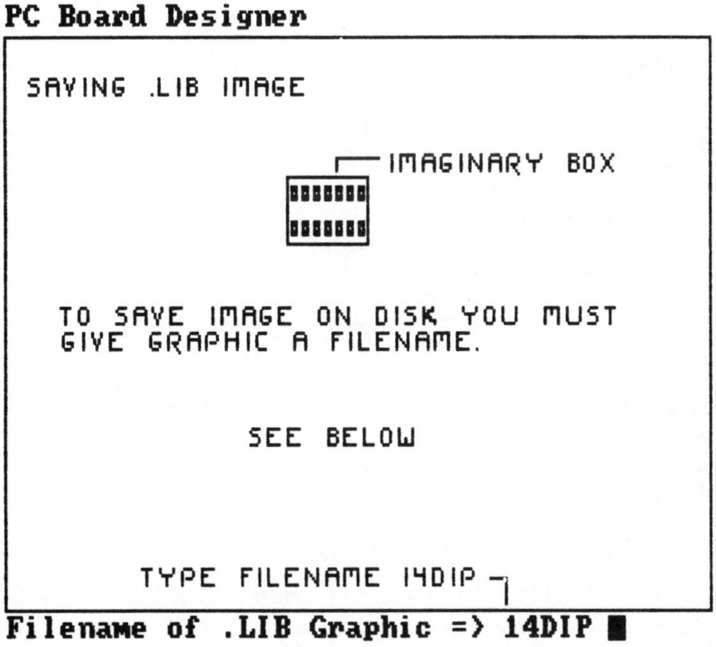

PC Board Designer

```
SAVING .LIB IMAGE


                        ┌─ IMAGINARY BOX
                   ▪▪▪▪▪▪▪
                   ▪▪▪▪▪▪▪

   TO SAVE IMAGE ON DISK YOU MUST
   GIVE GRAPHIC A FILENAME.


            SEE BELOW



      TYPE FILENAME 14DIP ─┐
```
Filename of .LIB Graphic => 14DIP █

Fig. 1-44. Giving the new PC board image a name.

PC Board Designer

```
LOADING A .LIB FILE

TO LOAD A .LIB IMAGE PRESS THE
-L- KEY. YOU WILL THEN BE ASKED
IF IMAGE IS TO BE LOADED FROM THE
-1- .LIB OR -2- .PIX FILE.


RESPOND BY TYPING THE NO. I THEN
PRESS THE -ENTER- OR -RETURN-
KEY.


                SEE BELOW



        TYPE NO.I PRESS -ENTER- ┐
                                 │
```

Load from ⟨1⟩.LIB or ⟨2⟩.PIX =⟩ 1 ∎

Fig. 1-45. Recalling a PC board Image from the Library File.

arrow keys, where you want the 14-pin DIP pattern drawn. Then press the "L" key. You are then asked if the image will be loaded from a .LIB or .PIX file. This time, select .LIB by entering the number 1, then press <ENTER> or <RETURN> (see Fig. 1-45).

Figure 1-46 illustrates the computer monitor after the <ENTER> key has been pressed. You are asked to enter the filename of the image to be loaded. At this prompt, enter the following:

14DIP   <ENTER>

Drive A starts its search for the image. When found, the graphic is displayed on the screen at the location you have chosen.

The use of the "A" key to erase and redraw the now loaded image is the same as indicated with the Schematic Design Program.

Pre-Programmed Library Symbols

Figures 1-47 and 1-48 illustrate the four pre-programmed Library Symbols that are included in the complete Programming Disk available to you from TAB BOOKS.

SAMPLE1 (Fig. 1-47) shows an NAND gate. Symbols like this can be used to design digital electronic circuits. You can add AND, OR, NOR, and XOR gates.

PC Board Designer

```
LOADING A .LIB IMAGE

WHEN THE NO.1 BUTTON HAS BEEN
PRESSED AND -ENTERED- YOU ARE
THEN ASKED TO ENTER THE FILENAME
OF THE IMAGE YOU WISH LOADED.

    IN THIS EXAMPLE - TYPE 14DIP


        ▮▮▮▮▮▮▮
                 ─RECALLED .LIB
        ▮▮▮▮▮▮▮
                    IMAGE.




    TYPE 14DIP -ENTER- ┐
                       └
```

Enter Name of .LIB File => 14DIP ▮

Fig. 1-46. Before the image can be recalled from the disk, you must give its filename to the computer.

SAMPLE2 shows a transformer connected to a bridge rectifier. This graphic is very useful, especially if you design many circuits using on-board power supplies.

SAMPLE3 (Fig. 1-48) shows a 14-pin integrated circuit pattern. Other patterns may include 6-pin, 8-pin, and 16-pin.

SAMPLE4 shows a layout that represents the proper layout and pin spacing of a miniature audio transformer. This sample also includes the stationary graphic dots. When saving an image using PC Board Designer, it is a good idea to include these dots. They help in the proper placement of the pattern on the screen.

If you purchase the program disk from TAB BOOKS, you can load these samples by first loading the Schematic Designer program. Then press the "L" key. Enter the number 1 when asked if the image is to be loaded from a Library or Picture File. When you are asked to enter the filename of the .LIB image, type SAMPLE1 for the NAND gate or SAMPLE2 to display the power supply.

The third and fourth samples are to be used with the PC Board program. When it is loaded and running, press the "L" key. Make the proper responses so the image can be loaded from the Library Files. When prompted, enter SAMPLE3 to display the 14-pin DIP socket or SAMPLE4 for the audio transformer layout.

The program disk available from TAB BOOKS, also contains a fifth PC Board layout (see Fig. 1-49). This sample demonstrates the complexities of PCB

Schematic Designer

SAMPLE LIBRARY ELECTRONIC SYMBOLS

  IF YOU DECIDE TO PURCHASE THE CEA PROGRAM DISK AVAILABLE FROM
TAB BOOKS INC. YOU WILL HAVE THE SAMPLE .LIB SYMBOLS AS SEEN
BELOW. READY FOR USE.

SAMPLE 1

SAMPLE 2

TO LOAD YOUR OWN TYPE -SAMPLE1- OR -SAMPLE2-

Fig. 1-47. Two sample electronic symbols included on the CAE Programming Disk available from TAB BOOKS, Inc.

PC Board Designer

SAMPLE .LIB SYMBOLS

IF YOU PURCHASE A PRE-PROGRAMMED
COMPUTER DISK FROM TAB BOOKS INC.
YOU WILL HAVE THE SAMPLE .LIB
SYMBOLS AS SEEN BELOW.

SAMPLE 3

SAMPLE 4

TO LOAD YOUR OWN TYPE -SAMPLE3-
                OR   -SAMPLE4-

Fig. 1-48. Two PC board patterns included on the CAE Programming Disk available from TAB BOOKS, Inc.

PC Board Designer

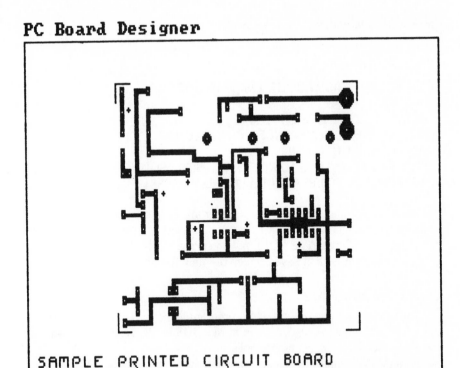

SAMPLE PRINTED CIRCUIT BOARD

D=Draw   T=IC Pads   C=Circular Pads

Fig. 1-49. Sample printed circuit board layout included on the CAE Programming Disk available from TAB BOOKS, Inc. (filename SAMPLE5).

artwork designs but it is easy to draw using your computer. To display this layout, make the correct responses to load a Picture File (.PIX) from disk. When prompted for its filename, enter SAMPLE5 and then press <ENTER> or <RETURN>.

USING SCHEMATIC DESIGNER TO DRAW PICTURES

Many of the figures and pictures in this book have been drawn using a standard IBM PC computer. You can achieve the same results by slightly modifying the Schematic Designer program.

Modifications

The drawing program is almost identical to Designer, so to save time in programming, let's reload this program. Insert the disk containing the Electronic Schematic Designer program in Drive A and type LOAD "DESIGNER". Then press the <ENTER> key. When loaded, make the following changes:

    Delete Lines 10 to 150
    Delete Lines 680 to 1050
    Delete Line 290
    Delete Line 420

Change the indicated lines to read as shown:

```
  10   REM                Draw Program
  20   REM
  30   REM    (C)OPYRIGHT 1987 TAB BOOKS INC.
  40   REM
 200   LOCATE 1,1:PRINT"Drawing Program"
1990   GOSUB 2300:A$="CLEAR": GOTO 1210
1140   CLOSE:GOTO 260
1230   F=0:LOCATE 25,1:PRINT SPACE$(80);:SOUND 800,3:GOTO 260
2070   PSET (X,Y),0:BSAVE"DATA4.PIX",0,16384
```

When you're done, do not run the program. First save the new program. Remove the Designer disk from Drive A and insert a formatted (but empty) disk in its place. Type SAVE "DRAW" and press <ENTER>. The modified Designer program is then saved under the new filename, "DRAW".

Using the Program

For proper operation of any CAE program listed in this book, a Graphic Utility program must be loaded when in MS-DOS or PC-DOS. It is assumed that this procedure has been accomplished.

With the disk containing the program in Drive A, type RUN "DRAW" and press <ENTER>. At this time, the reset screen for the program must be saved on Disk. With the computer screen completely empty of any graphic material (except the frame and program title), press the "S" key. In the lower left corner of the screen you are asked to enter a filename. Type CLEAR and press the <ENTER> key.

This command can then be called upon at any time by pressing the "R" key. It clears the screen of any unwanted graphics, just like in the Designer Program.

Using DRAW

The DRAW commands associated with this program are the same as those described in the Schematic Designer section of this book except for the "I" (Insert) and "H" (Help) options. A complete DRAW listing can be found in Listing 1-5 if you want to experiment with the program by adding some of your own ideas.

Listing 1-5. Listing of the Modified Designer program.

```
 10 REM                Drawing Program
 20 REM
 30 REM        (C)opyright 1987 Tab Books Inc.
160 CLS
170 KEY OFF
180 SCREEN 2,,0,0
190 LINE(0,10)-(639,190),1,B
```

```
200 LOCATE 1,1:PRINT"Drawing Program"
210 LOCATE 1,50:PRINT"(C)opyright 1987 Tab Books Inc."

220 DEF SEG=&HB800
230 DIM B(1500)
240 X=320:Y=90:C=1:L=1:S=1
250 GOTO 1230
260 A$=INKEY$
270 ON ERROR GOTO 650
280 IF A$ <>"" THEN SOUND 800,2
300 IF A$="R"OR A$="r" THEN GOSUB 2300:S=1:LOCATE 25,
    1:INPUT;"REALLY ERASE (Y/N) ";Q$:IF Q$="Y"OR Q$="y"TH
    EN GOTO 1990 ELSE GOSUB 2300:GOTO 1230
310 IF A$="J"OR A$="j" GOTO 1830
320 IF A$="F" OR A$="f" THEN GOSUB 2300:GOTO 2070
330 IF A$="D"OR A$="d" THEN S=S*-1
340 IF A$="E"OR A$="e" THEN L=L*-1:IF L=-1 THEN A1=X:
    A2=Y: ELSE A3=X:A4=Y:LINE(A1,A2)-(A3,A4),0,BF
350 IF A$="T"OR A$="t" THEN PSET(X,Y):CIRCLE (X,Y),3,
    3:S=1
360 IF A$="P"OR A$="p" THEN L=L*-1:S=1:IF L=-1 THEN A
    1=X:A2=Y ELSE A3=X:A4=Y:LINE(A1,A2)-(A3,A4)
370 IF A$="G"OR A$="g" THEN L=L*-1:PSET(X,Y),0:S=1:IF
     L=-1 THEN A1=X:A2=Y ELSE A3=X:A4=Y:B=0:GOSUB 2300:LO
    CATE 25,1:PRINT"Recording Picture - Please Stand By";
    :GET(A1,A2)-(A3,A4),B:SOUND 800,2:GOSUB 2300:GOTO 232
    0
380 IF A$="A"OR A$="a" THEN  A1=X:A2=Y :PUT(A1,A2),B,
    XOR:SOUND 800,2
390 IF A$="S"OR A$="s" GOTO 1070
400 IF A$="L" OR A$="l" THEN GOTO 2340
410 IF A$="W" OR A$="w" GOTO 1240
430 IF A$="1" THEN C=1:F=0:S=1
440 IF A$="2" THEN C=0:F=0
450 IF A$="C" OR A$="c" THEN GOTO 1740
460 ON KEY (11) GOSUB 610
470 ON KEY (12) GOSUB 550
480 ON KEY (13) GOSUB 520
490 ON KEY (14) GOSUB 580
500 KEY(11)ON:KEY(12)ON:KEY(13)ON:KEY(14)ON
510 GOTO 260
520 IF X>=639 THEN GOSUB 2430;:RETURN ELSE P=POINT(X+
    1,Y):PSET(X+1,Y),C
530 IF S=-1 THEN PSET(X,Y),C ELSE PSET(X,Y),F
540 X=X+1:SOUND 200,1:F=P:RETURN
550 IF X=0 THEN GOSUB 2440;:RETURN ELSE P=POINT(X-1,Y
    ):PSET(X-1,Y),C
560 IF S=-1 THEN PSET(X,Y),C ELSE PSET(X,Y),F
570 X=X-1:SOUND 300,1:F=P:RETURN
580 IF Y>=190 THEN GOSUB 2420;:RETURN ELSE P=POINT(X,
    Y+1):PSET(X,Y+1),C
590 IF S=-1 THEN PSET(X,Y),C ELSE PSET(X,Y),F
600 Y=Y+1:SOUND 400,1:F=P:RETURN
610 IF Y=10 THEN GOSUB 2410;:RETURN ELSE P=POINT(X,Y-
    1):PSET(X,Y-1),C
620 IF S=-1 THEN PSET(X,Y),C ELSE PSET(X,Y),F
```

```
630 Y=Y-1:SOUND 500,1:F=P:RETURN
640 END
650 PSET(X,Y),0:DEF SEG=&HB800:IF ERR=53 GOTO 2460 EL
    SE RUN 230
660 END
670 LOCATE 1,37:PRINT SPACE$(44)
1060 END
1070 REM SAVE SCHEMATIC
1080 PSET(X,Y),0
1090 GOSUB 2300
1100 LOCATE 25,1:INPUT;"Enter Filename of .PIX Graphi
     c to be SAVED (No extension needed) ",A$
1110 IF A$="" GOTO 1230
1120 GOSUB 2300
1130 BSAVE A$+".PIX",0,16384
1140 CLOSE:GOTO 260
1150 REM LOAD SCHEMATIC
1160 PSET(X,Y),0
1170 GOSUB 2300
1180 LOCATE 25,1:INPUT;"Enter Filename of .PIX Graphi
     c to be LOADED (No extension needed) ",A$
1190 IF A$="" GOTO 1230
1200 GOSUB 2300
1210 BLOAD A$+".PIX",0
1220 CLOSE
1230 F=0:LOCATE 25,1:PRINT SPACE$(80);:SOUND 800,3:GO
     TO 260
1240 GOSUB 2300
1250 LOCATE 25,1:PRINT "Character Insert Mode.        =
     => Hit COMMA ',' to Exit";:S=1
1260 B$=INKEY$:IF B$="" THEN 1260
1270 IF X>620 AND B$<>"," THEN GOSUB 2390:GOTO 1260
1280 PSET(X,Y)
1290 SOUND 800,2
1300 IF B$="1" THEN DRAW "U5":X=X+5:GOTO 1260
1310 IF B$="2" THEN DRAW "C0;R4;C1;L4;U3;R4;U2;L4":PS
     ET(X,Y-3),0:PSET(X+4,Y-3),0:PSET(X+4,Y-5),0:X=X+9:GOT
     O 1260
1320 IF B$="3" THEN DRAW "R3;U3;L2;R2;U2;L3":PSET(X+3
     ,Y),0:PSET(X+3,Y-3),0:PSET(X+3,Y-5),0:X=X+9:GOTO 1260

1330 IF B$="4" THEN DRAW "C0;U5;C1;D2;R4;U2;D5":X=X+9
     :GOTO 1260
1340 IF B$="5" THEN DRAW "R4;U3;L4;U2;R3":PSET(X+4,Y),
     0:PSET(X+4,Y-3),0:X=X+9:GOTO 1260
1350 IF B$="6" THEN DRAW "C0;U5;C1;D5;R4;U3;L4":PSET(
     X,Y),0:PSET(X+4,Y),0:PSET(X+4,Y-3),0:X=X+9:GOTO 1260
1360 IF B$="7" THEN DRAW "C0;U5;C1;R4;D5":X=X+9:GOTO
     1260
1370 IF B$="8" THEN DRAW "U5;R4;D2;L4;R4;D3;L4":PSET(
     X,Y),0:PSET(X+4,Y),0:PSET(X+4,Y-3),0:PSET(X,Y-3),0:PS
     ET(X,Y-5),0:PSET(X+4,Y-5),0:X=X+9:GOTO 1260
1380 IF B$="9" THEN DRAW "C0;R4;C1;U5;L4;D2;R4":PSET(
     X,Y-5),0:PSET(X,Y-3),0:PSET(X,Y-5),0:PSET(X+4,Y-5),0:
     X=X+9:GOTO 1260
1390 IF B$="0" THEN DRAW "U5;R4;D5;L4":PSET(X,Y),0:PS
```

```
     ET(X,Y-5),0:PSET(X+4,Y),0:PSET(X+4,Y-5),0:X=X+9:GOTO
     1260
1400 IF B$="/" THEN DRAW "R1;U1;R1;U1;R1;U1;R1;U1;R1;
     U1":X=X+9:GOTO 1260
1410 IF B$="-" THEN DRAW "C0;U2;C1;R4":X=X+9:GOTO 126
     0
1420 IF B$="A" OR B$="a" THEN DRAW "U5;R5;D5;U3;L4":P
     SET(X,Y-5),0:PSET(X+5,Y-5),0:X=X+9:GOTO 1260
1430 IF B$="B" OR B$="b" THEN DRAW "U5;R4;D2;L4;R4;D3
     ;L4":PSET(X+4,Y),0:PSET(X+4,Y-3),0:PSET(X+4,Y-5),0:X=
     X+7:GOTO 1260
1440 IF B$="C" OR B$="c" THEN DRAW "R4;L4;U5;R4":PSET
     (X,Y),0:PSET(X,Y-5),0:X=X+9:GOTO 1260
1450 IF B$="D" OR B$="d" THEN DRAW "U5;R4;D5;L4":PSET
     (X+4,Y),0:PSET(X+4,Y-5),0:X=X+9:GOTO 1260
1460 IF B$="E" OR B$="e" THEN DRAW "R5;L5;U3;R2;L2;U2
     ;R5":X=X+9:GOTO 1260
1470 IF B$="F" OR B$="f" THEN DRAW "U3;R2;L2;U2;R4":X
     =X+8:GOTO 1260
1480 IF B$="G" OR B$="g" THEN DRAW "C0;U5;R4;C1;L4;D5
     ;R4;U2;L2":PSET(X,Y),0:PSET(X,Y-5),0:PSET(X+4,Y),0:X=
     X+9:GOTO 1260
1490 IF B$="H" OR B$="h" THEN DRAW "U5;D2;R5;U2;D5":X
     =X+9:GOTO 1260
1500 IF B$="I" OR B$="i" THEN DRAW "C0;R1;C1;U5":X=X+
     6:GOTO 1260
1510 IF B$="J" OR B$="j" THEN DRAW "U2;D2;R4;U5":PSET
     (X,Y),0:PSET(X+4,Y),0:X=X+9:GOTO 1260
1520 IF B$="K" OR B$="k" THEN DRAW "U5;D2;R2;U1;R2;U1
     ":X=X+5:PSET(X,Y):DRAW "U1;L2;U1;L2":X=X+5:GOTO 1260
1530 IF B$="L" OR B$="l" THEN DRAW "U5;D5;R4":X=X+8:G
     OTO 1260
1540 IF B$="M" OR B$="m" THEN DRAW "U5;R3;D2;U2;R3;D5
     ":X=X+10:GOTO 1260
1550 IF B$="N" OR B$="n" THEN DRAW "U5;F5;U5":X=X+9:G
     OTO 1260
1560 IF B$="O" OR B$="o" THEN DRAW "U5;R4;D5;L4":PSET
     (X,Y),0:PSET(X,Y-5),0:PSET(X+4,Y),0:PSET(X+4,Y-5),0:X
     =X+9:GOTO 1260
1570 IF B$="P" OR B$="p" THEN DRAW "U5;R5;D3;L3":PSET
     (X,Y-5),0:PSET(X+5,Y-5),0:PSET(X+5,Y-2),0:X=X+9:GOTO
     1260
1580 IF B$="Q" OR B$="q" THEN DRAW "U5;R5;D6;U1;L5":P
     SET(X,Y),0:PSET(X,Y-5),0:PSET(X+5,Y-5),0:X=X+9:GOTO 1
     260
1590 IF B$="R" OR B$="r" THEN DRAW "U5;R5;D3;L3;F3":P
     SET(X,Y-5),0:PSET(X+5,Y-5),0:PSET(X+5,Y-2),0:X=X+9:GO
     TO 1260
1600 IF B$="S" OR B$="s" THEN DRAW "R4;U3;L4;U2;R4":P
     SET(X+4,Y),0:PSET(X,Y-3),0:PSET(X+4,Y-3),0:PSET(X,Y-5
     ),0:X=X+9:GOTO 1260
1610 IF B$="T" OR B$="t" THEN DRAW "C0;U5;C1;R4;L2;D5
     ":X=X+8:GOTO 1260
1620 IF B$="U" OR B$="u" THEN DRAW "U5;D5;R6;U5":PSET
     (X,Y),0:PSET(X+6,Y),0:X=X+10:GOTO 1260
1630 IF B$="V" OR B$="v" THEN PSET(X,Y),0:LINE (X,Y-5
```

```
      )-(X+2,Y):LINE(X+2,Y)-(X+4,Y-5):X=X+8:GOTO 1260
1640 IF B$="W" OR B$="w" THEN DRAW "C0;U5;C1;D5;R3;U2
     ;D2;R3;U5":X=X+10:GOTO 1260
1650 IF B$="X" OR B$="x" THEN DRAW "C0;U5;C1;F5":PSET
     (X,Y):DRAW "E5":X=X+9:GOTO 1260
1660 IF B$="Y" OR B$="y" THEN DRAW "C0;U5;C1;D2;R5;L2
     ;D3;U3;R3;U2":PSET(X,Y-3),0:PSET(X+6,Y-3),0:X=X+10:G(
     TO 1260
1670 IF B$="Z" OR B$="z" THEN DRAW "C0;R5;C1;L5;C0;U5
     ;C1;R5;G5":X=X+9:GOTO 1260
1680 IF B$="." THEN PSET(X,Y):X=X+3:GOTO 1260
1690 IF B$=CHR$(32) THEN:PSET(X,Y),0:X=X+9:GOTO 1260
1700 IF B$=CHR$(44) THEN:PSET(X,Y),0: GOTO 1230
1710 IF A$="W" OR A$="w" GOTO 1260 ELSE 1720
1720 F=0:S=1:LOCATE 1,50:PRINT"(C)opyright 1987 Tab B
     ooks Inc.":GOTO 260
1730 END
1740 GOSUB 2300
1750 LOCATE 25,1:INPUT;"Enter Size of Circle Desired
     (1/2/3) ",B
1760 IF B>3 OR B<1 THEN GOTO 1230
1770 PSET(X,Y)
1780 ON B GOTO 1790,1800,1810
1790 CIRCLE(X+6,Y),5:S=1:GOTO 1230
1800 CIRCLE(X+11,Y),10:S=1:GOTO 1230
1810 CIRCLE(X+21,Y),20:S=1:GOTO 1230
1820 END
1830 GOSUB 2300:LOCATE 25,1:PRINT "Cursor Express ON"
     ;
1840 PSET(X,Y),0
1850 A$=INKEY$
1860 IF A$="J" OR A$="j" GOTO 1920
1870 X=STICK(0):Y=STICK(1)
1880 IF POINT(X*6,Y*1.8)=0 THEN 1890 ELSE X=X+1:Y=Y+1
     :GOTO 1870
1890 PSET(X*6,Y*1.8):FOR AA=1 TO 100:NEXT AA:PSET(X*6
     ,Y*1.8),0
1900 IF X*6>=0 AND X*6<14 AND Y*1.8>=0 AND Y*1.6<5 TH
     EN LOCATE 25,1:PRINT"No Joystick Connected to Port";:
     FOR T=1 TO 2000:NEXT:X=320:Y=90:GOTO 1230
1910 GOTO 1850
1920 X=INT(X*6):Y=INT(Y*1.8)
1930 IF X>600 THEN X=620
1940 IF X<0 THEN X=1
1950 IF Y<11 THEN Y=12
1960 IF Y>180 THEN Y=185
1970 A3=X:A4=Y:PSET(X,Y),1:S=1:GOTO 1230
1980 END
1990 GOSUB 2300:A$="CLEAR":GOTO 1210
2000 END
2010 A$="CLEARSCR":GOTO 1130
2020 END
2030 PSET(X,Y),0:A$="DATA":GOTO 1120
2040 END
2050 SOUND 800,2:LOCATE 25,1:INPUT;"Hit <ENTER> to Co
     ntinue...",AA$:RETURN
```

```
2060 END
2070 PSET(X,Y),0:BSAVE"DATA4.PIX",0,16384
2080 CLS:LOCATE 1,27:PRINT"Current Filenames on Disk"

2090 FILES
2100 LOCATE 25,1:INPUT;"When Ready - Hit <ENTER> ",ZZ
     $
2110 IF ZZ$="KILL" OR ZZ$="kill" THEN LOCATE 25,1:INP
     UT;"Which file shall I kill (must include extension)
     ",QQ$:IF QQ$="" THEN GOTO 2120 ELSE KILL QQ$:GOTO 208
     0:ELSE GOTO 2120
2120 CLS:BLOAD"DATA4.PIX",0:CLOSE:RUN 230
2130 END
2140 DEF SEG
2150 GOSUB 2300:SOUND 800,2
2160 LOCATE 25,1:INPUT;"Enter filename of .LIB Graphi
     c to be SAVED (No extension needed) ",SS$
2170 IF SS$="" THEN DEF SEG=&HB800:RUN 230
2180 BSAVE SS$+".LIB",VARPTR(B(0)),5200
2190 CLOSE:DEF SEG=&HB800:GOTO 1230
2200 END
2210 DEF SEG
2220 GOSUB 2300:SOUND 800,2
2230 LOCATE 25,1:INPUT;"Enter filename of .LIB Graphi
     c to be LOADED (No extension needed) ",SS$
2240 IF SS$="" THEN DEF SEG=&HB800:GOTO 1230
2250 PSET(X,Y),0
2260 BLOAD SS$+".LIB",VARPTR(B(0))
2270 PUT(X,Y),B
2280 CLOSE:DEF SEG=&HB800:GOTO 1230
2290 END
2300 LOCATE 25,1:PRINT SPACE$(80);:RETURN
2310 END
2320 LOCATE 25,1:INPUT;"Do you wish this Image be SAV
     ED in the Library (Y/N) ",ZZ$:IF ZZ$="Y" OR ZZ$="y" T
     HEN GOSUB 2140 ELSE GOTO 1230
2330 END
2340 GOSUB 2300:LOCATE 25,1:INPUT;"Do you wish to LOA
     D from <1> .LIB (Library) or <2> .PIX (Picture) file
     ";ZZ$
2350 IF ZZ$="1" THEN GOTO 2210
2360 IF ZZ$="2" THEN GOTO 1150
2370 IF ZZ$<>"1" OR ZZ$<>"2" THEN GOTO 1230
2380 END
2390 FOR I=1 TO 10:SOUND 800,1:SOUND 0,1:NEXT:RETURN
2400 END
2410 Y=190:RETURN
2420 Y=10:RETURN
2430 X=0:RETURN
2440 X=639:RETURN
2450 END
2460 GOSUB 2300:LOCATE 25,30:PRINT"=> File Not Found
     <=";:GOSUB 2390:FOR I=1 TO 2000:NEXT:IF ERL=2110 THEN
     GOTO 2120 ELSE RUN 230
2470 GOTO 2120
```

Chapter 2
PC Board
Designer Program

Now that you've used your computer to draw a schematic of a 12-volt power supply, let's take the finished graph and convert it into artwork that can be used to develop the final PC board, ready for component insertion and soldering.

The PC Board Designer can develop PC board artwork to a scale of 1:1. Also included is a program named GRAPH which displays a graph pattern on the computer monitor that is later printed on paper. This hard copy graph is used to place components and allows you to draw, by hand, what the board is to look like as a finished product. The graph pattern generated is an exact representation of the computer monitor using the PC board program.

The PC Board Designer has four parts: Introduction, Main A, Help and Main B. Like Schematic Designer, the Introduction acquaints you with the available commands used to produce quality PC Boards. As with the Schematic Designer program, the Introduction displays seven screens. When all have been displayed, the computer automatically loads and runs the Main A program. This program, saved under the filename "PCB", contains all Designer functional commands which are under keyboard control using the INKEY$ function.

Unlike expensive CAE system programs that require the use of a mouse and a mouse controller card, the Drawing Cursor can be moved by using the four arrow keys, joystick, or graphics tablet. (To use a joystick or graphics tablet, the Cursor Express option must be chosen.)

PC Board Designer

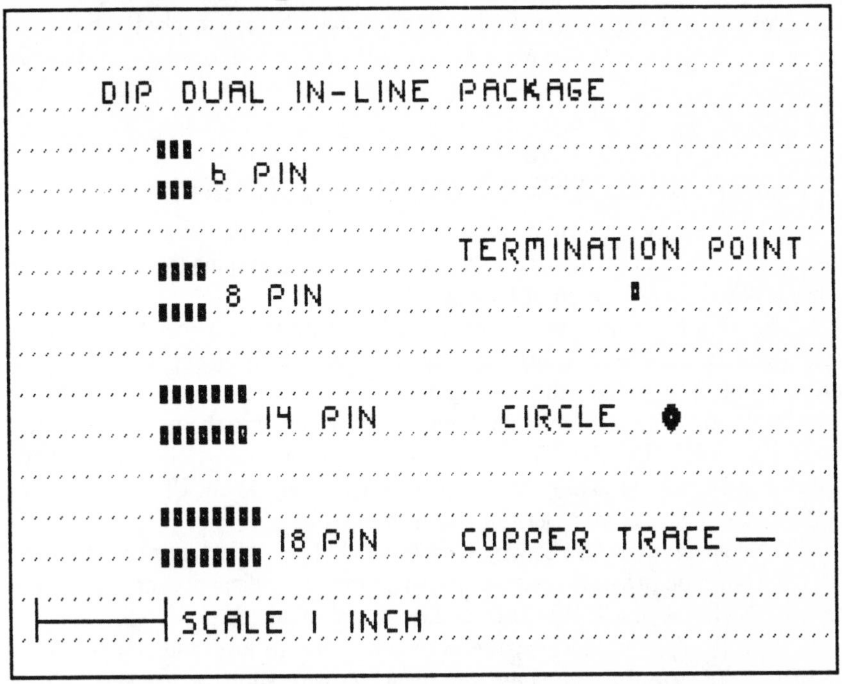

Fig. 2-1. Sample printout of the PC Board Designer's programmed shapes.

The PC Board Designer uses only three in-memory shapes (Fig. 2-1).

- Copper pad—Used to solder a component to the board. The spacing of the pads depends on the physical size or lead separation on the selected component. This component spacing is discussed in greater detail later.
- Solid line—Drawn to connect the pads. On the finished board, this line is the copper trace. The thickness of this line can be varied by moving the Drawing Cursor up or down one pixel and then drawing a second or third line parallel to the first.
- Circular pad—Used as an outside world connection point where wires are soldered to components mounted on a front panel or elsewhere.

From these basic shapes, all printed circuit figures can be generated.

Help Screen

If, while using the MAIN PROGRAM A (PCB), you need to refresh your memory regarding the available drawing modes, press the "H" key. Two Help screens are displayed describing the drawing commands. Before displaying a Help screen, the computer saves on disk the image which is on the screen under the filename DATA3. Upon completion of the five Help screens, the computer loads and runs the Main Program B.

Main Program B (Filename "PCB2")

Lines 1 to 17 reload the screen graphic saved before displaying the Help screen. The balance of the Main Program B contains all drawing commands available in the Main Program A which allows you to redesign, edit, or print a layout.

PROGRAMMING THE PC BOARD DESIGNER

With an empty but formatted disk (see your computer's instruction for the proper procedure on formatting disks) in Drive A, begin typing the Introduction. This program is presented in Listing 2-1.

Like all printed program material that must be transformed to computer language by using the keyboard, care must be taken in programming. Care taken now will save time in the debugging of the final product.

When you're done, don't run the program. First save the program on disk by typing SAVE "INTRO2". Then hit the <ENTER> or <RETURN> key. Drive A will start, indicating that the program is being saved. Upon completion of the save function, you can run the Introduction.

The computer displays copyright credits and plays a short musical interlude. The Introduction program contains seven screens. To display each, just press the <ENTER> and <RETURN> key when required.

After the seventh screen, the computer tries to load and run the main Designer program, but the computer responds with an error message: FILE NOT FOUND. This is the next program to be entered.

Listing 2-1. PC Board Designer Introduction program listing.

```
10 REM Printed Circuit Board Designer *INTRODUCTION*
20 REM
30 REM                 by: Steve Sokolowski
40 REM
50 REM                   (C)opyright 1987
60 REM
70 REM     This program is protected under the laws of
80 REM     the United States of America. Any
90 REM     publication or reproduction in any form -
100 REM    without the expressed written consent of
110 REM    the author or Tab Books Inc. is prohibited.
120 REM
130 REM      ==> SAVE UNDER FILENAME "INTRO2" <==
140 CLS
150 KEY OFF
160 CLEAR 5000
170 SCREEN 1
180 COLOR 1,3
190 FOR T=1 TO 500:NEXT T
200 LOCATE 10,8:PRINT"Computer-Aided Engineering"
210 LOCATE 12,16:PRINT"PC Board"
220 LOCATE 14,13:PRINT"Design Program"
230 LOCATE 25,6:PRINT"(C)opyright 1987 TAB Books Inc."
```

```
240 SOUND 523.25,10:SOUND 659.26,10:SOUND 587.33,5:SO
    UND 698.46,25
250 SOUND 493.88,10:SOUND 587.33,10:SOUND 523.25,5:SO
    UND 0,5:SOUND 523.25,20
260 FOR A=1 TO 2500:NEXT A
270 SCREEN 2
280 CLS
290 LOCATE 1,17:PRINT "Program designed for IBM PC's
    and Compatibles"
300 LOCATE 5,25:PRINT "Minimum Computer Requirements:
    "
310 LOCATE 8,28:PRINT "Color Monitor"
320 LOCATE 9,28:PRINT "128K Memory"
330 LOCATE 10,28:PRINT "One Disk Drive"
340 LOCATE 11,28:PRINT "Graphics Printer"
350 LOCATE 12,28:PRINT "Optional Joystick"
360 LOCATE 13,28:PRINT "MS-DOS or PC-DOS (Basica vers
    ion 2.11 or later)"
370 LOCATE 14,28:PRINT "320 x 200 Color Graphics Card
    "
380 GOSUB 1360
390 PRINT "In the DRAW MODE - you have the following
    options to input graphic"
400 PRINT "commands. They are as follows:":PRINT:PRIN
    T
410 PRINT "D=Draw R=Reset E=Erase I=Insert S=Save C=C
    ircle L=Load W=Wording P=Print Line"
420 PRINT "F=Filenames G=Get Section of Schematic  A=
    Put Graphic on Screen  T=Term.Point":PRINT
430 PRINT "DRAW - To activate, hit the 'D' key. This
    will allow you to draw a line.
440 PRINT "       To de-activate, just hit the 'D' a
    second time. You are now able to"
450 PRINT "       move the Drawing Cursor without lea
    ving a trace.":PRINT
460 PRINT "RESET - By hitting the 'R' key - you will
    clear the image on the screen."
470 PRINT "       The contents of the memory will re
    main.":PRINT
480 PRINT "Get Option - Saves desired graphic in comp
    uter memory. You are asked if this"
490 PRINT "            image will be saved in the Li
    brary File. You respond by typing"
500 PRINT "            Y (Yes) or N (No). If you ans
    wer Yes, you will then be asked to"
510 PRINT "            give this new image a name. R
    espond by entering a Filename. Then"
520 PRINT "            press the <ENTER> Key. The im
    age will now be saved on Disk. You"
530 PRINT "            may recall this image at any
    time by using the 'L' (LOAD) option."
540 PRINT "            The GET option requires two d
    iagonal X/Y coordinates to be entered."
550 PRINT "            Do this by pressing the 'G' k
    ey twice at the desired locations."
```

```
560 GOSUB 1360
570 PRINT "ERASE - This option erases a section of yo
    ur graphic. The 'E' option is used"
580 PRINT "          in the same manner as the 'G' opti
    on (two diagonal X/Y coordinates"
590 PRINT "          are needed). Instead of saving the
    image in computer memory, the"
600 PRINT "          ERASE option paints this graphic s
    ection to BLACK, thus erasing"
610 PRINT "          the image.":PRINT
620 PRINT "FILENAMES - The 'F' option allows you to d
    isplay ALL filenames saved on"
630 PRINT "          Disk, which is located in Driv
    e A. You may also DELETE files"
640 PRINT "          just by typing KILL to the pro
    mpt <Hit Enter to Continue>."
650 PRINT "          Then type in the filename you
    wish Deleted - then press <ENTER>."
660 PRINT "          NOTE - This filename MUST cont
    ain the extension"
670 PRINT "          (ex. .LIB - .BAS ect.)":PRINT
680 PRINT "SAVE - Used to SAVE the layout shown, on d
    isk. You are asked to give your"
690 PRINT "          design a filename. When entered - h
    it <ENTER>. The disk drive starts."
700 PRINT "          Your drawing is now being saved for
    future use.":PRINT
710 GOSUB 1360
720 PRINT "LOAD - LOADs a Complete Screen or Library
    symbol from Disk A. You enter"
730 PRINT "          the number 1 if you wish to LOAD an
    image from the Library, or"
740 PRINT "          enter the number 2 if you wish to L
    OAD an image from the Picture"
750 PRINT "          File. Then when asked, enter the FI
    LENAME of the image. When loaded,"
760 PRINT "          graphic will be displayed at the lo
    cation of the Drawing Cursor.":PRINT
770 PRINT "CIRCLE - This key draws a pre-programmed c
    ircular pad at any desired location"
780 PRINT "          on the screen. These circles are
    used to indicate wire connections"
790 PRINT "          that will be made to the PC Board
    from the outside source.":PRINT
800 PRINT "WORDING - Used to print letters & numbers
    at any location on the screen."
810 PRINT "          The ARROW keys can be used to mo
    ve the Drawing Cursor to any location"
820 PRINT "          so wording can be placed at a de
    sired point. To EXIT - just"
830 PRINT "          press the COMMA ',' Key. You wil
    l then be placed in the Draw Mode.":PRINT
840 PRINT "Screen Paint - When layout is complete and
    you are ready to make a printed"
850 PRINT "          copy, press the 'P' key. Th
    is option erases the stationary"
```

```
860 PRINT "               graphic dots by first paint
    ing the screen purple, then"
870 PRINT "               re-painting the screen to B
    LACK. The PC Board layout previously"
880 PRINT "               drawn will remain untouched
    . You may now press the Print"
890 PRINT "               or Shift/Print key to make
    a hard copy."
900 GOSUB 1360
910 PRINT "A Option  -  With an image in computer mem
    ory, (placed there by using the 'G'"
920 PRINT "               or 'L' option) the 'A' Key al
    lows the computer to Draw this in"
930 PRINT "               memory graphic at the indicat
    ed X/Y coordinates. By pressing the"
940 PRINT "               'A' Key for the second time,
    the computer will Erase the image"
950 PRINT "               just drawn but leaving any pr
    eviously drawn material untouched."
960 PRINT "               With image at desired locatio
    n - Press the F1 key.":PRINT
970 PRINT "Termination - This option draws a small re
    ctangular pad that can be used as"
980 PRINT "               copper pads for Intergrated
    Circuits or any other components.":PRINT
990 PRINT "Help     -  This option saves the schemat
    ic you are working on, under the"
1000 PRINT "               Filename 'DATA3'. The screen
    will clear then the HELP program"
1010 PRINT "               will be LOADED. This program
    lists the Computer Key Options"
1020 PRINT "               used with the CAE Programs.
    When the needed information is"
1030 PRINT "               known, your computer will re
    -load your present PC Board layout.":PRINT
1040 PRINT "Cursor Express - By pressing the 'J' Key,
    you are placed in the Cursor Express"
1050 PRINT "               Mode. If you have a Joys
    tick or Graphics Table connected to"
1060 PRINT "               the LEFT Joystick Port,
    you can now move the Drawing Cursor"
1070 PRINT "               around the screen faster
    then if the Arrow Keys were used."
1080 PRINT "               When at the desired loca
    tion, press the 'J' Key for the second"
1090 PRINT "               time. You will then be a
    ble to Draw at the new coordinates."
1100 GOSUB 1360
1110 LOCATE 4,1
1120 PRINT "Print   or        Used to print your schem
    atic on a Graphic Printer."
1130 PRINT "               Which button to press de
    pends on the type of computer you"
1140 PRINT "Shift/Print       have. Consult your BASIC
    Instruction Booklet for additional"
1150 PRINT "               information.":PRINT
```

```
1160 PRINT "No. 1 Button   By pressing this button, t
     he color of the Drawing Cursor"
1170 PRINT "              is changed to WHITE.":PRIN
     T
1180 PRINT "No. 2 Button   By pressing this button, t
     he color of the Drawing Cursor"
1190 PRINT "              is changed to BLACK. If us
     ed in conjunction with the 'D'"
1200 PRINT "              key, you can erase drawn l
     ines by re-coloring the line"
1210 PRINT "              BLACK."
1220 GOSUB 1360
1230 LOCATE 4,1
1240 PRINT "To EXIT from any required keyboard input
     (ex. Entering a Filename or Component"
1250 PRINT "Number) just press the <ENTER> Key withou
     t entering any information. Your"
1260 PRINT "computer will cancel that input and retur
     n you to the Drawing Mode.":PRINT
1270 PRINT "When requested to enter a filename of an
     image that will be LOADED or SAVED,"
1280 PRINT "you are NOT required to add the extension
     (ex. .LIB or .PIX). These"
1290 PRINT "extensions are automatically inserted by
     the computer.":PRINT
1300 PRINT "The extension .LIB indicates ALL Files th
     at were SAVED as a LIBRARY File.":PRINT
1310 PRINT "The extension .PIX indicates ALL Files th
     at were SAVED as an IMAGE File."
1320 PRINT "An Image File is a file that has SAVED th
     e entire contents of the screen"
1330 PRINT "on Disk."
1340 LOCATE 24,1:INPUT;"Hit <ENTER> to Load your Comp
     uter-Aided Engineering Program ",AA$:CLS:RUN"PCB"
1350 END
1360 LOCATE 24,1:INPUT;"Hit <ENTER> to Continue ",ZZ$
     :CLS:RETURN
```

Main Program A

Before entering the next program, you must first clear the Introduction program from memory. Do this by typing ''NEW'' and pressing <ENTER> or <RETURN> key. The resident program (the program already in computer memory) is erased. To verify that all memory is erased, type LIST and press <ENTER>. Your computer responds by displaying the OK prompt but no program listing is displayed.

The computer is now ready to accept the Main Program A. This program can be seen in Listing 2-2. When the program has been typed, save the program by re-inserting the disk that was previously used to save the Introduction program (INTRO2) into Drive A. Type SAVE ''PCB'' and press <ENTER>.

Listing 2-2. PC Board Designer Main program A listing.

```
10 REM        PRINTED CIRCUIT BOARD DESIGN   "Main A"
20 REM
30 REM                by: Steve Sokolowski
40 REM
50 REM                  (C)opyright 1987
60 REM
70 REM    This program is protected under the laws of
80 REM    the United States of America. Any
90 REM    publication or reproduction in any form -
100 REM    without the expressed written consent of
110 REM    the author or Tab Books Inc. is prohibited.
120 REM
130 REM        ==> SAVE UNDER FILENAME "PCB" <==
140 CLS
150 KEY OFF
160 SCREEN 1
170 COLOR 1,3
180 LOCATE 11,17:PRINT"PC Board"
190 LOCATE 15,14:PRINT"Design Program"
200 LOCATE 25,12:PRINT"(C)opyright    1987"
210 FOR T=1 TO 5500:NEXT T
220 CLS:COLOR 0,1
230 LINE(0,10)-(319,190),3,B
240 LOCATE 1,1:PRINT"PC Board Designer":LOCATE 1,25:P
    RINT"(C)opyright 1987"
250 FOR Y=15 TO 185 STEP 11
260     FOR X=5 TO 315 STEP 5:PSET(X,Y),2:NEXT X:NEXT
    Y
270 DEF SEG=&HB800
280 DIM B(2500)
290 X=155:Y=99:C=3:S=1:L=1:BB=1
300 GOTO 2080
310 A$=INKEY$
320 ON ERROR GOTO 700
330 IF A$ <>"" THEN SOUND 800,2
340 IF A$="R"OR A$="r" THEN GOSUB 890:S=1:LOCATE 25,1
    :INPUT;"Really Erase (Y/N) ";Q$:IF Q$="Y"OR Q$="y"THE
    N GOSUB 890:GOTO 1620 ELSE GOSUB 890:GOTO 2080
350 IF A$="H"OR A$="h" GOTO 1670
360 IF A$="F"OR A$="f" GOTO 1730
370 IF A$="J"OR A$="j" GOTO 1450
380 IF A$="D"OR A$="d" THEN S=S*-1
390 IF A$="E"OR A$="e" THEN L=L*-1:PSET(X,Y),0:IF L=-
    1 THEN A1=X:A2=Y: ELSE A3=X:A4=Y:LINE(A1,A2)-(A3,A4),
    0,BF
400 IF A$="T"OR A$="t" THEN PSET(X,Y):GOSUB 1650:S=1
410 IF A$="P"OR A$="p" THEN PSET(X,Y),0:PAINT (2,11),
    2,3:PAINT (2,11),0,3:SOUND 500,2
420 IF A$="G"OR A$="g" THEN L=L*-1:PSET(X,Y),0:IF L=-
    1 THEN A1=X+1:A2=Y ELSE A3=X:A4=Y-1:B=0:GOSUB 890:LOC
    ATE 25,1:PRINT"Recording Picture";:GET(A1,A2)-(A3,A4),
    B:SOUND 800,2:BB=1:GOSUB 890:GOTO 1950
430 IF A$="A"OR A$="a" THEN A1=X:A2=Y:PUT(A1,A2),B
440 IF A$="S"OR A$="s" GOTO 720
```

```
450 IF A$="L"OR A$="l" GOTO 1970
460 IF A$="W" OR A$="w" GOTO 910
470 IF A$="1" THEN C=3:S=1:F=0
480 IF A$="2" THEN C=0:F=0
490 IF A$="C" OR A$="c" THEN GOTO 1410
500 ON KEY (11) GOSUB 660
510 ON KEY (12) GOSUB 600
520 ON KEY (13) GOSUB 570
530 ON KEY (14) GOSUB 630
540 ON KEY (1) GOSUB 2050
550 KEY(11) ON:KEY(12) ON:KEY(13) ON:KEY(14) ON:KEY(1
    ) ON
560 GOTO 310
570 IF X>=319 THEN GOSUB 2090;:RETURN ELSE P=POINT(X+
    1,Y):PSET(X+1,Y),C
580 IF S=-1 THEN PSET(X,Y),C ELSE PSET(X,Y),F
590 X=X+1:SOUND 200,1:F=P:RETURN
600 IF X=0 THEN GOSUB 2100;:RETURN ELSE P=POINT(X-1,Y
    ):PSET(X-1,Y),C
610 IF S=-1 THEN PSET(X,Y),C ELSE PSET(X,Y),F
620 X=X-1:SOUND 300,1:F=P:RETURN
630 IF Y>=190 THEN GOSUB 2110;:RETURN ELSE P=POINT(X,
    Y+1):PSET(X,Y+1),C
640 IF S=-1 THEN PSET(X,Y),C ELSE PSET(X,Y),F
650 Y=Y+1:SOUND 400,1:F=P:RETURN
660 IF Y<=10 THEN GOSUB 2120;:RETURN ELSE P=POINT(X,Y
    -1):PSET(X,Y-1),C
670 IF S=-1 THEN PSET(X,Y),C ELSE PSET(X,Y),F
680 Y=Y-1:SOUND 500,1:F=P:RETURN
690 END
700 PSET(X,Y),F:DEF SEG=&HB800:IF ERR=53 THEN GOSUB 2
    140 ELSE RUN 280,R
710 END
720 REM SAVE ARTWORK
730 PSET(X,Y),F
740 GOSUB 890
750 LOCATE 25,1:INPUT;"Enter Name of .PIX File => ",A
    $
760 GOSUB 890
770 IF A$="" THEN GOTO 2080
780 BSAVE A$+".PIX",0,16384
790 CLOSE:GOTO 2080
800 REM LOAD ARTWORK
810 PSET(X,Y),F
820 GOSUB 890
830 LOCATE 25,1:INPUT;"Enter .PIX Name to be Loaded =
    > ",A$
840 GOSUB 890
850 IF A$="" THEN GOTO 2080
860 DEF SEG=&HB800:BLOAD A$+".PIX",0
870 CLOSE:GOTO 2080
880 END
890 LOCATE 25,1:PRINT SPACE$(80);:RETURN
900 END
910 GOSUB 890
```

```
920 LOCATE 25,1:PRINT "Character Insert. Hit Comma ',
    ' to Exit";:S=1
930 B$=INKEY$:IF B$="" THEN 930
940 IF X>=319 THEN X=0:IF X<0 THEN X=319:IF Y<=10 THE
    N Y=190:IF Y>=190 THEN Y=10
950 IF X>300 AND B$<>"," THEN GOSUB 2030:GOTO 930
960 PSET(X,Y)
970 SOUND 800,2
980 IF B$="1" THEN DRAW "U5":X=X+4:GOTO 930
990 IF B$="2" THEN DRAW "C0;R4;C3;L4;U3;R4;U2;L4":PSE
    T(X,Y-3),0:PSET(X+4,Y-3),0:PSET(X+4,Y-5),0:X=X+8:GOTO
    930
1000 IF B$="3" THEN DRAW "R3;U3;L2;R2;U2;L3":PSET(X+3
    ,Y),0:PSET(X+3,Y-3),0:PSET(X+3,Y-5),0:X=X+7:GOTO 930
1010 IF B$="4" THEN DRAW "C0;U5;C3;D2;R4;U2;D5":X=X+8
    :GOTO 930
1020 IF B$="5" THEN DRAW "R4;U3;L4;U2;R3":PSET(X+4,Y),
    0:PSET(X+4,Y-3),0:X=X+7:GOTO 930
1030 IF B$="6" THEN DRAW "C0;U5;C3;D5;R4;U3;L4":PSET(
    X,Y),0:PSET(X+4,Y),0:PSET(X+4,Y-3),0:X=X+7:GOTO 930
1040 IF B$="7" THEN DRAW "C0;U5;C3;R4;D5":X=X+8:GOTO
    930
1050 IF B$="8" THEN DRAW "U5;R4;D2;L4;R4;D3;L4":PSET(
    X,Y),0:PSET(X+4,Y),0:PSET(X+4,Y-3),0:PSET(X,Y-3),0:PS
    ET(X,Y-5),0:PSET(X+4,Y-5),0:X=X+7:GOTO 930
1060 IF B$="9" THEN DRAW "C0;R4;C3;U5;L4;D2;R4":PSET(
    X,Y-5),0:PSET(X,Y-3),0:PSET(X,Y-5),0:PSET(X+4,Y-5),0:
    X=X+7:GOTO 930
1070 IF B$="0" THEN DRAW "U5;R4;D5;L4":PSET(X,Y),0:PS
    ET(X,Y-5),0:PSET(X+4,Y),0:PSET(X+4,Y-5),0:X=X+9:GOTO
    930
1080 IF B$="/" THEN DRAW "R1;U1;R1;U1;R1;U1;R1;U1;R1;
    U1":X=X+9:GOTO 930
1090 IF B$="-" THEN DRAW "C0;U2;C3;R4":X=X+9:GOTO 930

1100 IF B$="A" OR B$="a" THEN DRAW "U5;R5;D5;U3;L4":P
     SET(X,Y-5),0:PSET(X+5,Y-5),0:X=X+8:GOTO 930
1110 IF B$="B" OR B$="b" THEN DRAW "U5;R4;D2;L4;R4;D3
     ;L4":PSET(X+4,Y),0:PSET(X+4,Y-3),0:PSET(X+4,Y-5),0:X=
     X+7:GOTO 930
1120 IF B$="C" OR B$="c" THEN DRAW "R4;L4;U5;R4":PSET
     (X,Y),0:PSET(X,Y-5),0:X=X+8:GOTO 930
1130 IF B$="D" OR B$="d" THEN DRAW "U5;R4;D5;L4":PSET
     (X+4,Y),0:PSET(X+4,Y-5),0:X=X+8:GOTO 930
1140 IF B$="E" OR B$="e" THEN DRAW "R5;L5;U3;R2;L2;U2
     ;R5":X=X+9:GOTO 930
1150 IF B$="F" OR B$="f" THEN DRAW "U3;R2;L2;U2;R4":X
     =X+7:GOTO 930
1160 IF B$="G" OR B$="g" THEN DRAW "C0;U5;R4;C3;L4;D5
     ;R4;U2;L2":PSET(X,Y),0:PSET(X,Y-5),0:PSET(X+4,Y),0:X=
     X+8:GOTO 930
1170 IF B$="H" OR B$="h" THEN DRAW "U5;D2;R5;U2;D5":X
     =X+9:GOTO 930
1180 IF B$="I" OR B$="i" THEN DRAW "C0;R1;C3;U5":X=X+
     5:GOTO 930
```

```
1190 IF B$="J" OR B$="j" THEN DRAW "U2;D2;R4;U5":PSET
     (X,Y),0:PSET(X+4,Y),0:X=X+8:GOTO 930
1200 IF B$="K" OR B$="k" THEN DRAW "U5;D2;R2;U1;R2;U1
     ":X=X+5:PSET(X,Y):DRAW "U1;L2;U1;L2":X=X+4:GOTO 930
1210 IF B$="L" OR B$="l" THEN DRAW "U5;D5;R4":X=X+8:G
     OTO 930
1220 IF B$="M" OR B$="m" THEN DRAW "U5;R3;D2;U2;R3;D5
     ":X=X+10:GOTO 930
1230 IF B$="N" OR B$="n" THEN DRAW "U5;F5;U5":X=X+9:G
     OTO 930
1240 IF B$="O" OR B$="o" THEN DRAW "U5;R4;D5;L4":PSET
     (X,Y),0:PSET(X,Y-5),0:PSET(X+4,Y),0:PSET(X+4,Y-5),0:X
     =X+8:GOTO 930
1250 IF B$="P" OR B$="p" THEN DRAW "U5;R5;D3;L3":PSET
     (X,Y-5),0:PSET(X+5,Y-5),0:PSET(X+5,Y-2),0:X=X+9:GOTO
     930
1260 IF B$="Q" OR B$="q" THEN DRAW "U5;R5;D6;U1;L5":P
     SET(X,Y),0:PSET(X,Y-5),0:PSET(X+5,Y-5),0:X=X+9:GOTO 9
     30
1270 IF B$="R" OR B$="r" THEN DRAW "U5;R5;D3;L3;F3":P
     SET(X,Y-5),0:PSET(X+5,Y-5),0:PSET(X+5,Y-2),0:X=X+9:GO
     TO 930
1280 IF B$="S" OR B$="s" THEN DRAW "R4;U3;L4;U2;R4":P
     SET(X+4,Y),0:PSET(X,Y-3),0:PSET(X+4,Y-3),0:PSET(X,Y-5
     ),0:X=X+8:GOTO 930
1290 IF B$="T" OR B$="t" THEN DRAW "C0;U5;C3;R4;L2;D5
     ":X=X+8:GOTO 930
1300 IF B$="U" OR B$="u" THEN DRAW "U5;D5;R6;U5":PSET
     (X,Y),0:PSET(X+6,Y),0:X=X+10:GOTO 930
1310 IF B$="V" OR B$="v" THEN PSET(X,Y),0:LINE (X,Y-5
     )-(X+2,Y):LINE(X+2,Y)-(X+4,Y-5):X=X+8:GOTO 930
1320 IF B$="W" OR B$="w" THEN DRAW "C0;U5;C3;D5;R3;U2
     ;D2;R3;U5":X=X+10:GOTO 930
1330 IF B$="X" OR B$="x" THEN DRAW "C0;U5;C3;F5":PSET
     (X,Y):DRAW "E5":X=X+9:GOTO 930
1340 IF B$="Y" OR B$="y" THEN DRAW "C0;U5;C3;D2;R5;L2
     ;D3;U3;R3;U2":PSET(X,Y-3),0:PSET(X+6,Y-3),0:X=X+10:GO
     TO 930
1350 IF B$="Z" OR B$="z" THEN DRAW "C0;R5;C3;L5;C0;U5
     ;C3;R5;G5":X=X+9:GOTO 930
1360 IF B$="." THEN PSET(X,Y),3:X=X+3:GOTO 930
1370 IF B$=CHR$(32) THEN PSET(X,Y),0:X=X+9:GOTO 930
1380 IF B$=CHR$(44) THEN PSET(X,Y),0:GOSUB 890:GOTO 2
     080
1390 IF A$="W" OR A$="w" THEN GOTO 930
1400 END
1410 REM CIRCLE PRINTER
1420 PSET(X,Y)
1430 CIRCLE(X,Y),5,3:PAINT(X+1,Y+1),3,3:PSET(X,Y),0:F
     =0:S=1:GOTO 310
1440 END
1450 GOSUB 890:LOCATE 25,1:PRINT"Cursor Express => ON
     <=";
1460 PSET(X,Y),F
1470 F=0
```

```
1480 A$=INKEY$
1490 IF A$="J" OR A$="j" GOTO 1550
1500 X=STICK(0):Y=STICK(1)
1510 IF X>=0 AND X<=14 AND Y>=0 AND Y<=5 THEN GOSUB 8
     90:LOCATE 25,1:PRINT"         Joystick Not Connected"
     ;:X=155:Y=99:PSET(X,Y),3:FOR I=1 TO 2200:NEXT:GOTO 20
     80
1520 IF POINT(X*2.8,Y*1.8)=0 THEN 1530 ELSE X=X+1:Y=Y
     +1:GOTO 1480
1530 PSET(X*2.8,Y*1.8),3:FOR AA=1 TO 30:NEXT AA:PSET(
     X*2.8,Y*1.8),0
1540 GOTO 1480
1550 SOUND 800,2:X=X*2.8:Y=Y*1.8:Y=INT(Y):X=INT(X)
1560 IF X<0 THEN X=5
1570 IF X>300 THEN X=315
1580 IF Y<12 THEN Y=12
1590 IF Y>190 THEN Y=185
1600 PSET(X,Y),3:A3=X:A4=Y:S=1:GOSUB 890:GOTO 2080
1610 END
1620 A$="CLS":GOTO 860
1630 END
1640 REM PAD PRINTER
1650 DRAW"C0;D2;C3;L1;U4;R2;D4;L1":PSET(X,Y+1),3:PSET
     (X,Y-1),3:F=0:RETURN
1660 END
1670 GOSUB 890:PSET(X,Y),F:BSAVE"DATA3.PIX",0,16384
1680 CLOSE
1690 RUN"HELP2.BAS"
1700 END
1710 SOUND 800,2:LOCATE 25,1:INPUT;"Hit <ENTER> to Co
     ntinue.....",AA$:CLS:CLOSE:RETURN
1720 END
1730 GOSUB 890:PSET(X,Y),F:BSAVE"DATA3.PIX",0,16384
1740 CLS:SCREEN 2:LOCATE 1,23:PRINT"Filenames already
     on Disk"
1750 FILES
1760 LOCATE 25,1:INPUT;"When ready - Hit <ENTER> ",ZZ
     $
1770 IF ZZ$="KILL" OR ZZ$="kill" THEN LOCATE 25,1:INP
     UT;"Which File shall I Kill (Must include Extension)
     ";QQ$:IF QQ$="" THEN GOTO 1780 ELSE KILL QQ$:GOTO 174
     0:ELSE GOTO 1780
1780 CLS:SCREEN 1:BLOAD"DATA3.PIX",0:CLOSE:RUN 280
1790 DEF SEG
1800 SOUND 800,2
1810 LOCATE 25,1:INPUT;"Filename of .LIB Graphic => "
     ,SS$
1820 IF SS$="" THEN DEF SEG=&HB800:GOSUB 890:GOTO 208
     0
1830 BSAVE SS$+".LIB",VARPTR(B(0)),5200
1840 DEF SEG=&HB800:GOSUB 890:SOUND 800,2:GOTO 2080
1850 END
1860 DEF SEG
1870 GOSUB 890
1880 LOCATE 25,1:INPUT;"Enter Name of .LIB File => ",
     SS$
```

```
1890 IF SS$="" THEN DEF SEG=&HB800:GOSUB 890:GOTO 208
     0
1900 GOSUB 890
1910 BLOAD SS$+".LIB",VARPTR(B(0))
1920 PUT(X,Y),B:BB=1
1930 DEF SEG=&HB800:GOTO 2080
1940 END
1950 LOCATE 25,1:INPUT;"Save in Library File (Y/N)";Z
     Z$:IF ZZ$="y" OR ZZ$="Y" THEN GOSUB 890:GOTO 1790 ELS
     E GOSUB 890:GOTO 2080
1960 END
1970 GOSUB 890:LOCATE 25,1:INPUT;"Load from <1>.LIB o
     r <2>.PIX => ",ZZ$
1980 A1=X:A2=Y
1990 IF ZZ$="1" THEN GOTO 1860
2000 IF ZZ$="2" THEN GOTO 800
2010 IF ZZ$<>"1" OR ZZ$<>"2" THEN GOSUB 890:GOTO 2080

2020 END
2030 FOR I=1 TO 10:SOUND 800,1:SOUND 0,1:NEXT:RETURN
2040 END
2050 IF BB=1 THEN PUT(X,Y),B,PSET
2060 SOUND 800,2:RETURN
2070 END
2080 LOCATE 25,1:PRINT" D=Draw    T=IC Pads    C=Circ
     ular Pads ";:SOUND 800,2:GOTO 310
2090 X=0:RETURN
2100 X=319:RETURN
2110 Y=10:RETURN
2120 Y=190:RETURN
2130 END
2140 GOSUB 890:LOCATE 25,1:PRINT"=> File Not Found <=
     ";:GOSUB 2030:FOR I=1 TO 2500:NEXT:IF ERL=1770 THEN G
     OTO 1780 ELSE RUN 280
```

Help Screens

Before programming Help, the resident PCB listing must be erased from memory by typing NEW and pressing the <ENTER> key. To verify that PCB has been erased, type LIST and then press <ENTER>. If no listing is displayed, the Help Screens can now be programmed.

The Help Screens, which can be found in Listing 2-3, includes five displays. To list each screen, just press the <ENTER> or <RETURN> key when needed.

When programming is completed, save the Help screens on the same disk that the other two PC Board Designer programs have been saved on, using the filename HELP2.

Main Program B

Since the Main Program B is almost identical to main Program A, you can reload "PCB" (Main Program A) and make the necessary corrections. To do

Listing 2-3. PC Board Designer Help program listing.

```
10 REM       PC Board Designer      * HELP *
20 REM
30 REM    ==> SAVE UNDER FILENAME "HELP2" <==
40 CLS
50 KEY OFF
60 SCREEN 2
70 LOCATE 1,33:PRINT"H E L P"
80 LOCATE 5,1
90 PRINT CHR$(24);:PRINT" - - - - - Moves Drawing Cur
   sor in the UP Direction"
100 PRINT CHR$(25);:PRINT" - - - - - Moves Drawing Cu
    rsor in the DOWN Direction"
110 PRINT CHR$(26);:PRINT" - - - - - Moves Drawing Cu
    rsor to the RIGHT"
120 PRINT CHR$(27);:PRINT" - - - - - Moves Drawing Cu
    rsor to the LEFT"
130 PRINT
140 PRINT"Key Board LETTER KEYS":PRINT
150 PRINT"D - - - - - Press the 'D' key to draw lines
    on the screen. In this mode,"
160 PRINT"          you can press any of the four A
    rrow keys and leave a trace of the"
170 PRINT"          movement. To EXIT, press the 'D
    ' key again."
180 PRINT
190 PRINT"R - - - - - By pressing the 'R' key, you wi
    ll be able to Clear the screen of"
200 PRINT"          ALL graphic material. In the lo
    wer left hand corner of the screen,"
210 PRINT"          you will be asked again if you
    wish to clear the monitor. Respond"
220 PRINT"          by entering a Y for Yes or N fo
    r No. Then press <ENTER>."
230 GOSUB 1180
240 PRINT"G - - - - - Saves desired graphic in comput
    er memory. You are asked if this"
250 PRINT"          image will be saved in the Libr
    ary File. You respond by typing Y"
260 PRINT"          for Yes or N for No. If you ans
    wer Yes, you will then be asked to"
270 PRINT"          give this new image a name. Res
    pond by entering a Filename. Then"
280 PRINT"          press the <ENTER> key. The imag
    e will now be saved on Disk. You may"
290 PRINT"          recall this image at any time b
    y using the 'L' (LOAD) option."
300 PRINT"          This option requires you to inp
    ut two X/Y diagonal coordinates."
310 PRINT"          Do this by pressing the 'G' key
    twice when in the desired location."
320 PRINT
330 PRINT"A - - - - - With an image in computer memor
    y, (placed there by using the 'G'"
340 PRINT"          or 'L' option) the 'A' key allo
    ws the computer to Draw this in"
```

```
350 PRINT"             memory graphic at the indicated
     X/Y coordinates. By pressing"
360 PRINT"             the 'A' key for a second time,
     the computer will Erase the image"
370 PRINT"             just drawn but leaving any prev
     iously drawn material untouched."
380 PRINT"             With image at desired location
     - Press the F1 Key."
390 PRINT
400 PRINT"E - - - - - This option ERASEs a section of
     your graphic. The 'E' option is used"
410 PRINT"             in the same manner as the 'G' o
     ption (two Diagonal X/Y coordinates"
420 PRINT"             are needed). Instead of saving
     the image in computer memory, the"
430 PRINT"             ERASE option paints this graphi
     c section BLACK, thus erasing"
440 PRINT"             the image."
450 PRINT
460 GOSUB 1180
470 PRINT"S - - - - - SAVEs Complete Screen on Disk A
     - You enter Filename when requested."
480 PRINT
490 PRINT"C - - - - - This key draws a pre-programmed
     circular pad at any desired location"
500 PRINT"             on the screen. These circles ar
     e used to indicate wire connections"
510 PRINT"             that will be made to the PC Boa
     rd from the outside world."
520 PRINT
530 PRINT
540 PRINT"L - - - - - LOADs a Complete Screen or Libr
     ary symbol from Disk A. You enter"
550 PRINT"             the number 1 if you wish to LOA
     D an image from the Library, or"
560 PRINT"             enter the number 2 if you wish
     to LOAD an image from the Picture"
570 PRINT"             File. Then when asked, enter th
     e Filename of the image. When loaded,"
580 PRINT"             the graphic will be displayed a
     t the location of the Drawing"
590 PRINT"             Cursor."
600 PRINT
610 PRINT"W - - - - - Used to print letters and numbe
     rs at any location on the screen."
620 PRINT"             Hit the Comma ',' key to EXIT."

630 PRINT
640 PRINT"P - - - - - When ready to make a printed co
     py of the PC Board layout, press"
650 PRINT"             the 'P' key. This option erases
     the stationary graph dots by"
660 PRINT"             first painting the screen purpl
     e, then re-painting the screen to"
670 PRINT"             Black. The PC Board layout prev
     iously drawn will remain untouched."
```

```
680 PRINT"            You may now press the Print or
    Shift/Print to make a hard copy."
690 PRINT
700 GOSUB 1180
710 LOCATE 2,1
720 PRINT"J - - - - By pressing the 'J' key, you ar
    e placed in the Cursor Express Mode."
730 PRINT"            If you have a Joystick or Graph
    ic Table connected to the LEFT"
740 PRINT"            Joystick Port, you can now move
    the Drawing Cursor around the"
750 PRINT"            screen faster then if the Arrow
    Keys were used. When at the desired"
760 PRINT"            location, press the 'J' key for
    the second time. You will now be"
770 PRINT"            able to Draw, Erase or Insert C
    omponents at the new coordinates."
780 PRINT
790 PRINT"T - - - - This option draws a small recta
    ngular pad that can be used as"
800 PRINT"            copper pads for Intergrated Cir
    cuits or any other components."
810 PRINT
820 PRINT"Print or  - Used to print your schematic on
    a graphic Printer."
830 PRINT"            Which button to press depends o
    n the type of computer you have."
840 PRINT"Shift/Print Consult your BASIC Instruction
    Booklet for additional information."
850 PRINT
860 PRINT"F - - - - The 'F' option allows you to di
    splay ALL filenames saved on Disk A."
870 PRINT"            You may also DELETE Files just
    by typing - KILL - to the prompt"
880 PRINT"            <Hit Enter to Continue>. Then t
    ype in the filename you wish to"
890 PRINT"            Delete - then press <ENTER>. NO
    TE - this filename MUST contain the"
900 PRINT"            extension (ex. .LIB - .BAS ect.)"

910 GOSUB 1180
920 PRINT"No. 1 Button  - By pressing this button, t
    he color of the Drawing Cursor"
930 PRINT"                is changed to WHITE."
940 PRINT
950 PRINT"No. 2 Button  - By pressing this button, t
    he color of the Drawing Cursor"
960 PRINT"                is changed to BLACK. If us
    ed in conjunction with the 'D'"
970 PRINT"                key, you can erase drawn l
    ines by re-coloring the line"
980 PRINT"                Black."
990 PRINT
1000 PRINT"To exit from any required keyboard input (
    Ex. Entering a Filename or Component"
```

```
1010 PRINT"Number) just press the <ENTER> Key without
     entering any information. Your"
1020 PRINT"computer will cancel that input and return
     you to the Drawing Mode."
1030 PRINT
1040 PRINT"When requested to enter a filename of an i
     mage that will be LOADED or SAVED,"
1050 PRINT"you are NOT required to add the extension
     (ex. .LIB or .PIX). These"
1060 PRINT"extensions are automatically inserted by t
     he computer."
1070 PRINT"Extensions are required ONLY if you intend
     to KILL a File when the 'F' option"
1080 PRINT"is being used."
1090 PRINT
1100 PRINT"The extension .LIB indicates ALL Files tha
     t have been SAVED as a Library File."
1110 PRINT
1120 PRINT"The extension .PIX indicates ALL Files tha
     t were SAVED as an Image File."
1130 PRINT"An image File is a file that has SAVED the
     entire contents of the screen on"
1140 PRINT"Disk."
1150 GOSUB 1180
1160 GOTO 1200
1170 END
1180 LOCATE 25,1:INPUT;"Hit <ENTER> to Continue ....."
     ,AA$:CLS:RETURN
1190 END
1200 CLS:RUN "PCB2.BAS"
```

this, type LOAD ''PCB'' and then press <ENTER>. When the program is loaded, type DELETE 10 - 260, and press the <ENTER> or <RETURN> key.

The delete command erases only the section of the program indicated. In this case, lines 10 through 260 are deleted from the resident program but the balance is left untouched, so the necessary program changes can now be made.

Refer to Listing 2-4. This is a listing of new programming lines that have to be made in order for proper program operation. Enter these lines as they appear. When you're done, save the program under the filename ''PCB2''.

Loading the Graph Paper Program

The last program to be entered into the computer is the Graph Paper program. This program allows your computer to print a graph pattern on paper using a dot matrix printer or equivalent. This pattern is the exact copy of the PC Board Main Screen and is used to place electronic components properly and to draw by hand the proper interconnecting copper traces.

The Graph Paper Program can be found in Listing 2-5. This 26-line program should take very little time to enter.

Listing 2-4. PC Board Designer Main Program B listing.

```
1 REM      PRINTED CIRCUIT BOARD DESIGN   "Main B"
2 REM
3 REM               by: Steve Sokolowski
4 REM
5 REM                  (C)opyright 1987
6 REM
7 REM    This program is protected under the laws of
8 REM    the United States of America. Any
9 REM    publication or reproduction in any form -
10 REM   without the expressed written consent of
11 REM   the author or Tab Books Inc. is prohibited.
12 REM
13 REM      ==> SAVE UNDER FILENAME "PCB2" <==
14 CLS
15 KEY OFF
16 SCREEN 1
17 BLOAD"DATA3.PIX",A:CLOSE
```

Listing 2-5. Graph Paper program listing.

```
10 REM    CAE Program    Printed Circuit Board Designer
20 REM
30 REM                Graphic Paper Printer Program
40 REM
50 REM
60 REM                   (C)opyright 1987
70 REM
80 REM
90 REM    This program is protected under the laws of
100 REM   the United States of America. Any
110 REM   publication or reproduction in any form -
120 REM   without the expressed written consent of
130 REM   the author or Tab Books Inc. is prohibited.
140 REM
150 REM          ==> SAVE UNDER FILENAME "GRAPH" <==
160 CLS
170 KEY OFF
180 CLEAR 5000
190 SCREEN 1
200 LINE(0,10)-(319,190),3,B
210 LOCATE 1,1:PRINT"CAE Program":LOCATE 1,26:PRINT"P
    C Board Design"
220 FOR Y=15 TO 185 STEP 11
230     FOR X=5 TO 315 STEP 5:PSET(X,Y),3:NEXT X:NEXT
    Y
240 SOUND 900,2
250 LOCATE 25,10:PRINT"Graph Paper Program"
260 GOTO 260
```

When you're done, save it on disk under the filename "GRAPH". Printing the graph and using this printout is discussed in greater detail later.

MAKING BACK-UP COPIES

As with all computer software, back-up copies of all valuable data and programming should be made. MS-DOS and PC-DOS provide a means of copying disks easily with a utility named DISKCOPY.

If you are in BASIC, type SYSTEM and press <ENTER> or the <RETURN> key. Insert the DOS disk in Drive A and type DISKCOPY. When it is loaded, you are asked to switch between the Source Disk (the disk containing the CAE programs) and the Target Disk (a formatted disk which will be programmed with the CAE material) a few times until all information is recorded on the Target Disk. You may be required to switch between the two disks as many as nine times but if a computer is available with two disk drives this procedure is very much simplified.

If you have two drives, while in MS-DOS or PC-DOS, type DISKCOPY A:B. When the program is loaded, you are prompted to insert the Source Disk into Drive A and a formatted Target Disk into Drive B. Then press any key when you are ready. Without any disk switching, the material contained on the Source Disk is transferred automatically to the Target Disk.

I recommend that you make a number of copies of each program disk, especially if you plan to modify and program to suit your own needs. This prevents losing hours of typing time if you damage or accidentally erase the disk.

If you decide to purchase the complete CAE Program Disk from TAB BOOKS, you should also make a number of back-up copies of this master. Additional information on making back-ups, and program manipulation of the complete CAE computer disk, can be found at the end of this chapter.

PC BOARD DESIGNER COMMANDS

The main PC Board Designer Program has 13 useful commands that control what your computer draws. Each is now discussed in detail.

Reset

Before the rest (R) option can be used, you must save on disk a reset memory image file. This option clears the contents of the screen. It works just like the CLS computer command. Whatever is contained on the screen is lost.

While in BASICA, type RUN "PCB" and then press <ENTER> to load the program. A frame is drawn and copyright credits are displayed. The center of the monitor is empty except for a graph paper pattern. Press the "S" key (Save Drawing on Disk). In the lower left corner, you are prompted to enter a filename. Type CLS. With the PC Designer disk in Drive A press the <ENTER> key. The drive turns indicating that the contents of the screen are now being saved on disk. With this disk in Drive A, you can call upon the "R" option any time you want to clear the screen of all graphic material.

With the screen cleared, you can start drawing. (Refer to Fig. 2-2).

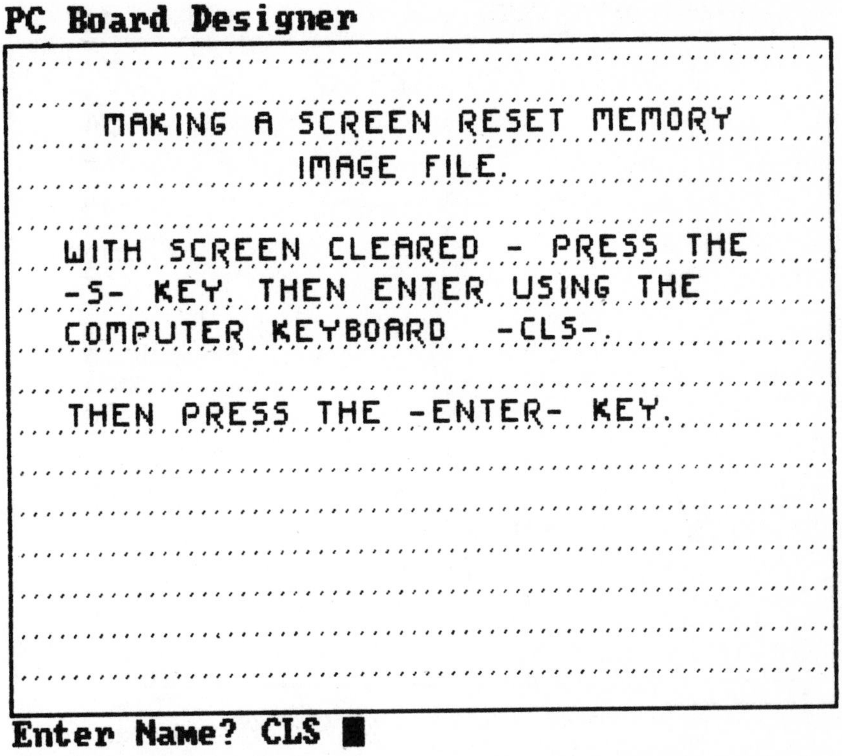

PC Board Designer

```
.....................................................
....... MAKING A SCREEN RESET MEMORY .......
................. IMAGE FILE. .......................
.....................................................
... WITH SCREEN CLEARED - PRESS THE .......
... -S- KEY. THEN ENTER USING THE .........
... COMPUTER KEYBOARD  -CLS-. ..............
.....................................................
... THEN PRESS THE -ENTER- KEY. ..........
.....................................................
.....................................................
.....................................................
.....................................................
.....................................................
.....................................................
.....................................................
```

Enter Name? CLS ■

Fig. 2-2. Making a RESET image screen for the PC Board Designer Program.

Arrow Keys

The CAE program allows the use of the four arrow keys to move the Drawing Cursor to any location on the screen (within the limits of the frame). The use of the arrow keys is a substitute for using an expensive mouse for cursor control. Press the up arrow key. The flashing dot moves up. Also, you will hear beeps as the dot moves up the screen. The frequency of the beeps depends on the direction the dot is moving. Press the down arrow key. The dot moves in the downward direction. (See Fig. 2-3). As with the Schematic Designer, you may find, if you are using an IBM compatible, that the beeps generated by the computer are too loud. This volume can be adjusted with the BASIC command SOUND. A list of program changes that include lowering the audio volume can be found in the section marked "Program Modifications."

Drawing a Line

To draw a line, press the "D" key once. Now press the arrow key for the direction in which you wish to draw a line. The Drawing Cursor now leaves a trace. Try the other three arrow keys.

To exit from this mode, hit the "D" key a second time. Now press any arrow key. The Drawing Cursor does not leave any trace. Use this option to draw the interconnecting lines between component pads. (See Fig. 2-4).

PC Board Designer

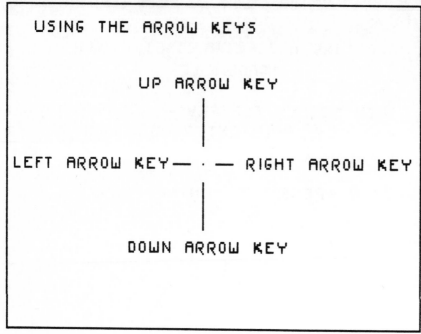

Fig. 2-3. Using the arrow keys to move the Drawing Cursor.

PC Board Designer

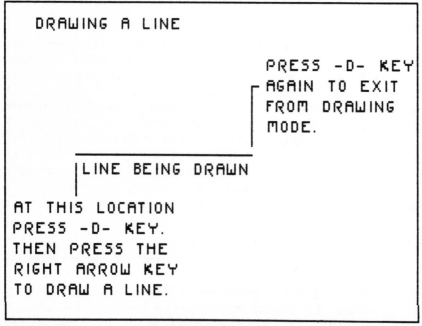

Fig. 2-4. Drawing a line using the PC Board Designer Program.

PC Board Designer

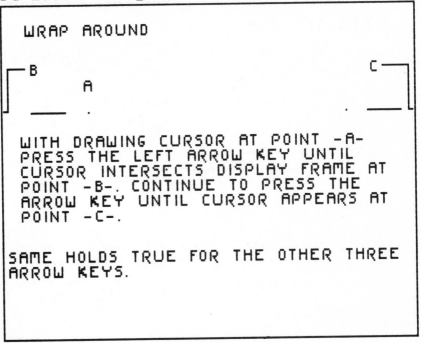

Fig. 2-5. Drawing Cursor wrap around.

Cursor Wrap Around

As with the first CAE program, a Drawing Cursor Wrap Around Feature is also incorporated in the PC Board Designer. Wrap Around describes a feature that allows the Drawing Cursor to be moved to its outermost limits; in this case, the left section of the screen. The cursor is automatically returned to the right portion of the screen.

An example of Wrap Around can be seen in Fig. 2-5. This figure demonstrates that the Drawing Cursor can be moved to the left by pressing the left arrow key. Then, when the cursor reaches the left display frame, it re-appears at the right. Wrap Around can be used with any of the four arrow keys.

This feature can also be used when inserting text on the PC Board layout while in the Wording Option.

Erasing a Line

If you made a mistake in the direction you wish to draw a line, recovery is quite simple. The cursor comes in two colors, white and black. The "1" key is used to change the dot's color to white while the "2" key is used to change the color to black. To erase a mistake, just change the dot's color to black (which is the monitor's background color), to erase the line.

Refer to Fig. 2-6 and clear the screen by tapping the "R" key. Draw a line to the right by pressing the "D" key once, then pressing the right arrow

PC Board Designer

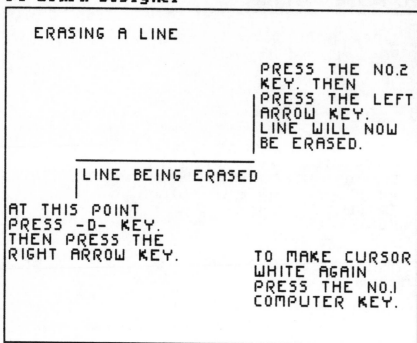

ERASING A LINE

PRESS THE NO.2
KEY. THEN
PRESS THE LEFT
ARROW KEY.
LINE WILL NOW
BE ERASED.

LINE BEING ERASED

AT THIS POINT
PRESS -D- KEY.
THEN PRESS THE
RIGHT ARROW KEY.

TO MAKE CURSOR
WHITE AGAIN
PRESS THE NO.I
COMPUTER KEY.

Fig. 2-6. Erasing a line using the PC Board Designer Program.

key. Remove your finger from the arrow key. Press the "2" key. The line will now be erased by backtracking the move to the right by pressing the left arrow key. Notice that the line is being erased.

To change the color of the dot to WHITE again hit the "1" key.

Drawing an IC Pad

Figure 2-7 shows how to draw the pads needed for a 6-pin DIP (Dual In-Line Package) IC. Using one of the four arrow keys, move the Drawing Cursor over one of the colored stationary graph dots. Then press the "T" key. A copper trace pad is instantly drawn. Now, using the right arrow key, move the cursor to the next colored graph dot. Press the "T" key again. A second pad is drawn at that location. Proceed with this operation for the third pad. Now, using the down arrow key, move the cursor to the next lower row of colored graph dots. Proceed to draw the next three copper pads. The computer screen will show a trace for a 6-pin IC. For IC's using more then 6 pins, just continue to draw pads for the number of required leads. Then using the "D" option, interconnect these pads for a complete board.

Cursor Express

With the addition of a joystick or graphics tablet and by enabling Cursor Express, you can move the Drawing Cursor hundreds of times faster around

PC Board Designer

```
. . . . . . . . . . . . . . . . . . . . . . . . . . . . . . . . . . . . . . . . . . . . . . . . . . . . . . . . .
. . . . . . . . . . . . . . . . . . . . . . . . . . . . . . . . . . . . . . . . . . . . . . . . . . . . . . . . .
  DRAWING AN IC PAD
. . . . . . . . . . . . . . . . . . . . . . . . . . . . . . . . . . . . . . . . . . . . . . . . . . . . . . . . .
. . . . . . . . . . . . . . . . . . . . . . . . . . . . . . . . . . . . . . . . . . . . . . . . . . . . . . . . .
                                              ▮▮▮
                                              ▮▮▮ b PIN IC
. . . . . . . . . . . . . . . . . . . . . . . . . . . . . . . . . . . . . . . . . . . . . . . . . . . . . . . . .
  MOVE DRAWING CURSOR TO A
  GRAPH DOT. THEN PRESS THE
  -T- KEY. MOVE DOT TO NEXT
  DOT - PRESS -T- KEY AGAIN.
  THEN MOVE CURSOR TO THE NEXT
  LOWER LEVEL OF DOTS. USE THE
  -T- KEY TO DRAW THE NEXT 3 PADS
  YOUR DRAWING SHOULD BE THE SAME
  AS PICTURED ABOVE.
```

Fig. 2-7. Using the PC Board Designer to draw the pads for a 6-pin IC.

the screen compared to using the slower arrow keys. Just connect the DIN plug of your joystick (or graphics tablet) to the left joystick port. To activate Cursor Express, hit the "J" key one time. Now move the joystick in different directions. The cursor zooms across the screen.

To exit from Cursor Express, press the "J" key a second time. You can now draw or insert IC pads at the new location.

If you are using an IBM machine, your computer must be equipped with a serial interface card in order to be able to take advantage of Cursor Express. This card can be purchased for as little as $29.00.

If the CAE Programs are running on a compatible computer similar to the Tandy 1000, chances are that an interface is already incorporated into the machine. If this is the case, just plug the joystick or graphics tablet into the appropriate connector.

Circle

To draw a circle, move the flashing cursor to the appropriate location and then press the "C" key. Instantly, a circle is drawn and then filled in white with a colored center to indicate where a hole is to be drilled. (See Fig. 2-8.)

Saving the Layout on Disk

Now that you have an understanding of how to draw component pads and copper traces, a means of saving the artwork on disk must be discussed. To

PC Board Designer

```
CIRCLE OPTION -C-



          ● — DRAWN BY PRESSING
               THE -C- KEY.

THE CIRCLE OPTION IS USED TO
INDICATE OUTSIDE CONNECTION
TO PC BOARD.

JUST MOVE CURSOR TO DESIRED
LOCATION. THEN PRESS THE -C- KEY.
```

Fig. 2-8. Using the circle option.

save the layout, refer to Fig. 2-9 and press the "S" key. In the lower left corner, you are asked to give the image a filename. Type the PCB's name (it must be less than 8 characters in length). Then, making sure the PC Board Designer Program is in Drive A, press the <ENTER> key. The computer is now saving the PCB layout on disk under the .PIX (Picture) filename you have chosen. This process takes about five or ten seconds depending on the complexity of the graphic.

An image saved on disk requires a large amount of space. About six layouts can be saved on one disk. Keep an eye on the available disk space when using the SAVE option.

Loading a Graphic

The next option to be examined is LOAD. With prints already saved on disk, a layout can be instantly displayed at any time. (Refer to Fig. 2-10.) Press the "L" key. In the lower left corner of the screen, you are asked whether the computer is to load a graphic from the .LIB (Library) or the .PIX (Picture) File. For this example, enter the number <2>. This will load a picture from the .PIX file.

After pressing the <ENTER> or <RETURN> key, the computer prompts you to enter the filename of the desired graphic (see Fig. 2-11). Using the keyboard, enter the filename of a previously saved pattern, and press

PC Board Designer

```
SAVING LAYOUT ON DISK

   WITH LAYOUT DISPLAYED ON SCREEN
   PRESS THE -S- KEY.
   YOU WILL THEN BE ASKED TO ENTER
   THE NAME OF THE IMAGE.

   WHEN COMPLETE   PRESS THE
   -ENTER- KEY.

   LAYOUT WILL THEN BE SAVED AS A
   .PIX FILE.




   ENTER FILENAME HERE ─┐
                        │
```

Enter Name of .PIX File => ■

Fig. 2-9. Saving an image in the Picture (.PIX) File.

PC Board Designer

```
LOADING A GRAPHIC

WITH SCREEN CLEARED OR DISPLAYING
AN IMAGE -PRESS THE -L- KEY.
YOU WILL THEN BE ASKED IF THE NEW
WILL BE LOADED FROM THE LIBRARY
OR PICTURE FILE.




        SEE BELOW



SELECT NO.1 OR 2 THEN ENTER ─┐
                             │
```

Load from <1>.LIB or <2>.PIX => ■

Fig. 2-10. Giving the .PIX File a name.

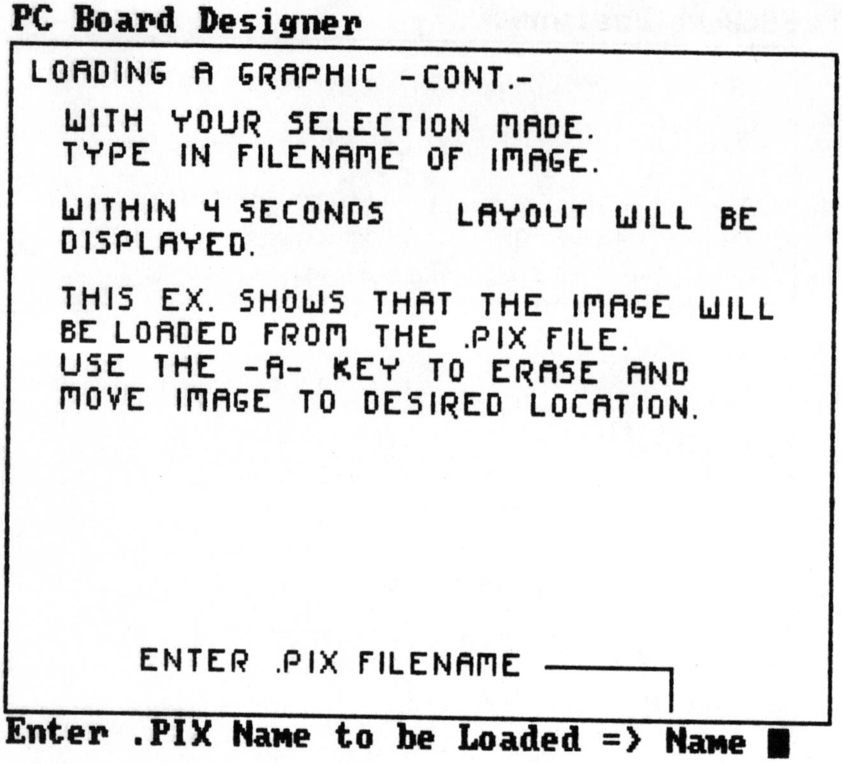

PC Board Designer

```
LOADING A GRAPHIC -CONT.-

WITH YOUR SELECTION MADE.
TYPE IN FILENAME OF IMAGE.

WITHIN 4 SECONDS    LAYOUT WILL BE
DISPLAYED.

THIS EX. SHOWS THAT THE IMAGE WILL
BE LOADED FROM THE .PIX FILE.
USE THE -A- KEY TO ERASE AND
MOVE IMAGE TO DESIRED LOCATION.




              ENTER .PIX FILENAME ─────────┐
                                           │
```

Enter .PIX Name to be Loaded => Name ■

Fig. 2-11. Recalling a .PIX File from disk.

<ENTER> or <RETURN>. Drive A starts and within two to four seconds the layout is displayed on the monitor, ready to be edited or printed on paper.

This option is also used to load an image that has been saved as a .LIB (Library) File. Techniques on using this option have already been discussed in the section entitled "Adding Your Own Symbols to the Schematic Designer and PC Board Designer Programs." Return to those pages to refresh your memory on this option.

Wording Option

PC Board Designer also allows you to enter a number of characters (using the computer keyboard) at any location on the screen. Characters supported by PC Board Designer are as follows:

ABCDEFGHIJKLMNOPQRSTUVWXYZ

1234567890

. – /

space bar

To activate the Wording option, press the "W" key. In this mode, you can still use the arrow keys to move the Drawing Cursor to the desired location

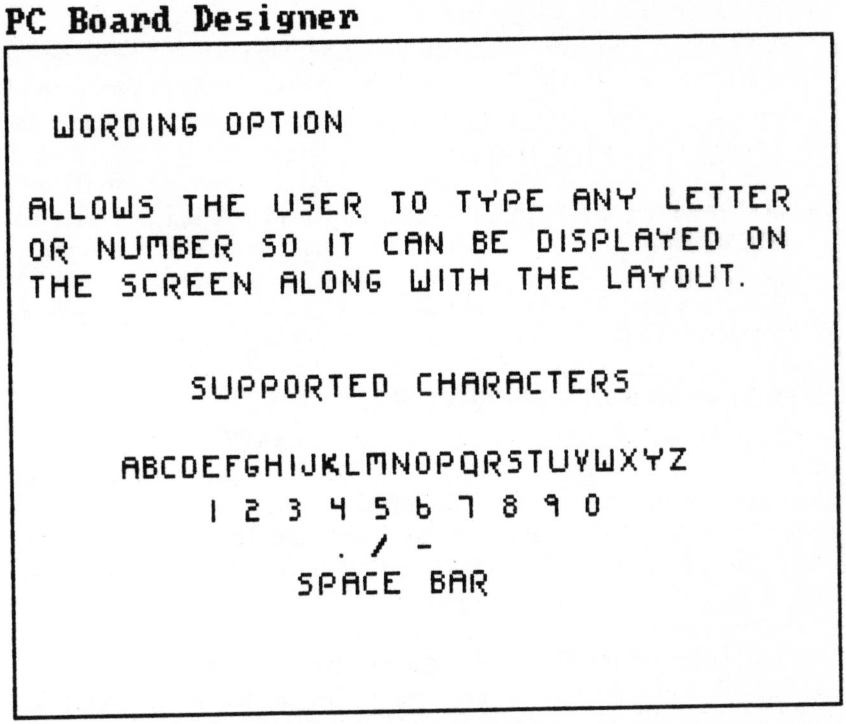

PC Board Designer

```
WORDING OPTION

ALLOWS THE USER TO TYPE ANY LETTER
OR NUMBER SO IT CAN BE DISPLAYED ON
THE SCREEN ALONG WITH THE LAYOUT.


        SUPPORTED CHARACTERS

   ABCDEFGHIJKLMNOPQRSTUVWXYZ
        1 2 3 4 5 6 7 8 9 0
              . / -
           SPACE BAR
```

Fig. 2-12. Using the PCB Designer's Wording Option.

(see Fig. 2-12). To exit from Wording, just hit the comma key. (Note: Cursor Express does not operate in this mode.)

Print Option

With a layout on the screen, a hard copy printout can be made at any time. Before printing, the now-unwanted graph paper pattern must be erased while leaving the finished layout untouched.

By pressing the "P" key, the computer screen is painted the same color as the graphic dots, thus erasing them. Then the screen is painted black. This painting leaves the layout (colored in white) untouched.

To make a hard copy, press the <PRINT> and/or <SHIFT> <PRINT> keys (for the IBM Computer press the <CRTL> and/or the <PrtSc> keys). (The key to be pressed to make a hard copy of the layout depends on the type of computer being used. Refer to your computer instruction booklet for proper usage.) Make sure the graphics printer is on line. The printer begins to draw the layout in a scale of 1:1.

You should save the PC Board layout (with graph paper pattern) using the SAVE option before pressing the "P" key. This guarantees you a PC board layout along with the necessary graph paper pattern if future modifications are required. (The graphic Dot Pattern cannot be redrawn on the screen once it has been erased with the "P" key.

Erase Option

The ERASE option (not to be confused with erasing a line) is used to remove any portion of the layout from the screen. Just as with the DRAW option, sections of the image can be erased by re-coloring that portion black, which is the background color of the monitor.

With a graphic on the screen, use the arrow keys to move the Drawing Cursor to the upper left section of the pattern you want to erase. Then press the "E" key. Now move the cursor to the diagonal location of the graphic to be erased. Press the "E" key for a second time. Note that the layout that is to be erased is located within an imaginary box that is drawn using these two X, Y coordinates. This section is now erased by the computer.

Save Graphics in Computer Memory

Using the same principle as discussed with the ERASE option (diagonal X,Y coordinates), a section of the layout can be saved in computer memory so that it can be redrawn at a later time. Use this option to move sections of the layout to another portion of the screen or save a section of the layout so it can be used within a completely different PC board design. This option also allows you to save a pattern in the Library File so that it can be recalled at any time.

With your monitor showing a print, use the arrow keys to move the cursor to the upper left corner of the layout you want saved in memory. Then press the "G" (Get) key. Now move the cursor to the diagonal location of the first (lower right section). Then press the "G" key for the second time.

At this time, the computer saves the print located within the imaginary box that is drawn using the two X, Y coordinates. You are asked if this new image should be saved in the .LIB File. Enter the letter "N" for no.

Both CAE programs were written to operate on a computer using 128K of memory, so only a designated amount of memory is allowed for this option. If the computer does not take any time at all to save a large print, the area of the layout was too large for the memory. Break up this print into smaller sections so the limited computer memory can handle it.

See Fig. 2-13 for an example of the ERASE and GET options. They both use the same principle.

Placing Memory Graphics On Screen

Now that a graphic is in memory using the "G" option, move the Drawing Cursor using the arrow keys (or Cursor Express) to any other location on the screen, making sure there is enough room on the monitor to draw the new print. (If not enough screen space is available, the computer beeps. No graphic is displayed, but the image already displayed remains untouched.)

If the above conditions are met, press the "A" key. The computer draws the entire print that was saved in memory using the "G" option. This print can be redrawn any number of times without losing it from memory.

To relocate the saved graphic, press the "A" key a second time. The previously-drawn layout is erased leaving the resident image untouched. This

PC Board Designer

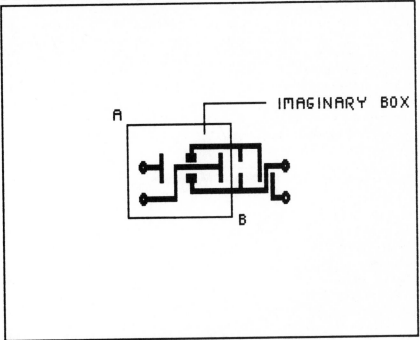

Fig. 2-13. Putting an image inside computer or to erase the image.

is called the XOR (Exclusive OR) Option. When the loaded image is in the desired position, press the F1 key. This redraws the image as a preset graphic.

File Option

With a number of .LIB and .PIX files on a disk, you may want to display the filenames and see how much disk space is available. Without exiting from a running PC Board Program, press the "F" key. At this time, the computer saves the monitor's layout on disk under the filename DATA. All listings located on Disk A are then displayed on the screen, along with the available disk space. Figure 2-14 is an example of this display. Note that free disk space is listed in bytes.

At the bottom of the screen, you are asked to press the <ENTER> key to continue the CAE program. If you type the word KILL at this prompt, you can delete any file you choose. At the prompt "Which File Shall I Kill?" type the name of the file you want to delete. Remember to add the appropriate extension (for example CLEARSCR.BAS); otherwise, a "File Not Found" error will occur.

Now, when the <ENTER> key is pressed, the computer lists all files again. This time, the file CLEARSCR.BAS is missing. The amount of available disk space has increased.

```
                    Current Filenames on Disk
A:\
1-29    .BAS    DRAW    .BAS    CLEARSCR.BAS      1-30    .BAS
1-31    .BAS    1-32    .BAS    PRI               1-34    .BAS
1-33    .BAS    1-35    .BAS    1-36    .BAS      1-37    .BAS
2-27    .BAS    2-28    .BAS    2-30    .BAS      2-31    .BAS
1-15B   .BAS
   108544 Bytes free
```

When Ready - Hit <ENTER> ■

Fig. 2-14. Sample screen display of the File option.

If you want to delete another file, type the word KILL to the prompt ''Hit <ENTER> to Continue''. If not, press the <ENTER> key. The computer then reloads the previously-saved PC board artwork.

USING THE GRAPH PROGRAM

It is a good idea to first draw by hand what the finished PC board should look like. To do this, you need graph paper with the proper spacing, which is impossible to find due to the unique pin spacing of the vertical lines.

To rectify this problem, the Graph Program was developed. The program draws a graph paper design on screen. When it's printed, copies can easily be made. To use this program, a Graphic Utility has to have been loaded while in MS-DOS or PC-DOS. (See ''Booting-up the Computer System'' in Chapter 1 for an explanation of this procedure.) Figure 2-15 shows a sample printout of GRAPH.

Figures 2-16 and 2-17 show the needed component spacing for a common electronic component, the resistor. The lead spacing can easily be translated into the correct spacing needed for other electricial components like capacitors or diodes.

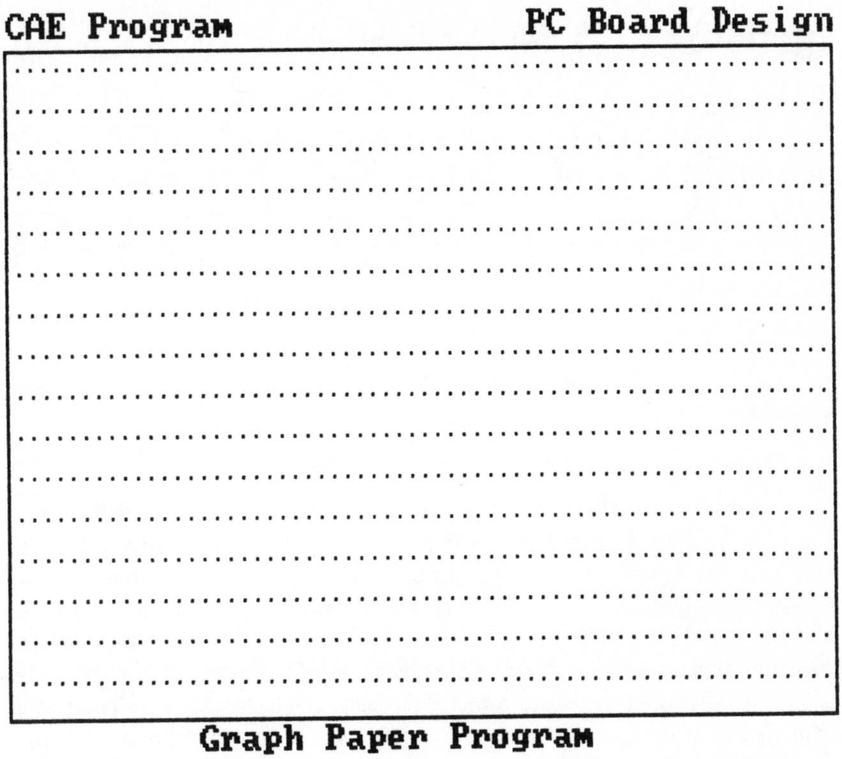

CAE Program **PC Board Design**

Graph Paper Program

Fig. 2-15. Sample printout of the Graph program.

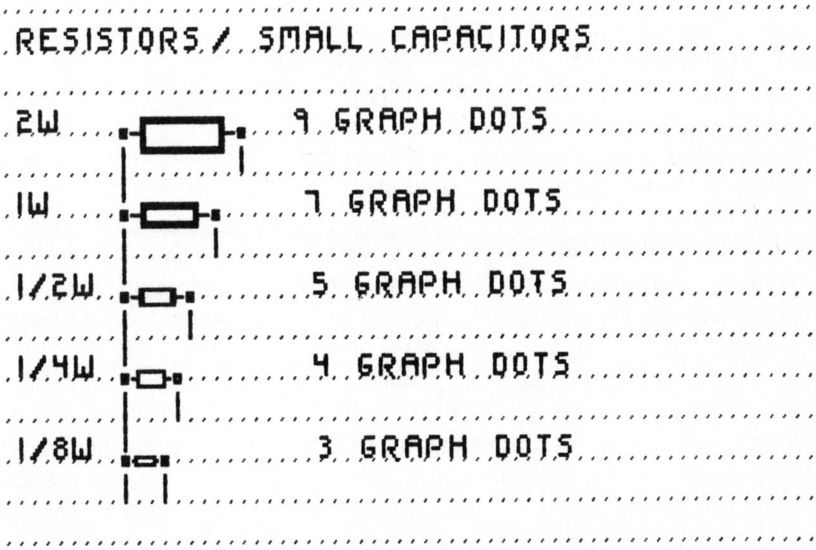

Fig. 2-16. Graphic display of the horizontal lead spacing for resistors and other small components.

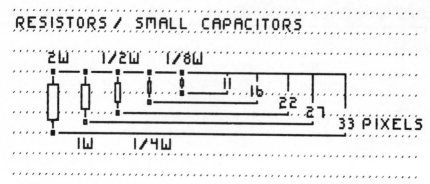

Fig. 2-17. Graphic display of the vertical lead spacing for resistors and other small components.

The resolution of Screen Mode 1 is 320 pixels across by 200 pixels down. If the pixels were arranged in an order of 320 by 320, we could simulate an electronic perf-board on the screen of the computer. If this was the case, all electronic components as well as integrated Circuits could be drawn by the computer in both the horizontal and the vertical direction. However, the available resolution of Screen 1 (320 by 200 pixels), ICs can only be drawn on the horizontal axis. Items like resistors, capacitors, and diodes which have wire leads protruding from them can be mounted in either the horizontal or vertical axis.

Figure 2-16 shows the horizontal lead spacing of common resistors of assorted sizes ranging from the smallest (⅛ watt) to the largest (2 watt).

For example, if a project requires the use of a ¼ watt resistor, Fig. 2-16 indicates that the horizontal lead spacing of this component should be four graphic dots. (Each dot is spaced .1 in. apart.) The total length needed by the 1/4 watt resistor is .1 × 4 or .4 inch. This spacing can also be used for other small components like signal diodes and capacitors.

Likewise, a 1 watt resistor needs the spacing of 7 graphic dots or .7 inch. Other components such as high current diodes and large value capacitors can also use this type of spacing.

Figure 2-17 shows the vertical lead spacing of the same resistor assortment. Instead of counting the printed stationary dots on the graph paper, you must count the number of pixels that the Drawing Cursor moves in either the upward or downward direction while pressing the arrow keys.

Suppose you want to figure the spacing needed for a 2 watt resistor which will be drawn on the vertical axis. Press the "T" key at the desired location to draw a copper pad, then press the up arrow key and count the number of times the pixel moves. As soon as you have reached the 33rd pixel, release the up arrow key and hit the "T" key for the second time. This gives you the exact lead spacing required by the 2 watt resistor.

If you want to place a ¼ watt resistor, count 16 pixels in the upward direction, then hit the ' T'' key. Do likewise for the other components.

DESIGNING A PC BOARD
FOR A 12 VOLT POWER SUPPLY

Figure 2-18 is a schematic of a 12-volt power supply that will be used to demonstrate step-by-step how to prepare a PC board layout. Using a copy of the graph paper printed using the graph program, first draw by hand a rough draft of the component placement and interconnecting copper traces. (See Fig. 2-19.) Remember to keep in mind the needed component spacing for horizontally and vertically mounted parts. To refresh your memory, refer back to Figs. 2-16 and 2-17.

Transformer T1 (16 Vac output) is a very large item. Since the cost of a PC board is quite high, the transformer will be mounted elsewhere in a cabinet, so at this time it can be ignored.

The bridge rectifier (D1 to D4) uses four diodes located on the horizontal axis. The needed spacing for this type of mounting is 4 stationary dots for each (see Fig. 2-16).

Filter capacitor C1 (radial type) uses a vertical spacing of 11 pixels. This spacing can be compared to the number needed to mount a ⅛ watt resistor. If you want to use an axial type of filter capacitor, the spacing between copper pads must be greater to accommodate this type of capacitor (see Fig. 2-17).

The 12 volt voltage regulator, REG1, can be mounted on the horizontal axis with 3 copper pads spaced .1 inch apart, the same as an Integrated Circuit.

To review, here is the pin spacing needed for the PC board:

- Bridge rectifier (4 diodes) horizontal mounting, 4 graphic dots
- Filter capacitor (radial type) vertical mounting of 11 pixels
- Voltage regulator (IC type) horizontal mounting of 3 graphics dots

12 VOLT POWER SUPPLY

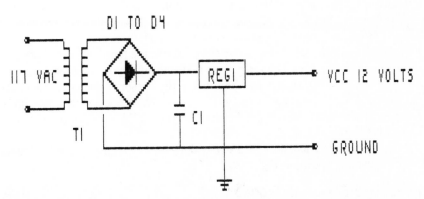

Fig. 2-18. Schematic of the power supply which will be used to design the PC board.

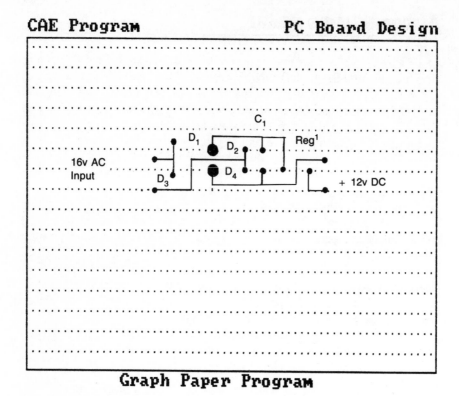

Fig. 2-19. Using the Graph Paper to draw by hand the finished PC board layout of the power supply.

With the needed spacing in mind, load and RUN the PC Board Designer Program. Using the "T" option, begin laying out the board.

With PC Board Designer loaded and running, let's start laying out the component pads. Referring to Fig. 2-20, move the Drawing Cursor to the approximate location shown to start laying out the four diodes incorporated with the bridge rectifier (D1 to D4), then press the "T" key. Instantly a rectangular box is drawn with a black center. This is a copper pad.

Using the right arrow key, move the cursor to the fourth stationary graphic dot, and press the "T" key again. This is the necessary spacing for diode D1.

Again, using the right arrow key, move the cursor to the next stationary graphic dot, then press the "T" key. Press the right arrow key until the cursor is over the fourth stationary graphic dot. Hit the "T" key again. At this time, you have drawn the spacing for diode D2.

Using the procedure described above, draw the copper pads for the additional components as shown in Fig. 2-20.

Adding PC Board Traces

Referring to Fig. 2-21, use the "D" (Draw) option to connect the copper pads as shown. The thick copper traces can be drawn by drawing one line and

PC Board Designer

```
. . . . . . . . . . . . . . . . . . . . . . . . . . . . . . . . . . . . . . . . . . . . . . . . . . . . . . .

..COMPONENT. LAYOUT. . . . . . . . . . . . . . . . . . . . . . . . . . . . .

. . . . . . . . . . . . . . . . . . . . . . . . . . . . . . . . . . . . . . . . . . . . . . . . . . . . . . .

                          DI  D2  CI
. . . . . . . . . . . . . . . . . . . I   II   I . . . . . . . . . . . . . . .

. . . . . . . . . . . . . . . . I   II   I  I  III REGI . . . . . . .

                          D3. D4 . . . . . . . . . . . . . . . . .

. . . . . . . . . . . . . . . . . . . . . . . . . . . . . . . . . . . . . . . . . . . . . . . . . . . . . . .

. . . . . . . . . . . . . . . . . . . . . . . . . . . . . . . . . . . . . . . . . . . . . . . . . . . . . . .

DI.-D4. HORIZONTAL. SPACING. OF .4 .DOTS. . .

CI. VERTICIAL. SPACING .OF .II .SCREEN .PIXELS.

REGI .HORIZONTAL .SPACING. OF .3 .DOTS. . . . .

. . . . . . . . . . . . . . . . . . . . . . . . . . . . . . . . . . . . . . . . . . . . . . . . . . . . . . .

. . . . . . . . . . . . . . . . . . . . . . . . . . . . . . . . . . . . . . . . . . . . . . . . . . . . . . .
```

Fig. 2-20. Having the computer draw the copper pads for the power supply components.

PC Board Designer

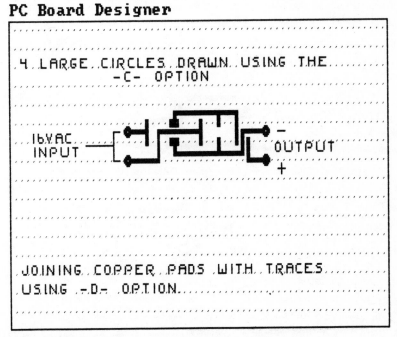

Fig. 2-21. Adding the copper traces and adding the input/output pads.

then pressing the up or down arrow key to move the Cursor one pixel element up or down. Draw a second line parallel to the first. The traces shown in Fig. 2-21 use three parallel lines.

Using the "C" Option

With the traces drawn, the "C" (Circle) option is used to create the copper circles that connect the 16-volt ac transformer to the board as well as the 12-volt dc output to a project. Connect these copper circles to the main layout as shown.

Adding Corner Brackets

To finish the layout, you must indicate the size of the finished product. This can be done by adding brackets to the four corners of the design (Fig. 2-22). You need not completely encase the layout in a box; just indicate the corners.

Finishing Touches

Before a hard copy of the layout is made, the now unwanted graphic paper pattern of the screen must be removed. This is accomplished by pressing the "P" key. When pressed, the monitor is colored the same as the dots, erasing them. Then the screen is repainted black. This removes any unwanted graphic material from the screen but leaves the layout untouched.

PC Board Designer

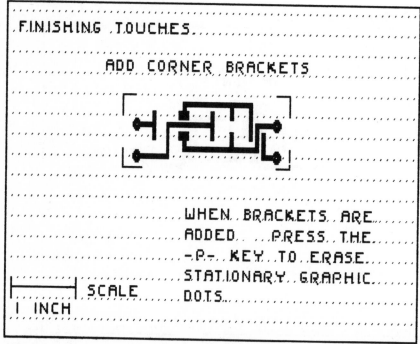

Fig. 2-22. Adding the corner brackets to the finished layout.

Printing

Now with the artwork in a printable condition, press the <PRINT> and/or the <SHIFT> <PRINT> key(s). (This depends on the type of computer you have.) With a graphics printer on line, the 12-volt power supply PC board is drawn on paper.

This is the artwork that is sent to a manufacturer to produce the finished product. (See Fig. 2-23.)

Artwork Scale Considerations

The PC Board Designer Program was written to produce artwork with a scale of 1:1. With so many types of computers, printers and Graphic Utility programs on the market today, your finished artwork may not be exactly on a 1:1 scale, but this is not a problem.

As you can see in Fig. 2-23, you can include a scale (located in the lower left corner). This can be easily drawn by using the "D" option and drawing a vertical line at one of the colored stationary graph points. Count 10 graph dots, then draw a second vertical line at this location. The spacing between these two vertical lines is 10 stationary graph dots or one inch (10 dots × .1 = 1 inch).

If your artwork is too small or too large, a PC Board manufacturer can enlarge or reduce the size of the camera negative needed to make a PC board

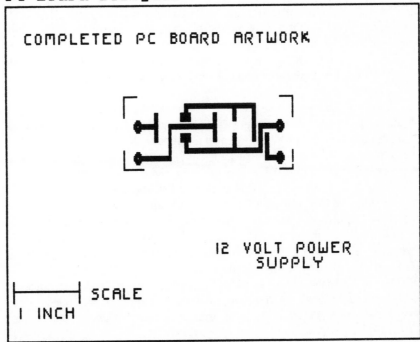

Fig. 2-23. Sample PC board artwork that will be sent to a manufacturer to produce the final product.

using the scale as a reference. All you must do is to inform him of this discrepancy when ordering the board.

The scale illustrated in the lower left corner of Fig. 2-23 would make a great addition to the Library (.LIB) File. This way the scale can be easily added to all PC board layouts just by pressing a few keys.

THE FINISHED PC BOARD

Upon the completion of your computer artwork, the easiest way to get a finished product is to send the layout along with a diagram indicating the size of the holes to be drilled to a PCB manufacturer. Purchasing a manufactured PCB is just like buying a car. Shop around for the best possible price. Manufacturers charge their customers by the total area of the board in square inches. The price can range from $.20 to $.50 a square inch.

To find the cost of a board, let's go back to elementary arithmetic.

Price per board = width × length × cost per square inch

But be careful - some manufacturers also charge you an additional $.01 to $.02 for each hole drilled in the board. Other manufacturers charge nothing.

Request price quotes from a number of firms before sending them the artwork. When you find a company you like, stick with them. You will have fewer problems with future purchases.

When you have chosen a company, send them the artwork, and indicate that the scale of the pattern is 1:1 and to drill all holes .018 in. This is the standard hole size used with ICs, ¼ watt resistors and small capacitors. Within two weeks the finished product will be delivered to your door. What could be easier?

Another method that can be used to make your own PCBs is the photoresist method. It is a professional method of fabricating and it should not be considered by the beginner.

This method uses a special printed circuit board with a light-sensitive coating on the copper side. When light is passed through the PCB negative artwork (that is in direct contact with the copper) a chemical change takes place. After exposure to light for a predetermined length of time, the board is then immersed into a chemical solution that hardens the area of the PCB on which electrical connections are to be made. (This trace is called the land.)

The board is then placed in the etching solution where the unused copper is removed. After the board is rinsed in clean water and dried, you can begin to drill the holes where needed. A drill with a carbon-tipped bit is strongly recommended. If any other drill bit is used, you run the risk of lifting the delicate PCB pads and destroying the board.

Complete kits using this method of PCB fabrication are available from large electronic houses for about $50.00. In case this method suits your needs, I will now discuss what is involved to transfer your computer artwork to a finished board.

In order to produce a board directly from the computer artwork you have just designed, inspect it under a strong light looking for breaks or bridges in the land (bridges occur when two or more land traces intersect at a point where electrical connections are not to be made). When you are satisfied that the artwork is clean, bring the artwork to a photographer and ask for a negative print of the page. This negative is just like a negative of a photograph. All areas that are clear will become black and all areas that are black will become clear.

Place the photographic negative on the sensitized copper board (wording side up) and expose to a strong light source located 12 inches form the PCB. The amount of time needed for proper exposure is found by experimentation.

The instruction booklet that comes with the photo etching kit will give you more precise timing. Refer to Fig. 2-24 and 2-25 which further illustrate the photoresist method of PC board fabrication.

After the board is developed and dried you can now remove the unwanted copper by using the etching solution. When etching is complete and the board is rinsed and dried, the material is ready for drilling (using a carbon-tipped drill bit) and component mounting.

When mounting components on a finished PC board, neatness counts. Don't insert the components in such a way that the device is suspended in the air. All parts should be in physical contact with the PC board material. (See Fig. 2-26.) There is one exception to this statement.

Power components such as power resistors or power transistors generate heat. This heat must be dissipated in the air; otherwise, the operation of the component deteriorates.

There are two ways to do this. The first is by using heat sinks. Heat sinks are metal devices that resemble bird wings which are fastened to the power component. The heat generated by the part is transferred to the heat sink through a silicon compound placed between the two devices. With the heat now being transferred to the heat sink, the bird-like wings dissipate the unwanted heat into the air. This heat dissipation keeps the operating temperature of the electronic component at an acceptable level. Heat sinks are available commercially through electronic mail-order houses and they come in a variety of sizes and shapes to accommodate a large number of components.

Another way to dissipate the heat is to mount all heat-generating components so that the body of the device is not in physical contact with the board. But don't exaggerate this spacing. Refer to Fig. 2-27 for an example of this.

When all components are mounted and soldered, check the board for any unwanted solder bridges (two copper traces are shorted together by using too much solder), component polarity, and proper values.

When you are sure all is OK apply the voltage to the project and check it for proper operation.

SOLDERING TECHNIQUES

Whichever circuit board technique you employ, whether you decide to make your own or have a professional etch the board, good soldering practices are essential for reliable operation of any project. If you are an electronics novice, please read the following carefully and practice soldering scrap wire together before attempting to solder any components to a PC board.

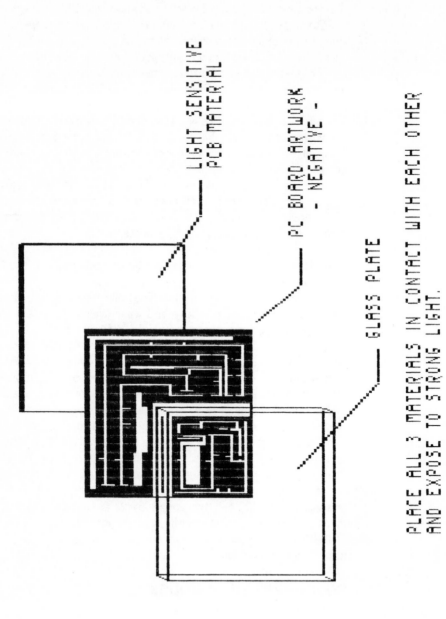

LIGHT SENSITIVE
PCB MATERIAL

PC BOARD ARTWORK
- NEGATIVE -

GLASS PLATE

PLACE ALL 3 MATERIALS IN CONTACT WITH EACH OTHER
AND EXPOSE TO STRONG LIGHT.

Fig. 2-24. Photo-etching a PC board.

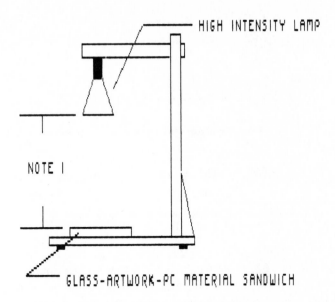

NOTE I - CHECK INSTRUCTION BOOKLET FOR PROPER DISTANCE.

Fig. 2-25. Exposing a PC board to UV light.

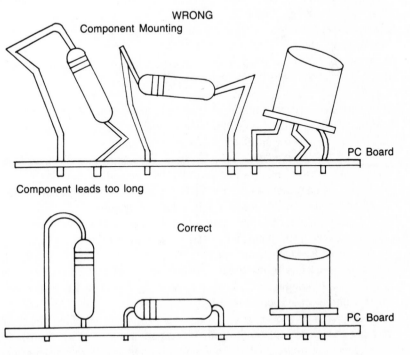

Fig. 2-26. The do's and don'ts on component mounting.

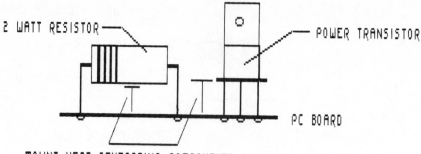

MOUNT HEAT GENERATING COMPONENTS SLIGHTLY ABOVE PC BOARD TO ALLOW FOR NATURAL COOLING.

Fig. 2-27. The proper method of munting power components on a PC board.

If you don't own a soldering iron, you should purchase a soldering pencil with a maximum wattage from 25 to 40 watts. Do not purchase a soldering gun. (See Fig. 2-28.) The high wattage associated with a gun can destroy delicate integrated circuits and other heat sensitive components with its high heating level.

The tip of the soldering pencil, when first used, must be tinned with standard electrical solder. When the iron is first used, dab a small amount of solder on the tip when the iron reaches normal operating temperature. Then after a few seconds, using a damp cloth, wipe off the excess solder. After repeating this procedure a few time, you will notice that the irons' tip becomes shiny.

Without tinning, a coat of oxidation is formed on the tip. If this oxidation is not removed, soldering any component is impossible because the solder only beads up on the tip, and there is no transfer of heat from the iron to the component. When this happens, a cold solder joint is made and you may run the risk of burning-out the component.

Acid core solder should never be used for soldering electronic components since this is a corrosive material and will damage electronic parts. A high quality rosin core solder should be used. This type of solder can be purchased from an electronic store or an electronic mail-order house.

To ensure a permanent bond between the solder and the wire lead of a component, grease, oil, paint, or any other foreign matter that may be covering the lead must be removed before soldering. To help remove this unwanted material, use a steel wool pad or a light faced sandpaper.

A major pitfall for the first-time solderer is melting the solder with the iron and then allowing this liquidified solder to flow over the component. This is a Mortal Sin of Electronics and should never be done. Using this method only produces headaches trying to troubleshoot a project that refuses to operate, not because of component failure or improperly designed PC board, but due to intermittent operation caused by cold solder joints (see Fig. 2-29).

The proper way to solder a component is to bring the tip of the iron in contact with both the wire lead and its pad. When both are heated by the iron, dab a small amount of solder on the component's copper pad. Remove the solder but leave the iron in place for an additional second or two. This additional heat allows

113

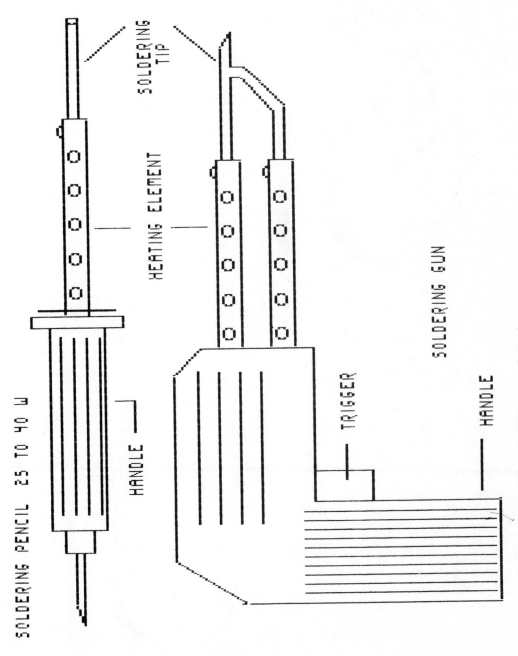

SOLDERING PENCIL 25 TO 40 W

SOLDERING TIP

HEATING ELEMENT

HANDLE

TRIGGER

SOLDERING GUN

HANDLE

Fig. 2-28. A typical soldering pencil (top) and soldering gun (bottom).

114

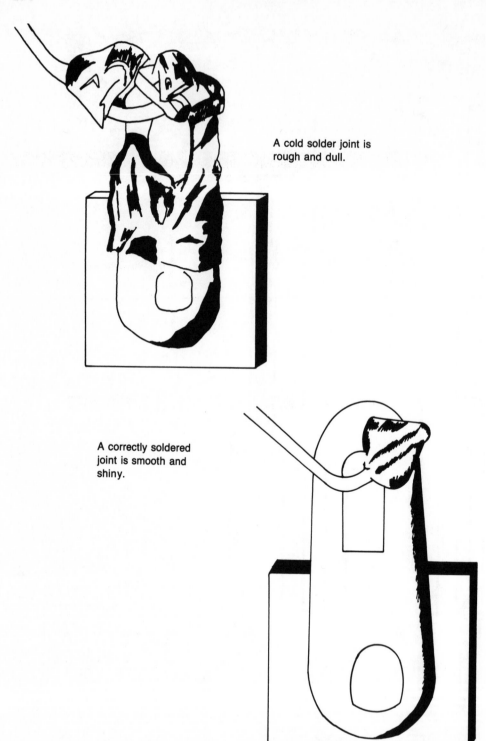

A cold solder joint is rough and dull.

A correctly soldered joint is smooth and shiny.

Fig. 2-29. Cold solder joint (top) vs. a correctly soldered joint (bottom).

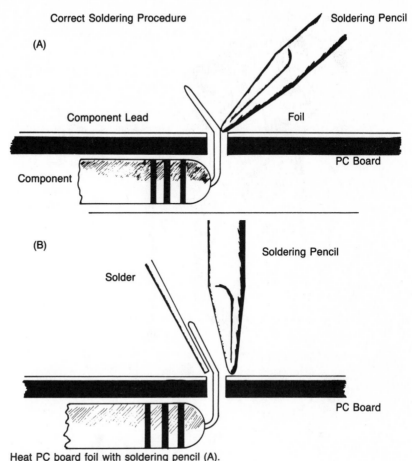

Correct Soldering Procedure

(A)

Component Lead

Component

(B)

Solder

Soldering Pencil

Foil

PC Board

Soldering Pencil

PC Board

Heat PC board foil with soldering pencil (A).
With connection heated apply solder.
Let solder flow over PC board foil and component lead.
Leave soldering pencil in contact with connection to avoid cold solder joints.

Fig. 2-30. Correct method of soldering electronic components.

the solder to flow over the connection point preventing a cold solder joint. The proper soldering procedure can be seen in Fig. 2-30. After soldering, the connection should appear smooth and shiny, while a poor connection is dull and rough.

After soldering a component, the tip of the iron should be cleaned with a damp sponge or cloth to remove excess solder. (See Fig. 2-31.)

You should always keep the soldering iron clean.

Soldering Heat-Sensitive Components

Integrated circuits are very sensitive to heat. For this reason, you should solder the leads of an IC quickly to avoid excessive heat that can destroy the component, not to mention destroying the bonding of the copper to the PC board material making the board useless. The use of another type of heat sink is recommended for soldering all heat sensitive components.

Always clean the tip of the soldering iron using wet sponge placed in a shallow metal plate or a wet cloth.

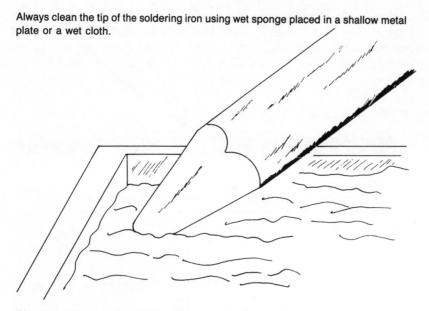

Fig. 2-31. Always clean the tip of the soldering iron to prevent oxidation from forming.

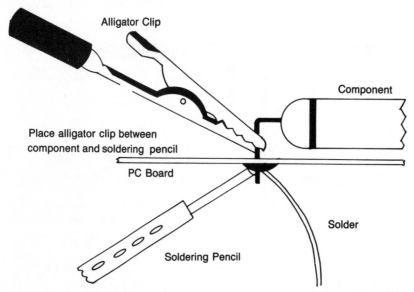

Fig. 2-32. Using an alligator clip as a heat sink to protect heat-sensitive components.

The heat sink is clamped to a component lead to conduct the heat away from the delicate internal circuitry of the part. Heat sinks should also be used when soldering diodes and transistors since these devices are also sensitive to the destructive power of high heat.

Figure 2-32 shows how a common alligator clip can be used as heat sink. The alligator clip is placed between the component and the soldering iron. By attaching the clip at this location, the destructive heat can be absorbed, thus preventing the abnormally high temperature created by soldering from being transferred to the component by its wire leads. Needless to say, after using an alligator clip as a heat sink, it will be very hot to the touch and can cause skin burns if you do not exercise caution when removing it.

CAE PROGRAM MODIFICATIONS

Both the Schematic and the PC Board Designing programs were written to be used on a computer with as little as 128K of memory. Due to the large number of programming lines, the Schematic Designer takes full advantage of this amount of memory.

In order to save as much internal memory as possible, when typing the program, do not use unnecessary spaces between commands and screen-printed prompts. The use of one unnecessary space takes up 1 byte of computer memory. This may not seem a lot, but if a number of unnecessary letters and/or spaces are included this can lead to a rather large amount of wasted memory.

This section is devoted to program modifications that you can make to get the most out of the CAE software. These modifications require additional memory to implement, so the first change that is discussed is to delete or erase all the unnecessary REM (Remark) statements.

Deleting the REM (Remark) Statements

To a computer, memory is a precious commodity and worth saving. Listing 2-6 compares the amount of memory (in bytes) between the standard program format to the same program which the REM statements have been deleted. From Listing 2-6, the amount of memory saved is very substantial. It may be worth the trouble.

Listing 2-6. Required memory for CAE programs.

```
Required Computer Memory for CAE Programs

Program    Memory     Memory      Memory
                      without     Saved
                      REM

Intro       9253       8841        412
Designer   11070      10450        620
Help        6184       6063        121
Data2      10984      10382        602
Draw        7487       7379        108

Intro2      8330       7776        554
PCB         8042       7431        611
Help2       6681       6560        121
PCB2        7787       7201        586
Graph        782        222        560

        All Memory Listed in BYTES
```

Listing 2-7 presents the line numbers of each line that contains unnecessary REM statements. As presented in this listing, these lines can be erased by using the delete command or just by entering the line number with no other information.

Both ways of erasing program lines are used to erase program lines from the DESIGNER listing as shown below.

DELETE 10-150   <ENTER> or <RETURN> Key
        1050   <ENTER> or <RETURN> key
        1150   <ENTER> or <RETURN> Key

Line 1070 in the Designer, Data2, and the Draw Programs and lines 720 and 800 in the PCB and PCB2 programs are REM statements that are part of the actual running program. These lines should not be erased.

Listing 2-7. Listing of REM line numbers for CAE programs.

```
           REM (Remark) Listings

Schematic Designer

Intro      10   20   30   40   50   60   70   80
           90  100

Designer   10   20   30   40   50   60   70   80
           90   100  110  120  130  140  150
           1050 1150

Help       10   20   30

Data2      1    2    3    4    5    6    7    8
           9    10   11   12   13   14   15
           1050 1150

Draw       10   20   30   1150

PC Board Designer

Intro 2    10   20   30   40   50   60   70   80
           90   100  110  120  130

PCB        10   20   30   40   50   60   70   80
           90   100  110  120  130
           1410 1640

Help2      10   20   30

PCB2       1    2    3    4    5    6    7    8
           9    10   11   12   13
           1410 1640

Graph      10   20   30   40   50   60   70   80
           90   100  110  120  130  140  150
```

If your computer has 216K, 512K, or even 620K of memory, the savings in computer memory made by this operation may be trivial and not worth the time. It's up to you.

Sound Modifications

As mentioned earlier, the volume in the program tones and musical interludes, if you're using an IBM compatible machine, is very loud. This is because the SOUND command used with an IBM computer has only two parameters, frequency and duration. An example of this statement is:

SOUND 800,1

The number 800 indicates that the computer is to emit a tone at a frequency of 800 Hz. The number 1 indicates that this tone shall be emitted for one computer clock tick (18.2 clock ticks equals one second in time). Using BASICA, this duration can be between .0015 to 65535 ticks.

The IBM computer makes use of these two parameters, while a compatible (like the Tandy 1000) has a third: volume. Using this third parameter, the volume of each sound statement can be under computer control.

The format of a sound statement used in a IBM-compatible computer is:

SOUND 800,1,10

The number 800 again indicates the frequency of the tone, the number one indicates the duration, and the 10 indicates the volume of the tone. The volume parameter can be in the range of 0 to 15 where 0 is the lowest volume and 15 the highest. The Default Volume is 8.

To make the CAE programs compatible with an IBM machine and clones, the third parameter was deliberately omitted. If you have a compatible computer that allows the use of the third sound parameter, see Listing 2-8, which shows the program line number for all CAE programs that contains a sound statement.

Using the EDIT Command, one can insert the needed volume parameter. The following sound statement should be inserted in each program line as seen in Listing 2-8.

SOUND 800,1,10

For those program lines that make use of different duration times (like the musical interludes on both Introductions), Insert the volume parameter (10) into the existing text. Remember to include the comma before the number 10, or a syntax error will result.

For more information on using the EDIT command, refer to the Reference Booklet that came with your computer.

Adding Commands for a Second Disk Drive

As presented, both CAE programs make use of one disk drive. Drive A saves and loads all program material, and Library and Picture files. The

Listing 2-8. Listing of SOUND line numbers for the CAE programs (used for modifications).

```
                    SOUND  Modifications

Schematic  Designer  Program

Intro         150   180   210   240   290   330

Designer      280   370   380   540   570   600
              630   1230  1290  2050  2150  2220
              2390

Data2         280   370   380   540   570   600
              630   1230  1290  2050  2150  2220
              2390

Draw          280   370   380   540   570   600
              630   1230  1290  2050  2150  2220
              2390

Help                      NONE

PC  Board  Designer  Program

Intro2        240   250

PCB           330   410   420   590   620   650
              680   970   1550  1710  1800  1840
              2030  2060  2080

PCB2          330   410   420   590   620   650
              680   970   1550  1710  1800  1840
              2030  2060  2080

Help2                     NONE

Graph         240
```

modifications presented allow the use of Drive B to load and save all Library and Picture files. The main CAE program disk can be kept in Drive A without the fear of erasing any information.

The reset memory image files (CLEAR, CLS, and CLEARSCR) must be before any disk drive modifications take place. These screen clearing images will be called upon from Drive A. If these images were saved on disk at Drive B, when called by the program, an error will occur.

If you purchase the complete CAE programming disk from TAB BOOKS Inc., these reset memory image files have already been programmed on the disk, so no additional files have to be created. You can just type the listed modifications and save the new program under its original filename.

When using this modification, place a new but formatted disk into Drive B and the CAE program disk into Drive A. Then, when saving an image in the

Listing 2-9. Required Schematic Designer modifications for a two drive system.

```
                Modifications for a 2 Drive System

Schematic Designer Program

Changes for the DESIGNER and DATA2 Programs

1130 BSAVE"B:"+A$+".PIX",0,16384
1210 IF A$="CLEARSCR" THEN BLOAD A$+".PIX",0 ELSE BLOAD"B:"
     +A$+".PIX",0
2090 FILES+"B:"
2110 IF ZZ$="KILL" OR ZZ$="kill" THEN LOCATE 25,1:INPUT;"Which
     file shall I Kill? (must include extension)",QQ$:IF QQ$=
     "" THEN GOTO 2120 ELSE KILL"B:"+QQ$:GOTO 2080 ELSE GOTO
     2120
2180 BSAVE"B:"+SS$+".LIB",VARPTR(B(0))
2260 BLOAD"B:"+SS$+".LIB",VARPTR(B(0))

Changes for the DRAW Program
Same as above except for the following:

1210 IF A$="CLEAR" THEN BLOAD A$+".PIX",0 ELSE BLOAD"B:"+A$+"
     .PIX",0
```

Listing 2-10. Required PC Board Designer modifications for a two drive system.

```
                Modification for 2 Disk Drive Systems

PC Board Designer Program

Changes for the PCB and PCB2 Program

780  BSAVE"B:"+A$+".PIX",0,16384
860  DEF SEG=&HB800:IF A$="CLS" THEN BLOAD A$+".PIX",0 ELSE
     BLOAD"B:"+A$+".PIX",0
1750 FILES+"B:"
1770 IF ZZ$="KILL" OR ZZ$="kill" THEN LOCATE 25,1: INPUT;
     "Which File shall I Kill? (must include extension)"
     ,QQ$:IF QQ$="" GOTO 1780 ELSE KILL"B:"+QQ$:GOTO 1740
     ELSE GOTO 1780
1830 BSAVE"B:"+SS$+".LIB",VARPTR(B(0))
1910 BSAVE"B:"+SS$+".LIB",VARPTR(B(0))
```

Library or Picture File, this .LIB or .PIX File is created on the disk located in Drive B. The only time Drive A is used is to recall the screen reset image, the file that erases unwanted schematics or PC board layouts from the monitor screen.

Listing 2-9 contains all modifications needed in the DESIGNER, DATA2, and DRAW programs, while Listing 2-10 contains the modification needed for the PCB and PCB2 programs.

Chapter 3
CAE Program
Screen Displays

To help with the programming and text placement of your CAE system, the following pages provide printouts of each program screen. Compare these printouts with your computer monitor display and make the necessary changes (if any) to your program.

Schematic Designer Program

Introduction (Filename "INTRO")

Computer-Aided Engineering Program

for

Electronic Schematic Design

Fig. 3-1. Schematic Designers title screen.

Program designed for IBM PC's and Compatibles

Minimum Computer Requirements:

    Black & White Monitor
    128K Memory
    One Disk Drive
    Graphics Printer
    Optional Joystick
    MS-DOS or PC-DOS (BASICA Version 2.11 or later)
    620 x 200 Graphic Card

Hit <ENTER> to Continue

Fig. 3-2. Introduction screen display #1.

In the DRAW MODE you have the following options to input graphic commands. They are as follows:

D=Draw R=Reset E=Erase I=Insert S=Save C=Circle L=Load W=Wording P=Print Line
F=Filenames G=Get Section of Schematic A=Put Graphic on Screen T=Term.Point

DRAW - To activate, hit the 'D' key. This will allow you to draw a line.
       To de-activate, just hit the 'D' a second time. You are now able to
       move the Drawing Cursor without leaving a trace.

RESET - By hitting the 'R' key you will clear the image on the screen.
        The contents of the memory will remain.

Get Option - Saves desired graphic in computer memory. You are asked if this
             image will be saved in the Library File. You respond by typing
             Y (Yes) or N (No). If you answer Yes, you will then be asked to
             give this new image a name. Respond by entering a Filename. Then
             press the <ENTER> Key. The image will now be saved on Disk. You
             may recall this image at any time by using the 'L' (LOAD) option.
             This option requires you to input two X/Y diagonal locations.
             Do this by pressing the 'G' key twice at the desired coordinates.

Hit <ENTER> to Continue

Fig. 3-3. Introduction screen display #2.

ERASE - This option erases a section of your graphic. The 'E' option is used
        in the same manner as the 'G' option (two diagonal X/Y coordinates
        are needed). Instead of saving the image in computer memory, the
        ERASE option paints this graphic section to BLACK, thus erasing
        the image.

INSERT - Using the 4 ARROW keys you can move the Drawing Cursor to any section
         of the screen. When in a section you wish a pre-programmed drawing to
         be placed - just hit the 'I' key. You will then be asked to enter the
         Item number that is associated with the electronic symbol. Then hit
         <ENTER>. The symbol chosen will be drawn at that location.

FILENAMES - The 'F' option allows you to display ALL filenames saved on
            Disk, which is located in Drive A. You may also DELETE files
            just by typing KILL to the prompt <Hit Enter to Continue>.
            Then type in the filename you wish Deleted - then press <ENTER>.
            NOTE - This filename MUST contain the extension.
            (ex. .LIB - .BAS ect.)

Hit <ENTER> to Continue

Fig. 3-4. Introduction screen display #3.

SAVE - Used to SAVE the schematic shown, on disk. You are asked to give your
schematic a filename. When entered hit <ENTER>. The disk drive starts.
Your drawing is now being saved for future use.

LOAD - LOADs a Complete Screen or Library symbol from Disk A. You enter
the number 1 if you wish to LOAD an image from the Library, or
enter the number 2 if you wish to LOAD an image from the Picture
File. Then when asked, enter the FILENAME of the image. When loaded,
graphic will be displayed at the location of the Drawing Cursor.

CIRCLE - This key allows you to draw any one of three programmed circles
on the screen. These circles are used to draw additional symbols not
included in the program library.

WORDING - Used to print letters & numbers at any location on the screen.
The ARROW keys can be used to move the Drawing Cursor to any location
so wording can be placed at a desired point. To EXIT just
press the COMMA ',' Key. You will then be placed in the Draw Mode.

Hit <ENTER> to Continue

Fig. 3-5. Introduction screen display #4.

PRINT LINE - Used to draw diagonal lines. This option needs two X/Y coordinates.
Move the Drawing Cursor to the desired location. Then press the
'P' Key once. Now move the Cursor to the second X/Y coordinate.
Press the 'P' Key again. The computer now connects these two
locations using a straight line.

A Option - With an image in computer memory, (placed there by using the 'G'
or 'L' option) the 'A' key allows the computer to draw this in
memory graphic at the indicated X/Y coordinates. By pressing the
'A' key for the second time, the computer will erase the image
just drawn but leaving any previously drawn material untouched.

Termination - This option draws a small circle at the end of a line to indicate
a connection to this point from the outside world.

Help   - This option saves the schematic you are working on under the
filename 'DATA'. The screen will clear then the HELP program will
be LOADED. This program lists the Computer Key Options used with
the CAE programs. When the needed information is known, your
computer will re-load your present schematic drawing.

Hit <ENTER> to Continue

Fig. 3-6. Introduction screen display #5.

Cursor Express - By pressing the 'J' key, you are placed in the Cursor Express
                 Mode. If you have a joystick or graphics tabletconnected to
                 the left joystick port, you can now move the Drawing Cursor
                 around the screen faster then if the arrow keys were used.
                 When at the desired location, press the 'J' key for the second
                 time. You will then be able to Draw, Erase or Insert components
                 at the new coordinates.

Print   or   - Used to print your schematic on a graphic printer.
                 Which button to press depends on tne type of computer you
Shift/Print   have. Consult your BASIC Instruction Booklet for additional
                 information.

No. 1 Button - Press this button to change the color of the Drawing Cursor
                 to WHITE.

No. 2 Button - Press this button to change the color of the Drawing Cursor
                 to BLACK. Use this button in conjunction with the 'D' key
                 to erase lines by re-coloring the line black.

Hit <ENTER> to Continue

Fig. 3-7. Introduction screen display #6.

To EXIT from any required keyboard input (ex. Entering a Filename or Component
Number) just press the <ENTER> key without entering any information. Your
computer will cancel that input and return you to the Drawing Mode.

When requested to enter a filename of an image that will be LOADED or SAVED,
you are NOT required to add the extension (ex. .LIB or .PIX). These
extensions are automatically inserted by the computer.

The extension .LIB indicates all Files that were saved as a library File.

The extension .PIX indicates all Files that were saved as an image File.
An image file is a file that has saved the entire contents of the screen
on disk.

Hit <ENTER> to load your Computer-Aided Engineering Program

Fig. 3-8. Final Introduction screen.

Main Schematic Designer Program (Filename ''DESIGNER'')

Schematic Designer

D=Draw R=Reset E=Erase I=Insert S=Save C=Circle L=Load W=Wording P=Print Line

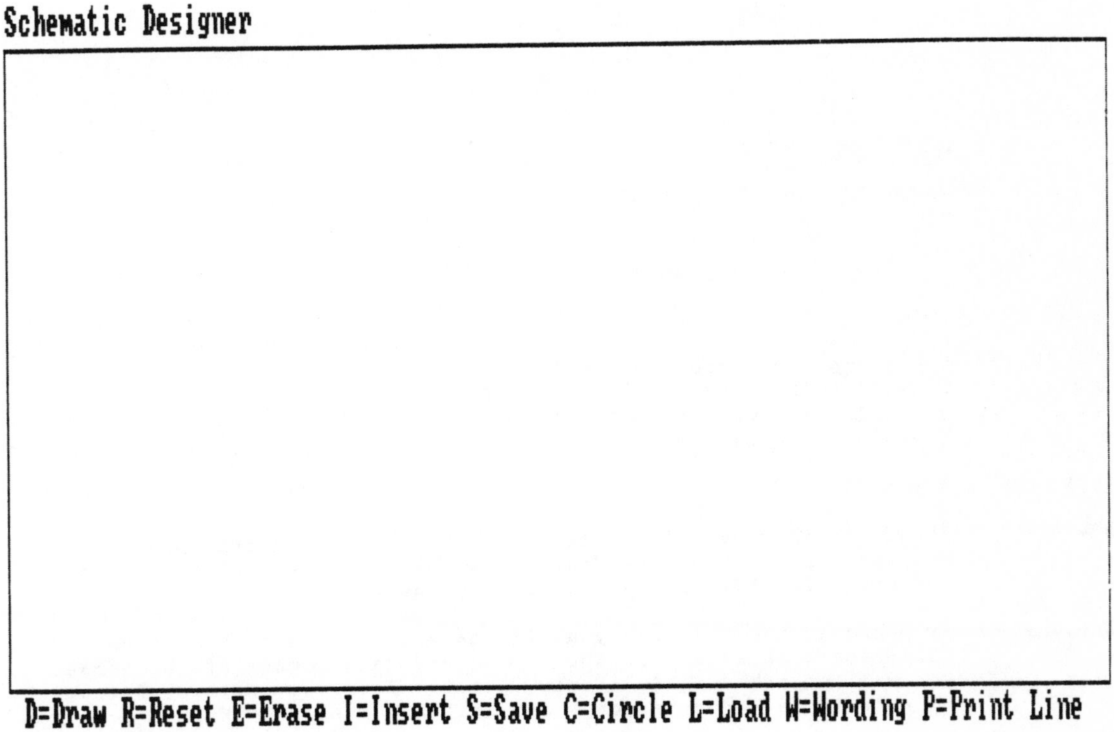

Fig. 3-9. Main Program screen display.

```
                         Current Filenames on Disk
A:\
  INTRO   .BAS      DESIGNER.BAS       HELP    .BAS       DATA2   .BAS
  DRAW    .BAS      GRAPH   .BAS       SAMPLE1 .LIB       CLEARSCR.PIX
  DATA    .PIX      SAMPLE2 .LIB       CLEAR   .PIX       SAMPLE5 .PIX
  PCB     .BAS      INTRO2  .BAS       HELP2   .BAS       PCB2    .BAS
  DATA3   .PIX      CLS     .PIX       SAMPLE3 .LIB       SAMPLE4 .LIB
    151552 Bytes free



        When Ready - Hit <ENTER>
```

Fig. 3-10. Disk Filename screen display.

```
                         H E L P



  ↑ - - - - - Moves Drawing Cursor in the UP Direction
  ↓ - - - - - Moves Drawing Cursor in the DOWN Direction
  → - - - - - Moves Drawing Cursor to the RIGHT
  ← - - - - - Moves Drawing Cursor to the LEFT

Keyboard LETTER KEYS

D - - - - - Press the 'D' key to draw lines on the screen. In this mode,
            you can press any of the four arrow keys and leave a trace of the
            movement. To EXIT, press the 'D' key again.

R - - - - - By pressing the 'R' key, you will be able to clear the screen of
            ALL graphic material. In the lower left hand corner of the screen,
            you will be asked again if you wish to clear the monitor. Respond
            by entering a Y for Yes or N for No. Then press <ENTER>.




 Hit <ENTER> to Continue .....
```

Fig. 3-11. Help screen display #1.

G - - - - - Saves desired graphic in computer memory. You are asked if this
image will be saved in the Library File. You respond by typing Y
for Yes or N for No. If you answer Yes, you will then be asked to
give this new image a name. Respond by entering a filename. Then
press the <ENTER> key. The image will now be saved on disk. You may
recall this image at any time by using the 'L' (LOAD) option.
This option requires you to input two diagonal X/Y coordinates.
Do this by pressing the 'G' key twice when at the desired locations.

A - - - - - With an image in computer memory, (placed there by using the 'G'
or 'L' option) the 'A' key allows the computer to draw this in
memory graphic at the indicated X/Y coordinates. By pressing
the 'A' key for a second time, the computer will Erase the image
just drawn but leaving any previously drawn material untouched.

E - - - - - This option ERASEs a section of your graphic. The 'E' option is used
in the same manner as the 'G' option (two diagonal X/Y coordinates
are needed). Instead of saving the image in computer memory, the
ERASE option paints this graphic section BLACK, thus erasing
the image.

I - - - - - INSERTS component of your choosing at any location on screen.
Enter number of component to be inserted.

Hit <ENTER> to Continue .....

Fig. 3-12. Help screen display #2.

S - - - - - SAVEs complete screen on Disk A - You enter filename when requested.

C - - - - - Leads you to a sub-routine that allows you to choose any one of
three pre-programmed circle sizes.

L - - - - - LOADs a complete screen or library symbol from Disk A. You enter
the number 1 if you wish to LOAD an image from the library, or
enter the number 2 if you wish to LOAD an image from the picture
file. Then when asked, enter the filename of the image. When loaded,
the graphic will be displayed at the location of the Drawing
Cursor.

W - - - - - Used to print letters and numbers at any location on the screen.
Hit the Comma ',' key to EXIT.

P - - - - - Used to draw diagonal lines - Needs two X/Y coordinates. Move the
Drawing Cursor to the desired location. Then press the 'P' key once.
Now move the cursor to the second X/Y coordinates. Press the 'P' key
again. Your computer now connects these two locations using a
straight line.

Hit <ENTER> to Continue .....

Fig. 3-13. Help screen display #3.

J - - - - - By pressing the 'J' key, you are placed in the Cursor Express mode. If you have a joystick or graphic tablet connected to the left joystick port, you can now move the Drawing Cursor around the screen faster then if the arrow Keys were used. When at the desired location, press the 'J' key for the second time. You will now be able to draw, erase or insert components at the new coordinates.

T - - - - - Draws a small circle - used to indicate a termination point on the schematic. (ex. connection to the outside world)

Print - - - Used to print your schematic on a graphic Printer.
or   Which button to press depends on the type of computer you have.
Shift/Print Consult your BASIC Instruction Booklet for additional information.

F - - - - - The 'F' option allows you to display all filenames saved on Disk A. You may also delete files just by typing - KILL - to the prompt <Hit Enter to Continue>. Then type in the filename you wish to Delete - then press <ENTER>. NOTE - This filename MUST contain the extension (ex. .LIB - .BAS etc.)

Hit <ENTER> to Continue .....

Fig. 3-14. Help screen display #4.

To exit from any required keyboard input (Ex. entering a filename or component number) just press the <ENTER> key without entering any information. Your computer will cancel that input and return you to the drawing mode.

When requested to enter a filename of an image that will be loaded or saved, you are NOT required to add the extension (ex. .LIB or .PIX). These extensions are automatically inserted by the computer.
Extensions are required only if you intend to kill a File when the 'F' option is being used.

The extension .LIB indicates all Files that have been saved as a Library File.

The extension .PIX indicates all Files that were saved as an Image File.

An image file is a file that has saved the entire contents of the screen on disk.

Hit <ENTER> to Continue .....

Fig. 3-15. Final Help screen display.

Main "B" Program (Filename "DATA2")

Same as Figure 3-9

Drawing Program (Filename "DRAW")

Printed Circuit Board Designer (Filename "INTRO2")

Drawing Program

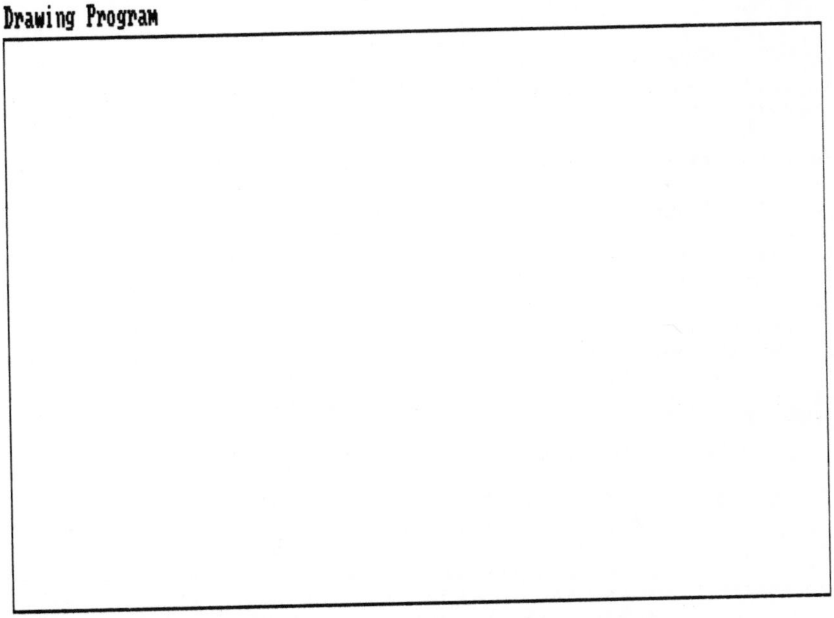

Fig. 3-16. Main screen display for the DRAW program.

Computer-Aided Engineering
PC Board
Design Program

Fig. 3-17. PCB Designer title screen (color).

Program designed for IBM PC's and Compatibles

Minimum Computer Requirements:

```
Color Monitor
128K Memory
One Disk Drive
Graphics Printer
Optional Joystick
MS-DOS or PC-DOS (BASICA version 2.11 or later)
320 x 200 Color Graphics Card
```

Hit <ENTER> to Continue

Fig. 3-18. Introduction screen display #1.

In the draw mode   you have the following options to input graphic
commands:

D=Draw R=Reset E=Erase I=Insert S=Save C=Circle L=Load W=Wording P=Print Line
F=Filenames G=Get Section of Schematic A=Put Graphic on Screen T=Term.Point

DRAW - To activate, hit the 'D' key. This will allow you to draw a line.
       To de-activate, just hit the 'D' a second time. You are now able to
       move the Drawing Cursor without leaving a trace.

RESET - By hitting the 'R' key   you will clear the image on the screen.
        The contents of the memory will remain.

Get Option - Saves desired graphic in computer memory. You are asked if this
             image will be saved in the Library File. You respond by typing
             Y (Yes) or N (No). If you answer Yes, you will then be asked to
             give this new image a name. Respond by entering a filename. Then
             press the <ENTER> Key. The image will now be saved on disk. You
             may recall this image at any time by using the 'L' (LOAD) option.
             The GET option requires two diagonal X/Y coordinates to be entered.
             Do this by pressing the 'G' key twice at the desired locations.

Hit <ENTER> to Continue

Fig. 3-19. Introduction screen display #2.

ERASE - This option erases a section of your graphic. The 'E' option is used
        in the same manner as the 'G' option (two diagonal X/Y coordinates
        are needed). Instead of saving the image in computer memory, the
        ERASE option paints this graphic section to black, thus erasing
        the image.

FILENAMES - The 'F' option allows you to display ALL filenames saved on
        disk, which is located in Drive A. You may also DELETE files
        just by typing KILL to the prompt <Hit Enter to Continue>.
        Then type in the filename you wish deleted - then press <ENTER>.
        NOTE - This filename must contain the extension
        (ex. .LIB - .BAS etc.)

SAVE - Used to save the layout on disk. You are asked to give your
       design a filename. When entered   hit <ENTER>. The disk drive starts.
       Your drawing is now being saved for future use.

Hit <ENTER> to Continue

Fig. 3-20. Introduction screen display #3.

LOAD - Loads a complete screen or library symbol from Disk A. You enter
       the number 1 if you wish to load an image from the Library, or
       enter the number 2 if you wish to load an image from the Picture
       File. Then when asked, enter the filename of the image. When loaded,
       graphic will be displayed at the location of the Drawing Cursor.

CIRCLE - This key draws a pre-programmed circular pad at any desired location
         on the screen. These circles are used to indicate wire connections
         that will be made to the PC board from the outside source.

WORDING - Used to print letters & numbers at any location on the screen.
          The arrow keys can be used to move the Drawing Cursor to any location
          so wording can be placed at a desired point. To **exit**   just
          press the comma ',' key. You will then be placed in the draw mode.

Screen Paint - When layout is complete and you are ready to make a printed
               copy, press the 'P' key. This option erases the stationary
               graphic dots by first painting the screen purple, then
               re-painting the screen to black. The PC board layout previously
               drawn will remain untouched. You may now press the Print
               or Shift/Print key to make a hard copy.

Hit <ENTER> to Continue

Fig. 3-21. Introduction screen display #4.

A Option   - With an image in computer memory (placed there by using the 'G'
                or 'L' option) the 'A' key allows the computer to Draw this in
                memory graphic at the indicated X/Y coordinates. By pressing the
                'A' key for the second time, the computer will erase the image
                just drawn leaving any previously drawn material untouched.
                With image at desired location press the F1 key.

Termination - This option draws a small rectangular pad that can be used as a
                copper pad for inte grated circuits or any other components.

Help   - This option saves the schematic you are working on under the
                filename 'DATA3'. The screen will clear then the HELP program
                will be loaded. This program lists the computer key options
                used with the CAE Programs. When the needed information is
                known, your computer will re-load your present PC board layout.

Cursor Express - By pressing the 'J' key, you are placed in the Cursor Express
                Mode. If you have a joystick or graphics tablet connected to
                the left joystick port, you can now move the Drawing Cursor
                around the screen faster then if the arrow keys were used.
                When at the desired location, press the 'J' key for the second
                time. You will then be able to draw at the new coordinates.

Hit <ENTER> to Continue

Fig. 3-22. Introduction screen display #5.

Print   or   Used to print your schematic on a graphic printer.
                 Which button to press depends on the type of computer you
Shift/Print   have. Consult your BASIC Instruction Booklet for additional
                 information.

No. 1 Button   By pressing this button, the color of the Drawing Cursor
                 is changed to white.

No. 2 Button   By pressing this button, the color of the Drawing Cursor
                 is changed to black. If used in conjunction with the 'D'
                 key, you can erase drawn lines by re-coloring the line
                 black.

Hit <ENTER> to Continue

Fig. 3-23. Introduction screen display #6.

To exit from any required keyboard input (ex. Entering a Filename or Component Number) just press the <ENTER> key without entering any information. Your computer will cancel that input and return you to the Drawing Mode.

When requested to enter a filename of an image that will be loaded or saved, you are NOT required to add the extension (ex. .LIB or .PIX). These extensions are automatically inserted by the computer.

The extension .LIB indicates all Files that were saved as a library File.

The extension .PIX indicates all Files that were saved as an image File. An image file is a file that has saved the entire contents of the screen on Disk.

Hit <ENTER> to load your Computer-Aided Engineering Program

Fig. 3-24. Final Introduction screen display.

Main PC Board Designer Program (Filename ''PCB'')

Title Screen (with Blue Background)	Fig. 3-25
Main Screen Display	Fig. 3-26
Disk Filename Screen Display	
Same as Fig. 3-10	

Help Screens (Filename ''HELP2'')

Help Screen Display #1	Fig. 3-27
Screen Display #2	Fig. 3-28
Screen Display #3	Fig. 3-29
Screen Display #4	Fig. 3-30
Screen Display #5	Fig. 3-31

PC Board

Design Program

Fig. 3-25. Main PCB Designer title screen (color).

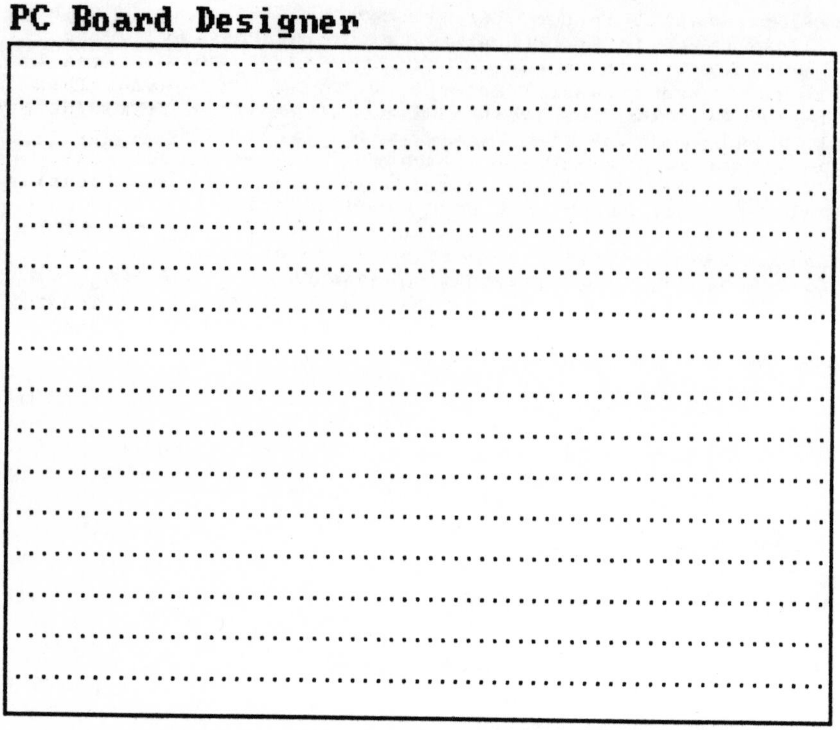

PC Board Designer

Fig. 3-26. Main PCB Designer screen display (color).

H E L P

↑ - - - - - Moves Drawing Cursor in the UP Direction
↓ - - - - - Moves Drawing Cursor in the DOWN Direction
→ - - - - - Moves Drawing Cursor to the RIGHT
← - - - - - Moves Drawing Cursor to the LEFT

Keyboard letter keys

D - - - - - Press the 'D' key to draw lines on the screen. In this mode,
            you can press any of the four arrow keys and leave a trace of the
            movement. To exit, press the 'D' key again.

R - - - - - By pressing the 'R' key, you will be able to clear the screen of
            all graphic material. In the lower left hand corner of the screen,
            you will be asked again if you wish to clear the monitor. Respond
            by entering a Y for Yes or N for No. Then press <ENTER>.

Hit <ENTER> to Continue .....

Fig. 3-27. Help screen display #1.

G - - - - - Saves desired graphic in computer memory. You are asked if this
image will be saved in the Library File. You respond by typing Y
for Yes or N for No. If you answer Yes, you will then be asked to
give this new image a name. Respond by entering a filename. Then
press the <ENTER> key. The image will now be saved on disk. You may
recall this image at any time by using the 'L' (LOAD) option.
This option requires you to input two X/Y diagonal coordinates.
Do this by pressing the 'G' key twice when in the desired location.

A - - - - - With an image in computer memory (placed there by using the 'G'
or 'L' option) the 'A' key allows the computer to draw this in
memory graphic at the indicated X/Y coordinates. By pressing
the 'A' key for a second time, the computer will Erase the image
just drawn but leaving any previously drawn material untouched.
With image at desired location press the F1 Key.

E - - - - - This option erases a section of your graphic. The 'E' option is used
in the same manner as the 'G' option (two diagonal X/Y coordinates
are needed). Instead of saving the image in computer memory, the
erase option paints this graphic section black, thus erasing
the image.

Hit <ENTER> to Continue .....

Fig. 3-28. Help screen display #2.

S - - - - - SAVEs complete screen on Disk A. You enter filename when requested.

C - - - - - This key draws a pre-programmed circular pad at any desired location
on the screen. These circles are used to indicate wire connections
that will be made to the PC Board from the outside world.

L - - - - - Loads a complete screen or Library symbol from Disk A. You enter
the number 1 if you wish to load an image from the Library, or
enter the number 2 if you wish to load an image from the Picture
File. Then when asked, enter the filename of the image. When loaded,
the graphic will be displayed at the location of the Drawing
Cursor.

W - - - - - Used to print letters and numbers at any location on the screen.
Hit the comma ',' key to EXIT.

P - - - - - When ready to make a printed copy of the PC board layout, press
the 'P' key. This option erases the stationary graph dots by
first painting the screen purple, then re-painting the screen
black. The PC board layout previously drawn will remain untouched.
You may now press the Print or Shift/Print to make a hard copy.

Hit <ENTER> to Continue .....

Fig. 3-29. Help screen display #3.

J - - - - - By pressing the 'J' key, you are placed in the Cursor Express Mode. If you have a joystick or graphic tablet connected to the left joystick Port, you can now move the Drawing Cursor around the screen faster then if the arrow keys were used. When at the desired location, press the 'J' key for the second time. You will now be able to draw, erase or insert components at the new coordinates.

T - - - - - This option draws a small rectangular pad that can be used as a copper pads for integrated circuits or any other components.

Print or - Used to print your schematic on a graphic printer.
Which button to press depends on the type of computer you have.
Shift/Print Consult your BASIC Instruction Booklet for additional information.

F - - - - - The 'F' option allows you to display all filenames saved on Disk A. You may also DELETE Files just by typing KILL to the prompt <Hit Enter to Continue>. Then type in the filename you wish to Delete and press <ENTER>. NOTE - This filename must contain the extension (ex. .LIB - .BAS etc.)

Hit <ENTER> to Continue .....

Fig. 3-30. Help screen display #4.

No. 1 Button - By pressing this button, the color of the Drawing Cursor is changed to white.

No. 2 Button - By pressing this button, the color of the Drawing Cursor is changed to black. If used in conjunction with the 'D' key, you can erase drawn lines by re-coloring the line black.

To exit from any required keyboard input (ex. Entering a Filename or Component Number) just press the <ENTER> key without entering any information. Your computer will cancel that input and return you to the Drawing Mode.

When requested to enter a filename of an image that will be loaded or saved, you are not required to add the extension (ex. .LIB or .PIX). These extensions are automatically inserted by the computer.
Extensions are required only if you intend to kill a file when the 'F' option is being used.

The extension .LIB indicates all files that have been saved as a Library File.

The extension .PIX indicates all files that were saved as an Image File. An image file is a file that has saved the entire contents of the screen on disk.

Hit <ENTER> to Continue .....

Fig. 3-31. Help screen display #5.

Main "B" Program (Filename "PCB2")

Same as Figure 3-26

Graph Paper Printing Program (Filename "GRAPH")

Main Screen Display   Fig. 3-32

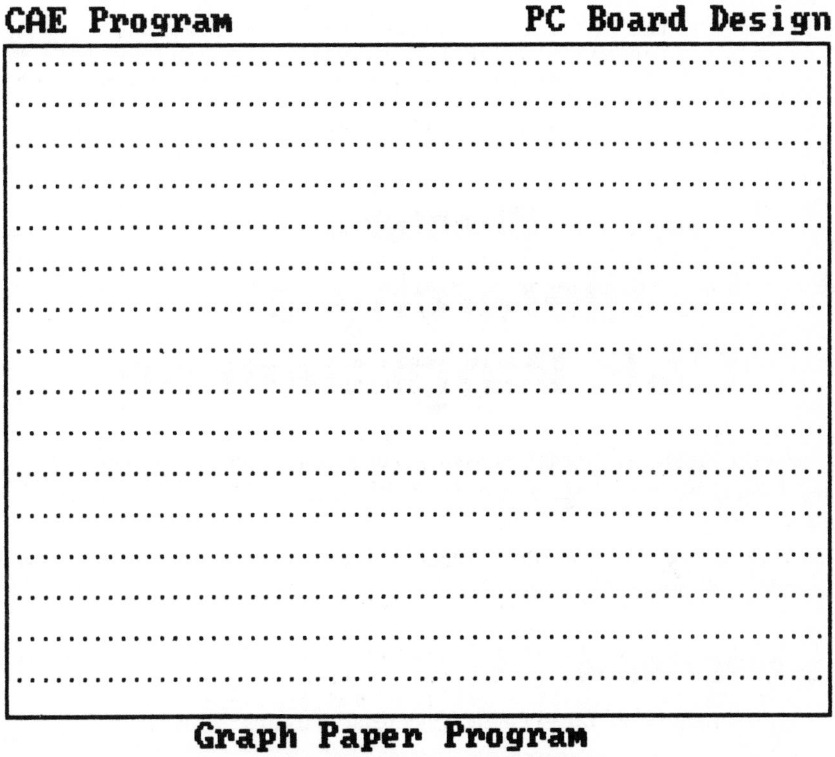

CAE Program   PC Board Design

Fig. 3-32. Main screen display for the Graph Paper Program.

Chapter 4
Hierarchy of
CAE Programming

The term "reserved words" is associated with all computer programming. These words are not to be used under any circumstances to describe a program, data file, or graphic print. If these were used, important program information would be erased from the disk, rendering the program useless until this information is reloaded on the disk.

RESERVE WORDS

Reserved Words for the Schematic Designer Program

INTRO.BAS	DESIGNER.BAS	DATA2.BAS
HELP.BAS	CLEARSCR.PIX	DATA.PIX
SAMPLE1.LIB	SAMPLE2.LIB	

Reserved Words for the Drawing Program

DRAW.BAS	CLEAR.PIX

Reserved Words for the PC Board Designer Program

INTRO2.BAS	PCB.BAS	DATA3.PIX
HELP2.BAS	CLS.PIX	PCB2.BAS
SAMPLE3.LIB	SAMPLE4.LIB	

Reserved Words for Graph Paper Program

GRAPH.BAS

BASIC ERROR CODES AND MESSAGES

Error Number	Error Message
1	NEXT without FOR
2	Syntax error
3	Return without GOSUB
4	Out of data
5	Illegal function call
6	Overflow
7	Out of memory
8	Undefined line number
9	Subscript out of range
10	Redimensioned array/duplicate definition
11	Division by zero
12	Illegal direct
13	Type mismatch
14	Out of string space
15	String too long
16	String formula too complex
17	Cannot continue
18	Undefined user function
19	No RESUME
20	RESUME without error
21	Unprintable error
22	Missing operand
23	Line buffer overflow
24	Device timeout
25	Device fault
26	FOR without NEXT
27	Out of paper
29	WHILE without WEND
30	WEND without WHILE
50	FIELD overflow
51	Internal error
52	Bad file number
53	File not found
54	Bad file mode
55	File already open
57	Device I/O error
58	File already exists
61	Disk full
62	Input past end

63	Bad record number
64	Bad file name
66	Direct statement in file
67	Too many files
68	Device unavailable
69	Communication buffer overflow
70	Disk write protected
71	Disk not ready
72	Disk media error
73	Advanced feature
74	Rename across disks
75	Path/file access error
76	Path not found
77	Dead lock

COMPUTER SCREEN RESOLUTIONS

Screen Mode 0 (Text Mode)

Color Set:	16
Graphics Resolution:	NOT AVAILABLE
Text Width:	40 or 80
Video Page Size:	If WIDTH = 40 – 2048 bytes
	If WIDTH = 80 – 4096 bytes

Screen Mode 1

Color Set:	4 (2 Palettes)
Graphics Resolution:	MEDIUM RESOLUTION
	320 pixels by 200 pixels
Text Width:	40
Video Page Size:	16384 bytes

Due to Screen Mode 1's resolution, proper pixel spacing (in the horizontal axis) and the four available colors, this screen is used with the PC Board Designer Program.

Screen Mode 2

Color Set:	2
Graphics Resolution:	HIGH RESOLUTION
	640 pixels by 200 pixels
Text Width:	80
Video Page Size:	16384 bytes

Due to the High Resolution of this screen, screen Mode 2 is used with the Electronic Schematic Designer Program.

Screen Mode 3

Color Set:	16
Graphics Resolution:	LOW RESOLUTION
	160 pixels by 200 pixels
Text Width:	20
Video Page Size:	16384 bytes

Screen Mode 4

Color Set:	4
Graphics Resolution:	MEDIUM RESOLUTION
	320 pixels by 200 pixels
Text Width:	40
Video Page Size:	16384 bytes

Screen Mode 5

Color Set:	16
Graphics Resolution:	MEDIUM RESOLUTION
	320 pixels by 200 pixels
Text Width:	40
Video Page Size:	32768 bytes

Screen Mode 6

Color Set:	4
Graphics Resolution:	HIGH RESOLUTION
	640 pixels by 200 pixels
Text Width:	80
Video Page Size:	32768 bytes

Due to the large amount of computer memory needed for video memory (32768 bytes), Screen Modes 5 and 6 can only be used with additional memory.

AVAILABLE COMPUTER COLORS

Color Set	Attributes
2 Colors	Black and white. The background color is black and the foreground is white. These colors cannot be changed.
4 Colors	One set or palette of four colors. Each of the four available colors is assigned a number. The colors and their corresponding numbers are:

Number	Color
0	Black
1	Cyan
2	Magenta
3	White

However, if you use Screen Mode 1, you have additional colors to choose from. They are:

Number	Palette 0	Palette 1
1	Green	Cyan
2	Red	Magenta
3	Brown	White

Color 0 is the current background color and is initially set to black. The background color can be changed to any of the 16 color set.

16 Colors

One palette with 16 colors. Each color is numbered as follows:

Number	Color	Number	Color
0	Black	8	Dark Gray
1	Blue	9	Light Blue
2	Green	10	Light Green
3	Cyan	11	Light Cyan
4	Red	12	Light Red
5	Magenta	13	Light Magenta
6	Brown	14	Yellow
7	Gray	15	White

Appendices

Appendix A

Summary of CAE Commands

This section offers information on booting-up IBM and IBM compatible computers, and provides a quick reference to the drawing commands of both programs.

BOOTING UP THE IBM COMPUTER

1. Place the IBM Disk Operating System (PC-DOS) disk into Drive A and close the locking latch on the door.
2. Turn on the power. This switch is located on the right side of the main computer housing.
3. When the A> prompt appears, type GRAPHICS and then press the <RETURN> key. This loads the IBM Graphics Utility Program that transforms the monitor's image into graphic data that can now be used to draw the picture on a dot matrix printer.
4. When the A> prompt appears again, type BASICA and press the <RETURN> key.
5. When BASIC is loaded, insert the CAE Programming Disk and type the following, depending on which program you wish to run:

To Run:		Type/Then Press <RETURN>
Schematic Designer	Introduction	INTRO
	Main Program	DESIGNER

PC Board Designer	Introduction	INTRO2
	Main Program	PCB
	Graph Paper Program	GRAPH
Drawing Program	Main Program	DRAW

BOOTING UP A COMPATIBLE COMPUTER

1. Insert the MS-DOS disk into Drive A and close the locking latch on the door.
2. Turn on the power. This switch can be found on the right side of the main computer housing.
3. When the A> prompt appears, type GRAPHICS and press the <ENTER> key. This action loads the Graphic Utility program.
4. Your version of MS-DOS may display four or five types of dot matrix printers that this version of MS-DOS supports. Select the number or letter that best describes the type of printer you have on line. If in doubt, enter the number or letter that indicates a standard resolution printer.
5. When the printer type is selected, press the <ENTER> key.
6. When the A> prompt appears, type BASICA and press the <ENTER> key.
7. When BASIC is loaded, insert the CAE Programming Disk and type the following, depending on which program you want to run:

To Run:		**Type/Then Press** **<ENTER>**
Schematic Designer	Introduction	INTRO
	Main Program	DESIGNER
PC Board Designer	Introduction	INTRO2
	Main Program	PCB
	Graph Paper Program	GRAPH
Drawing Program	Main Program	DRAW

ELECTRONIC SCHEMATIC
DESIGNER PROGRAM DRAW COMMANDS

Function	**Key to Press**	**Description of Command**
Draw	D	By pressing the "D" key, you can trace a line in the direction associated with the arrow key pressed
Cursor Movement	Arrow Keys	By pressing one of the arrow keys, the Drawing Cursor moves in the direction associated with the key pressed. Four directions of

movement are provided: up, down, left, and right. The program incorporates a wrap-around feature. If you come to the extreme right section of the frame, the cursor automatically reappears at the extreme left. This also holds true for the up and down arrow keys.

Screen Reset   **R**

An on-disk image used to clear the computer screen of all graphic material except the initial frame and copyright credits. All material on the screen is lost from memory. This is a user-generated Image File named CLEARSCR. With the screen empty, except for the initial title and copyright credits, press the "S" key. In response to the prompt, type CLEARSCR, and press <ENTER>. Screen Reset Image is saved on Disk.

Erase   **E**

Used to eliminate a section of a schematic so other material can be drawn in its place. To erase a section of the screen, move the Drawing Cursor to the upper left of the image, then press "E". Move the cursor to the lower right section, then press the "E" key for a second time. Using these two coordinates, the computer draws an imaginary box. Anything within this box is erased from the screen.

Insert   **I**

Used to indicate to the computer which of the 30 pre-programmed electronic symbols you want drawn.

Image Save   **S**

Saves all graphic material being displayed to disk.

Function requires user to enter, via keyboard, the name of the schematic. This display is saved as a Picture Image File with an extension .PIX.

Circle	C	Used to draw one of three programmed circles on the screen. Circle #3 is used to draw the FET and transistor symbols.
Image Load	L	Used to load a schematic previously saved using the "S" or the "G" option. By pressing the "L" key, you are asked if the image to be loaded will be loaded from a <1> Library (.LIB) or <2> Picture (.PIX) File. You respond by entering the number 1 or 2. Then press <ENTER>. At this time, you are asked the filename. Respond by entering the name of the image you wish displayed. When complete, press <ENTER>.
Wording	W	Used to print, via the computer keyboard, any combination of numbers or letters on the schematic like component values or any other required information. When typing characters, if you come close to the end of a line, the computer automatically warns you by sounding an alarm.
Print Line	P	Used to draw a line on the screen at any angle in respect to the horizontal. Computer requires user to input two X, Y coordinates. These coordinates are entered by pressing "P" two times. The computer then draws a line

		connecting these X, Y locations.
Memory Image	G	Used to place, in memory, an image that can be redrawn at any time using the "A" option. Function requires the user to input two X, Y coordinates, the second on the diagonal to the first. The image to be saved must be contained within an imaginary box drawn using the two X, Y coordinates. When saved in memory, your computer asks if this image should be saved in <1> Library (.LIB) or <2> Picture (.PIX) File. Respond appropriately. You are then asked to give the image a name. Enter a filename, then press <ENTER>. At this time, the graphic is saved as a Library or Picture File on Disk A.
Memory Image Print	A	Used to redraw a saved image using the "G" option. This function makes use of an XOR feature. By pressing the "A" key for the second time, the image just drawn can be erased, leaving the resident print untouched.
Termination Point	T	Used to draw a small circle at the end of a printed schematic line. This indicates a connection is to be made from this point to the outside world.
Help	H	Used to refresh the memory of the user regarding the available commands used with the Schematic Designer Program.
Filenames	F	By pressing the "F" key, you can inspect the contents

(filenames) of Disk A without exiting from a running program. When filenames are displayed, you can continue program execution by pressing the <ENTER> key or, if you wish, you can type KILL to delete any of the displayed files. To delete files, you must enter the filename and extension (for example, KILL "SAMPLE1.PIX").

Function	Key to Press	Description of Command
Hard Copy Print	SHIFT or SHIFT/PRINT	Used to print on paper the final schematic design. Printing may require the pressing of the <PRINT> or the <SHIFT> <PRINT> keys. Refer to the computer instruction book for proper usage.

PC BOARD DESIGNER PROGRAM DRAW COMMANDS

Function	Key to Press	Description of Command
Draw	D	By pressing the "D" key, the user can trace a line in the direction associated with the arrow key pressed.
Cursor Movement	Arrow Keys	By pressing one of the arrow keys, the Drawing Cursor moves in the direction associated with the key pressed. Four directions of movement are provided: up, down, left, and right. Program incorporates a wrap around feature. If you come to the extreme right section of the frame, the cursor automatically reappears at the extreme left. This also holds true for the up and down arrow keys.
Screen Reset	R	An on-disk image used to clear the computer screen of

all graphic material except for the initial frame and copyright credits. All material on the screen is lost from memory. This is a user-generated Image File named CLS. With screen empty, except for initial title and copyright credits, press the "S" key. Then, in response to the prompt, type CLS, then press <ENTER>. Screen Reset Image is saved on disk.

Erase	E	Used to eliminate a section of a layout so other material can be drawn in its place. Requires the input of two diagonal coordinates by pressing the "E" key twice.
Paint	P	Used to paint the colored graphic dots and repaint the computer monitor black. Layout is now ready to be printed.
Image Save	S	Saves all graphic material being displayed to disk. Function requires user to enter, via keyboard, the name of the PC board artwork. This artwork is saved with a .PIX (Picture) extension.
Circle	C	This key allows the user to draw one programmed circle on the screen. This is used to draw a circular copper trace that indicates a wire connection to the outside world.
Image Load	L	Used to load a schematic previously saved using the "S" or the "G" option. By pressing the "L" key, you are asked if the image to be loaded is loaded from a <1> Library (.LIB) or <2> Picture (.PIX) File. You re-

spond by entering the number 1 or 2. Then press <ENTER>. At this time, you are asked the filename. Respond by entering the name of the image you wish displayed. When complete, press <ENTER>.

| Wording | W | Used to print, via the computer keyboard, any combination of numbers or letters on the schematic. Such as, component values or any other information required to be present on the artwork. |

Wording W — Used to print, via the computer keyboard, any combination of numbers or letters on the schematic. Such as, component values or any other information required to be present on the artwork.

<Memory Image G — Used to place, in memory, an image that can be redrawn at any time using the A option. Function requires the user to input two X, Y coordinates. The second being on the diagonal to the first. The image to be saved must be contained within an imaginary box drawn using the two X, Y coordinates. When saved in memory, your computer will ask if this image will be saved in <1> Library (.LIB) or <2> Picture (.PIX) File. Respond appropriately. You are then asked to give the image a name. Enter a filename, then press <ENTER>. At this time, the graphic is saved as a Library or Picture File on Disk A.

Memory Image Print A — Used to redraw a saved image using the "G" option. This function makes use of an XOR feature. By pressing the "A" key for the second time, the image just drawn can be erased leaving the resident print untouched. When mem-

		ory image is at the desired location, press the F1 key. This redraws the picture as a PRESET drawing.
Termination	T	Draws a small box that is used to draw IC pads on the screen, or can be used to indicate outside world connections.
Help	H	Refreshes your memory regarding the available com mands used with the PC Board Designer Program.
Filenames	F	By pressing the "F" key, you can inspect the contents (filenames) of Disk A without exiting from a running pro gram. When filenames are displayed, you can continue program execution by pressing the <ENTER> key or, if you wish, you can type KILL to delete any of the displayed files. To delete files, you must enter filename and extension (for example, KILL "TRANS.LIB".
Hard Copy Print	SHIFT or SHIFT/PRINT	Prints on paper the final artwork design. Printing may require the pressing of the <PRINT> or the <SHIFT> <PRINT> keys. Refer to the computer instruction book for proper usage.

Appendix B

Making Back-Up
Copies of a Purchased
CAE Program Disk

A program disk containing both CAE programs is available from TAB BOOKS Inc. Please refer to the order coupon in back of this book for additional information and pricing.

If you wish to purchase the programming disk, I recommend that you read this section. It describes the procedure for making back-up copies and how to manipulate programming files so that each disk contains the required program and image files.

The machine language program that makes back-up copies of your disk is contained on the MS-DOS floppy. Upon initial start-up, the DOS prompt appears (A>). At this prompt, type DISKCOPY then press <ENTER>.

At this time, Drive A starts. When the program is loaded, the computer asks you to insert the source disk into drive A. When the main program floppy disk (purchased from TAB BOOKS Inc.) is loaded into Drive A, press <ENTER>. The computer now reads each of the 40 tracks. Depending on the amount of memory available in your computer, this reading stage can be completed in one disk insert.

If the computer has only 128K memory, the back-up program requires you to swap the source disk (program disk) with an empty formatted destination disk a number of times throughout the operation.

Whichever way you choose to make back-ups, three copies of the main program disk are needed. When the three copies are made, put the CAE Program Disk in a safe place. Work with the back-up copies only. If for any reason the copies are destroyed, you will still have the main program disk to make replacements.

The first of the three disks contains the Schematic Designer and associated programming material. The BASIC command KILL is used to delete the programs that are not needed.

With MS-DOS reloaded, type BASIC and press <ENTER>. When in BASIC, remove the MS-DOS disk from Drive A and replace it with one of the three back-up program floppies.

Type FILES. After a second or two, the following is displayed on the monitor.

```
A:\
HELP2     .BAS  PCB       .BAS  INTRO2    .BAS  CLS      .PIX
DATA3     .PIX  INTRO     .BAS  DESIGNER  .BAS  HELP     .BAS
PCB2      .BAS  DATA2     .BAS  CLEARSCR  .PIX  DATA     .PIX
GRAPH     .BAS  DRAW      .BAS  CLEAR     .PIX  SAMPLE1  .LIB
SAMPLE2   .LIB  SAMPLE3   .LIB  SAMPLE4   .LIB
   171008 Bytes free
```

As stated earlier, this disk is only for the Schematic Designer. So use the following format:

$$KILL \ \ ``filename.extension" \quad <ENTER>$$

To check to see if the file has been erased, just type FILES and press <ENTER> to display the current filenames on the disk. Continue to KILL the files named below for each of the three program disks. Then, if you wish, additional copies can be made of each disk. It is recommended that these three disks be placed in a safe place so that future copies can be made directly from them. This saves you the trouble of making additional copies of the master disk and then deleting files.

To make a Schematic Designer Disk, delete the following files using the KILL command.

```
HELP2     .BAS  PCB      .BAS  INTRO2  .BAS
CLS       .PIX  DATA3    .PIX  PCB2    .BAS
GRAPH     .BAS  DRAW     .BAS  CLEAR   .PIX
SAMPLE3   .LIB  SAMPLE4  .LIB
```

To make a PC Board Designer Disk, delete the following files using the KILL command.

```
INTRO     .BAS  DESIGNER  .BAS  DATA      .PIX
HELP      .BAS  DATA2     .BAS  CLEARSCR  .PIX
DRAW      .BAS  CLEAR     .PIX
SAMPLE1   .LIB  SAMPLE2   .LIB
```

To make a DRAW Program Disk, delete the following files using the KILL command.

HELP2	.BAS	PCB	.BAS	INTRO2	.BAS
CLS	.PIX	DATA3	.PIX	INTRO	.BAS
HELP	.BAS	DESIGNER	.BAS	PCB2	.BAS
DATA2	.BAS	CLEARSCR	.PIX	DATA	.PIX
GRAPH	.BAS				

To create additional disk space, you can also delete the following. They have no bearing on the normal operation of any program.

SAMPLE1 .LIB	SAMPLE2	.LIB	SAMPLE3	.LIB
	SAMPLE4	.LIB		

The filenames ending with the extension .PIX are Image Picture Files. These files contain all graphic and character images that appeared on the computer's monitor when the file was created.

All filenames ending with the extension .LIB are user-generated Image Library Files. This extremely useful operation increases the normal 30 pre-programmed electronic symbols in the Schematic Designer Disk to an unlimited number. (Naturally, disk space is required.) Unlike the .PIX file which saves the entire contents of the monitor, the .LIB function saves only a user-determined section.

While using the Schematic Designer program, press the ''L'' key (LOAD). Answer the .LIB or .PIX loading prompt by entering the number one for a Library Image Input. Then type the filename SAMPLE1 or SAMPLE2 (extension not needed). Sample 1 displays a Logic Gate (NAND) while Sample 2 displays an ac transformer already wired to a bridge rectifier.

While using the PC Board Designer program, press the ''L'' key and answer the prompts as indicated above, but type in the filenames SAMPLE3 or SAMPLE4. Sample 3 displays a complete 14-pin integrated circuit, while Sample 4 displays the proper pin spacing and drilling guide for an audio transformer.

The uses for this function are limited only by your imagination.

Glossary

Glossary

ABS(x)—Returns the absolute value of x.

**ASC(strings$)**—Returns the ASCII code the first character of string A$.

ATN(X)—Returns the arctangent of the number X.

AUTO [line], [increment]—Instructs the computer to automatically number each program line when the <ENTER> button is pressed. If a line number is already incorporated in the program, BASIC displays an asterisk (*) after the line in question. To turn off AUTO, press the <BREAK> key. Line is the starting line number (default is line 10). Increment is the increment to use when generating line numbers (default is 10 lines).

> Example: AUTO
>   AUTO 100,25

BEEP—Instructs the computer to generate an 800 Hz tone for ¼ second.

> Example: 10 BEEP
>   10 IF X>20 THEN BEEP

BLOAD "Filename",Starting Point—Used to load a saved graphic picture back into the computer monitor. Filename is the name of the graphic you have chosen (A$). Starting Point is the memory location of the upper left corner of the computer monitor.

BSAVE "Filename", Starting Point,Length—Used to save a graphic picture presently on the computer monitor to disk. Filename is the name you have chosen for the graphic (A\$). Starting Point is the memory location of the upper left corner of the monitor. Length is the number of memory locations you want to save on disk. This number is 16384.

CHAIN [Merge]pathname,[line],[ALL],[DELETE line-line]—Lets the current program load and execute another program without losing any user assigned variables or arrays. Schematic Designer Program makes use of this statement so that any image stored in memory using the GET option remains in memory when the help screens are called upon.

CIRCLE (Center Location),Radius—Used to draw a circle at any location on the computer monitor. Center location is an entered (X, Y) location where the circle is to be drawn. Radius indicates the size of the circle to be drawn.

CLEAR Memory Location—Frees memory for data without erasing the program currently in memory. Memory location specifies the highest memory location available for program use. With CAE programs, this memory is 5000.

CLOSE—Closes access to a disk file after it has been opened to load or save program data or graphic.

> Examples: 10 CLOSE
> 10 CLOSE 1,5,8

CLS—Clears the screen and returns the cursor to the home position at the upper left corner of the monitor.

> Example: 10 CLS

COLOR Foreground,Background—Sets the monitor's foreground and background color to any of the available colors used in the screen mode selected. If a black and white monitor is used, graphic characters may become light in color and hard to see. Use this command only with a color monitor.

CONT—Instructs the computer to resume program execution when stopped by pressing the <BREAK> key or when the program encounters a STOP or END statement.

> Example: CONT

COS(x)—Returns the cosine of the number X.

> Example: 10 PRINT COS(10.5)
> 30 AA = COS(Y*.0174533)

DATE\$ [= string]—Sets the date of the internal computer memory or retrieves the current date. String may be entered in the standard Month/Day/Year format (01/21/88).

> Example: 10 DATE\$ = "04/10/53"

DEF SEG [= address]—Assigns the current segment address. The segment address is used by BLOAD and by BSAVE in the CAE programs. To save an Image on Disk, the command 10 DEF SEG is used with the BSAVE command. To save an entire graphic, the command 10 DEF SEG = &HB800 is used with the BSAVE command. This DEF SEG address (&HB800) sets the video memory starting point to zero (0). This starting point is the upper left corner of the monitor. This memory location never changes, even if different Graphic Utilities are loaded while in MS-DOS.

DELETE line1-line2—This command is used to erase program lines. For example, if the statement DELETE 100-200 is used, the computer erases all lines between 100 and 200.

    Example: DELETE 10-200

DIM array(dimension)—Sets aside memory for the storage of contents in the array. Array is a variable name of a string, integer, single precision, or double precision variable name. With the CAE programs, this array (B) stores a selected monitor image.

DRAW "string"—Draws an image on the screen. String specifies 1 or more of the movement commands listed below using a ";" to separate drawing movements. Movement commands begin movement from the current graphic location which has been set at that location using the PSET(x,y) command. Movements listed (n = number of pixels to be turned on)

U(n)	Moves up n points
D(n)	Moves down n points
L(n)	Moves left n points
R(n)	Moves right n points
E(n)	Moves diagonally up and right n points
F(n)	Moves diagonally down and right n points
G(n)	Moves diagonally down and left n points
H(n)	Moves diagonally up and left n points

EDIT line—This command instructs the computer to enter the editing mode. BASIC displays the indicated line. Program changes can now be made. To exit from edit, press the <ENTER> key.

END—Ends program execution and closes all open files.

EOF (buffer)—Instructs the computer to automatically detect the end of a file. Buffer is the number assigned to the file when it was opened.

    Example: 10 IF EOF(1) THEN GOSUB 2000

ERASE array,array—This command erases one or more arrays from computer memory.

    Example: 10 ERASE B
                    10 ERASE G,U,I$

ERL—This command returns the number of a line in which an error has occurred.

Example: 20 ON ERROR GOTO 2000
1999 END
2000 PRINT"UNKNOWN ERROR IN LINE ";ERL
2010 INPUT;"Hit <ENTER> when Ready ";ZZ
2020 RESUME NEXT

ERR—Instructs the computer to display the error code if an error has occurred.

Example: 10 IF ERR=6 THEN 200 ELSE 500

FILES—This command instructs the computer to display all files saved on Disk A. The files command is used in both CAE Programs. This allows you to see the Picture and Library Image Files currently on disk without exiting the programs to do so. When all files have been displayed, press the <ENTER> key to continue program execution or type KILL to delete any one of the displayed files.

Example: 100 FILES

FOR variable = initial value TO final value NEXT variable—Establishes a program loop that allows a series of program statements to be executed at a given number of times. Variable must be either integer or single precision.

FRE (dummy argument)—Returns the number of bytes in memory not being used by BASIC. If you specify a number argument, BASIC returns the amount of unused memory. If a string ("55") is used, BASIC compresses the data before returning the amount of available memory.

Example: 10 PRINT FRE("55")
10 PRINT FRE(0)

GET(x1,y1) – (x2,y2),array—Transfers points from an area on the monitor to an array (B) so it can be placed at another location on the screen at a later time using the PUT command. GET must have a DIM statement to set aside computer memory for this array.

GOSUB line number—Branches to a subroutine beginning at the line indicated by line number. GOSUB must be used with a RETURN statement.

Example: 10 IF R=2 THEN GOSUB 500
499 END
500 PRINT "R=2":RETURN

GOTO line number—Branches program execution to a specified line.

Example: 10 IF R=2 THEN GOTO 500
499 END
500 PRINT "R=2":END

IF expression THEN statement ELSE statement—Tests a conditional expression and makes a decision regarding the flow of the program. If expression is TRUE, BASIC executes the THEN statement. If expression is FALSE, BASIC executes the matching ELSE statement or the next program line.

Example: IF A=1 THEN GOTO 200 ELSE 300
            IF A=1 THEN GOTO 200

INKEY$—Returns a one character string from a keyboard input without pressing the <ENTER> button. If no key is pressed, BASIC returns a null string.

Example: 10 A$=INKEY$: IF A$=" " THEN GOTO 10

INPUT;"prompt";variable—Accepts data from the keyboard and stores it in one or more variables. When reached, BASIC stops execution of the program and displays the prompt followed by a question mark indicating that the program is waiting for a keyboard input.

Example: INPUT"Enter Filename to be Saved";A$

If the prompt is followed by a comma, the question mark is not printed as part of the display. If INPUT is followed by a semi-colon, BASIC does not echo the <ENTER> key when you press it as part of the response.

INT (n)—Converts n to the largest integer that is less than or equal to n.

Example: 10 PRINT INT(79.565)

KEY number,string—Assigns or displays function key values. These keys are numbered as F1 - F2 - F3, etc. String is an expression assigned to the key indicated by its key number. This expression can contain a maximum of 15 characters.

KEY ON—Displays the current function key assignments on the bottom line of the monitor.

KEY OFF—This command erases the function key assignments from the monitor. NOTE: The key assignments are still activated.

KEY LIST—Displays all 15 characters of all 12 function key assignments on the screen.

KEY(number)action—Turns on, turns off, or temporarily halts key trapping for a specified key:

KEY ( ) ON	Enables key trapping
KEY ( ) OFF	Disables key trapping
KEY ( ) STOP	Temporarily suspends key trapping

Number can be a number in the range one to 20, indicating the number of the key to be trapped. The number of the four arrow keys using MS-DOS version 2.11, are as follows:

up Arrow Key	11	left Arrow Key	12
right Arrow Key	13	down Arrow Key	14

KILL pathname—Delete a filename from disk.

Example: KILL "DESIGNER.BAS"

The extension .BAS must also be included in this command or the computer will not erase this file from the disk. This command is used in both CAE programs to delete any Picture or Library Image File saved on disk.

LET variable = expression—Assigns the value expression to a variable.

Example: 10 LET A$ = "Computer Aided Design"

LINE (x1,y1) – (x2,y2)—Draws a line on the video display. (x1,y1) are the coordinates at which the line begins. (x2,y2) are the coordinates at which the line is to end. When entered, the computer connects these two coordinates with a line. In the CAE programs, both X, Y coordinates are entered by pressing the "P" key twice. This function uses the INKEY$ command.

LIST start-end line—Instructs the computer to list on screen or printer the program residing in memory. If you indicate the starting and end line, your computer displays or prints only the lines indicated within the indicated start and end line.

Example: LIST
             LIST 100-9000,LPT1:

LPT1: indicates that this listing is directed toward the printer.

LLIST start-end line—Lists program lines in memory to the printer. LLIST assumes a 132 character-wide printer. This can be changed by using the WIDTH statement.

LOAD"Filename"—Loads a BASIC program to computer memory from disk. While using this command, when loading is complete, you must type RUN then press the <ENTER> key to start program execution.

Example: LOAD"DESIGNER"   Type RUN then hit <ENTER>.

LOCATE row,column—Positions the cursor on the screen at the position indicated by row and column. Maximum row and column positions for SCREEN #2 is ROW 80 - COLUMN 25. For SCREEN #1 is ROW 40 - COLUMN 25.

Example: LOCATE 25,1

MERGE pathname—This command loads and merges a BASIC program currently in memory. Program lines in pathname are inserted into the resident program in sequential order. The program to be merged must be in ASCII format.

Example: MERGE "Program2.BAS"

The program "Program2.BAS" had to be saved using the command SAVE "Program2.BAS",A. "A" tells the computer to save this program in the ASCII format.

NEW—Erases or deletes the program currently in memory and resets all variables.

Example: NEW

ON ERROR GOTO line—Transfer control to line if an error occurs. You must execute an ON ERROR GOTO before the error is encountered.

Example: ON ERROR GOTO 600

ON n GOSUB line,line . . .—Looks at n and transfers program control to the subroutine indicated by the nth line listed. If n equals one, BASIC branches to the first line listed. If n equals two, BASIC branches to the second line listed and so on.

Example: 10 ON y GOSUB 100,200,300

Y is a number entered to the computer using the INPUT"prompt";Y command.
ON n GOTO line,line,line—This command instructs the computer to look at n and transfers program control to the nth line listed.

Example: 100 INPUT"ENTER A NUMBER";N
110 ON N GOTO 100,200,300,400,500,600

ON KEY number GOSUB line—Transfers program control to a subroutine beginning at line when you press a specified key. This command must be used with a KEY (x) ON statement.

Example: 10 ON KEY(11) GOSUB 2000

OPEN "mode",buffer,"Filename"—Establishes an input/output path for a file or device. As with our program, this device is Drive A. MODE can be any of the following:

O or OUTPUT	sequential output mode
I or INPUT	sequential input mode
A or APPEND	sequential output and extend mode
R or RANDOM	direct input/output mode

Example: To input data from disk, you must first open the file with OPEN"I",1,"Filename" and then this data must be entered into the computer by using INPUT#1,data variable.

INPUT #1,data variable.

The file must be closed by typing CLOSE. To save data on disk, you must first open the file with OPEN"O",1,"Filename". Then this data must be entered to the disk by using PRINT#1,data variable.

The file must be closed by typing CLOSE

PAINT(x,y)color,border—Fills in an area on the display with a selected color. (X,Y) are the coordinates at which the painting is to begin. Color can be either a number or string expression. If color is a number, it specifies a color number available in the current screen mode. If color is a string expression, it specifies the mask to be used for tiling in the form. Screen Mode 0 has 16 available colors, Screen Mode 1 has four colors with two palettes, Screen Mode 2 has two colors, Screen Mode 3 has 16 colors, and Screen Mode 4 has four available colors.

PLAY string—Plays the musical notes specified by string. String is an expression consisting of one or more single character musical commands.

A-G plays notes A through G of one musical scale. You can include an optional number sign (#) or plus sign (+) to indicate a sharp note or a minus sign (−) to indicate a flat note.

Ln sets the duration of the notes that follows. N may be a value in the range of 1 to 64 where:

1	indicates a whole note
2	indicates a half note
4	indicates a quarter note
8	indicates an eighth note
16	indicates a sixteenth note

On sets the current octave. There are 7 octaves, 0 through 6. Octave 3 starts with middle C. Default is Octave 4.

Nn	plays a note. N may be in the range of 0 to 84.
Pn	rests. N may be in the range of 1 to 64.
Tn	sets the number of quarter notes in 1 minute. N may be in the range of 32 to 255. Default equals 120 quarter notes in 1 minute.
	Plays a dotted note. BASIC plays the note one-half its length longer.
MF	plays the music in the foreground.
MB	plays the music in the background. A maximum of 32 notes and/or rests can play in background at a time.
MN	Each note plays ⅞ of the duration as set by the L option.
ML	sets Legato of the music. Each note plays the full duration as set by the L option.
MS	sets Staccato. Each note plays ¾ of the duration as set by the L option.

Example: 10 PLAY "L8ACDEP2G#DL16ACDEO4"

POINT(x,y)—Return the color number of a point on the monitor. (X,Y) are the coordinates of the point. In Screen Mode 2, an example is as follows:

IF POINT (24,35)=1 THEN GOTO 200

In the above example, if the pixel at coordinates (24,35) is white then GOTO line 200.
PRINT"expression";—Prints numeric or string data on the display.

> Example: 10 PRINT A$
>   20 PRINT "TAB BOOKS Inc."

You can also use the LOCATE command to position wording at any allowable location on the monitor. An example is as follows:

> Example: 10 LOCATE 25,1
>   20 PRINT "TAB BOOKS Inc.";

Using the above example, TAB BOOKS Inc. is printed at the lower left corner of the screen. The ";" at the end of the expression prevents an IBM computer from executing an automatic line feed. This line feed shifts the entire contents of the screen up one line. On some compatibles, this ";" is not needed.
PRINT buffer,data—Writes data items to disk drive after the file has been opened.

> Example: 10 OPEN"O",1,"Filename"
>   20 PRINT#1,DATA
>   30 CLOSE

PSET(x,y),color—Draws a point on the monitor at the location indicated by the X,Y coordinates. Color indicates the number of the color you wish the pixel to be colored. The color is limited to the available colors used with the screen mode indicated in your program.

> Example: 10 SCREEN 2
>   20 PSET(25,30),1   The 1 indicates the color white.

> Example: 10 SCREEN 2
>   20 PSET(25,30),0   The 0 indicates the color black

PUT(x,y),array,action—Transfers an image in an array to the screen. (X,Y) are the coordinates at which the upper left corner of the image is to be drawn. Array is the array variable that holds the image. In the CAE programs, this array is the variable B. Action sets the type of interaction between the transferred image and the image already on the screen. Action may be PSET,PRESET,AND,OR or XOR. The PC Board Design Program uses the XOR action. This statement is used with the GET command. The GET command stores an image in memory while the PUT command takes this image and places it within the boundaries of the screen. The memory used for GET and PUT is volatile. This means if you turn off your computer, the image stored by using the GET statement is lost from memory. Unless you make use of the "Q" option which saves the image on Disk.

Example: 10 PUT(25,30),B,PSET

REM—Inserts a remark line within the program. This is used as a flag to indicate computer action within a section of the program.

Example: 10 REM LOAD DATA TO DISK

RENUM—Renumbers the program currently in memory. Also changes all line numbers contained in GOTO, GOSUB, THEN ON/GOTO etc. commands

Example: RENUM

RESUME line
RESUME NEXT—Resumes program execution after an error-handling routine. RESUME line branches to a specified line number. RESUME NEXT branches to the statement following the point at which the error occurred.

Example: 10 ON ERROR GOSUB 100
             11 PRINT "TAB BOOKS Inc."
             99 END
             100 RESUME NEXT   Transfers execution to line 11

RETURN [line]—Returns control from a subroutine executed by a GOSUB to the specified line.

Example: 10 IF A = 5 THEN GOSUB 1000
             999 END
             1000 A = 10
             1010 RETURN

RUN
RUN line—Executes a program. Line is the program line at which BASIC begins execution.

Example: RUN "Designer"
             RUN 200

SAVE "Program Name",A—Saves a BASIC program on disk under the name you have chosen

Example: SAVE "Designer"
         SAVE "PCB",A

The "A" tells the computer to save this program in the ASCII format.

SCREEN mode—Sets the screen attributes to be used by all other graphic statements. Depending which graphics adapter you have installed on your computer, you may have seven screen modes to choose from (0 to 6). Each screen mode offers different graphic resolutions as well as the number of colors available with that mode.

Example: 10 SCREEN 2 (used with Schematic Designing Program)
             10 SCREEN 1 (used with the PC Board Designer Program)

SOUND tone,duration,volume—(Note: Volume notation not allowed on IBM). Generates a sound with the tone and duration specified. TONE is an integer in the range 1 to 1023, indicating the frequency in Hz.

Note	Frequency	Note	Frequency
Middle C	523.25	G	783.99
D	587.33	A	880.00
E	659.26	B	987.77
F	698.46	C	1046.50

Duration is an integer in the range 1 to 65535, specifying how long the computer is to produce the tone. Volume is an integer in the range 0 to 15 where 0 is the lowest volume and 15 is the highest.

Example: 10 SOUND 700,5,10

SPACE$(n)—Returns a string of n spaces. N must be in the range of 1 to 255.

Example: 10 PRINT SPACE$(80)

This example prints 80 spaces.

Example: 10 LOCATE 25,1:PRINT SPACE$(80)

This example prints 80 spaces at location 25,1.

STICK(action)—Returns the coordinates of the joystick or graphic tablet. Action may be one of the following:

0 returns the horizontal (x) coordinates for the left joystick
1 returns the vertical (y) coordinates for the left joystick.
2 returns the horizontal (x) coordinates for the right joystick
3 returns the vertical (y) coordinates for the right joystick
In the CAE Programs; Cursor Express uses this command

Example: 100 X = STICK(0): Y = STICK(1)

STOP—Stops execution of the program

SYSTEM—Returns the user to the DOS command level

TAB (n)—Spaces to position n on the display. N must be in the range of 1 to 255.

      Example: 10 PRINT TAB(20)''TAB BOOKS Inc.''

TIME$ [= string]—Sets or retrieves the current time.

      Examples: 10 TIME$ = ''14:30''
                     10 BB$ = TIME$

TIMER—Returns the number of seconds since midnight or since the last system reset.

      Examples: 10 PRINT TIMER
                     10 BB = TIMER

TRON

TROFF—Turns the trace function on or off. This trace allows you to follow program execution by line numbers. This helps you determine the area where a problem exists.

      Example: TRON
                  TROFF

VARPTR (variable)

VARPTR (buffer)—Returns the offset into BASIC's data segment of a variable or Disk buffer. When used with variable, VARPTR returns the address of the first byte of data identified with variable. When used with buffer, VARPTR returns the address of the file's control block.

      Example: 10 BLOAD ''BUFFER.LIB'',VARPTR(B(0))

WIDTH [LPRINT]

WIDTH buffer, size

WIDTH device,size—Sets the line width in number of characters for the display, printer, or communications channel. Buffer is the number assigned to the file in the OPEN statement. Device specifies the device that the character width is to be set. Device can be SCRN: (Screen), LPT1: (Printer), or COM1: or COM2: for communication channels. Size may be an integer in the range 0 to 255. This specifies the number of characters in a line. For the monitor display, size can be only 40 or 80 characters per line.

Index

Index

Other Bestsellers From TAB

☐ **HOW TO DESIGN SOLID-STATE CIRCUITS—2nd Edition—Mannie Horowitz and Delton T. Horn**

Design and build useful electronic circuits from scratch! The authors provide the exact data you need on every aspect of semiconductor design . . . performance characteristics . . . applications potential . . . operating reliability . . . and more! Four major categories of semiconductors are examined: Diodes . . . Transistors . . . Integrated Circuits . . . Thyristors. This second edition is filled with procedures, advice, techniques, and background information. All the hands-on direction you need to understand and use semiconductors in all kinds of electronic devices is provided. Ranging from simple temperature-sensitive resistors to integrated circuit units composed of multiple microcircuits, this new edition describes a host of the latest in solid-state devices. 380 pp., 297 illus.

Paper $19.95   **Hard $24.95**
Book No. 2975

☐ **HOW TO MAKE PRINTED CIRCUIT BOARDS, WITH 17 PROJECTS—Calvin Graf**

Now *you* can achieve the polished look of skillfully etched and soldered boards with the help of Calvin Graf. This book explains thoroughly and *in plain English*, everything you need to know to make printed circuit boards (PCBs). Key subjects include: getting from an electronic schematic to a PCB, etching a printed circuit board, cleaning, drilling, and mounting electronic parts, soldering, and desoldering project kits. 224 pp., 177 illus.

Paper $18.95   **Hard $23.95**
Book No. 2898

☐ **THE BENCHTOP ELECTRONICS REFERENCE MANUAL—Victor F.C. Veley**

One strength of this book lies in its unique format which divides the various topics into five subject areas that include direct-current principles, tubes, alternating-current principles, principles of radio communications, and solid-state devices. But, what really sets this electronics sourcebook apart from all the others is the wide range of information given on each of the 160 topics including basic principles and mathematical derivations. 672 pp., 82 illus.

Paper $27.95   **Hard $39.95**
Book No. 2785

☐ **THE CET STUDY GUIDE—2nd Edition—Sam Wilson**

Written by the Director of CET Testing for ISCET (International Society of Certified Electronics Technicians), Sam Wilson, this completely up-to-date and practical guide gives you a comprehensive review of all topics covered in the Associate and Journeyman exams. Example questions help you pinpoint your own strengths and weaknesses. There are two 75-question practice exams—with questions similar to, but not exactly like, the ones you will find on the CET test. Most important, the author has given the answers to all the questions and has even provided invaluable hints on how you can avoid careless errors when you take the actual CET exams. 336 pp., 179 illus.

Paper $16.95   **Hard $21.95**
Book No. 2941

☐ **HIGH PERFORMANCE INTERACTIVE GRAPHICS: MODELING, RENDERING AND ANIMATING FOR IBM PCs® AND COMPATIBLES—Lee Adams**

This comprehensive reference contains over 6000 lines of valuable source code and 44 breathtaking demonstration programs. Author Lee Adams helps you understand the concepts behind the programs. You'll learn modeling, rendering, and animating on IBM-compatible microcomputers in the context of a modular programming environment and properly structured BASIC code. 480 pp., 229 illus., 8 color pages.

Paper $22.95   **Book No. 2879**

☐ **BUILD YOUR OWN WORKING FIBEROPTIC, INFRARED AND LASER SPACE-AGE PROJECTS—Robert E. Iannini**

Here are plans for a variety of useful electronic and scientific devices, including a high sensitivity laser light detector and a high voltage laboratory generator (useful in all sorts of laser, plasma ion, and particle applications as well as for lighting displays and special effects). And that's just the beginning of the exciting space age technology that you'll be able to put to work! 288 pp., 198 illus.

Paper $18.95   **Hard $24.95**
Book No. 2724

Other Bestsellers From TAB

☐ **HOW TO DESIGN AND BUILD ELECTRONIC INSTRUMENTATION—2nd Edition—Joseph J. Carr**

One of the most useful books ever published on the design and construction of electronic circuitry has now been completely revised to include a wealth of applications devices . . . including the latest in microcomputer-based instrumentation and actual computer programs that are sure to make designing circuits less complicated. 518 pp., 328 illus.

Paper $19.95   **Book No. 2660**

☐ **IBM PC® GRAPHICS—John Clark Craig and Jeff Bretz**

Now, this practical and exceptionally complete guide provides the answers to questions and the programs you need to utilize your IBM PC's maximum potential. This is a collection of immediately useful programs covering a wide variety of subjects that are sure to captivate your interest . . . and expand your programming horizons. 272 pp., 138 illus., 8-page color section.

Paper$14.95   **Hard $16.95**
Book No. 1860

☐ **33 GAMES OF SKILL AND CHANCE FOR THE IBM PC®—Robert J. Traister**

Turn your IBM Personal Computer into a super computer arcade during its off-work hours! Here's a collection of challenging and entertaining games that can provide hours of enjoyment, *plus* help you extend your computing skills and build your programming knowledge. Includes brain teasers, games for amusement and relaxation, educational games, and games for every age level! 256 pp., 44 illus.

Paper$14.95   **Hard $18.95**
Book No. 1526

☐ **THE ENCYCLOPEDIA OF ELECTRONIC CIRCUITS—Rudolf F. Graf**

Here is every professional's dream treasury of analog and digital circuits—nearly 100 circuit categories . . . over 1,200 individual circuits designed for long-lasting applications potential. Adding even more to the value of this resource is the exhaustively thorough index which gives you instant access to exactly the circuits you need each and every time! 768 pp., 1,762 illus.

Paper $39.95   **Hard $60.00**
Book No. 1938

☐ **1001 THINGS TO DO WITH YOUR IBM PC®—Mark R. Sawusch and Tan A. Summers**

Here's an outstanding sourcebook of microcomputer applications and programs that span every use and interest from game playing and hobby use to scientific, educational, financial, mathematical, and technical applications. It provides a wealth of practical answers for anyone who's ever asked what can a personal computer do for me? Contains a gold mine of actual programs and printouts, and step-by-step instructions for using your micro. 256 pp., 47 illus.

Paper $10.95   **Hard $12.95**
Book No. 1826

☐ **BUILD YOUR OWN LASER, PHASER, ION RAY GUN AND OTHER WORKING SPACE-AGE PROJECTS—Robert E. Iannini**

Here's the highly skilled do-it-yourself guidance that makes it possible for you to build such interesting and useful projects as a burning laser, a high power ruby/YAG, a high-frequency translator, a light beam communications system, a snooper phone listening device, and much more—24 exciting projects in all! 400 pp., 302 illus.

Paper $16.95   **Book No. 1604**

Send $1 for the new TAB Catalog describing over 1300 titles currently in print and receive a coupon worth $1 off on your next purchase from TAB.

*Prices subject to change without notice.

━━━━━━━━━━━━━━━━━━━━━━━━━━━━━━━━━━

To purchase these or any other books from TAB, visit your local bookstore, return this coupon, or call toll-free 1-800-233-1128 (In PA and AK call 1-717-794-2191).

Product No.	Hard or Paper	Title	Quantity	Price

☐ Check or money order enclosed made payable to TAB BOOKS Inc.

Charge my ☐ VISA ☐ MasterCard ☐ American Express

Acct. No. _____ Exp. _____

Signature _____

Please Print
Name _____

Company _____

Address _____

City _____

State _____ Zip _____

Subtotal	
Postage/Handling ($5.00 outside U.S.A. and Canada)	$2.50
In PA add 6% sales tax	
TOTAL	

Mail coupon to:

TAB BOOKS Inc.
Blue Ridge Summit
PA 17294-0840   BC

How to Draw Schematics
and Design Circuit Boards with Your IBM PC

If you are intrigued with the possibilities of CAE as described in *How to Draw Schematics and Design Circuit Boards with Your IBM PC* (TAB Book No. 3034), you should definitely consider having the ready-to-run disk containing the software applications. This software is guaranteed free of manufacturer's defects. (If you have any problems, return the disk within 30 days, and we'll send you a new one.) Not only will you save the time and effort of typing the programs, the disk eliminates the possibility of errors that can prevent the programs from functioning. Interested?

Available on disk for IBM PC and compatibles with 128K and DOS 2.1 or greater at $24.95 for each disk plus $1.50 shipping and handling.

I'm interested. Send me:

_____disk for IBM PC or compatibles with 128K and DOS 2.1 or greater (6673S) Check/Money Order enclosed for $24.95 plus $1.50 shipping and handling for each disk ordered.

☐ VISA   ☐ MasterCard   ☐ American Express

Account No. _____   Expires _____

Name _____

Address _____

City _____ State _____ Zip _____

Signature _____

Mail To: **TAB BOOKS Inc.**
           Blue Ridge Summit, PA 17294-0850

OR CALL TOLL-FREE TODAY: **1-800-233-1128**
IN PENNSYLVANIA AND ALASKA CALL: **717-794-2191.**

(Pa. add 6% sales tax. Orders outside U.S. must be prepaid with international money orders in U.S. dollars.)
*Prices subject to change without notice.

TAB 3034